THE TROUBLE
WITH GENIUS

THE TROUBLE
WITH GENIUS

READING POUND, JOYCE,
STEIN, AND ZUKOFSKY

Bob Perelman

University of California Press
Berkeley · Los Angeles · London

University of California Press
Berkeley and Los Angeles, California

University of California Press, Ltd.
London, England

© 1994 by
The Regents of the University of California

Library of Congress Cataloging-in-Publication Data

Perelman, Bob.
  The trouble with genius : reading Pound, Joyce, Stein, and
Zukofsky / Bob Perelman.
    p.   cm.
  Includes bibliographical references and index.
  ISBN 0-520-08583-3 (alk. paper). — ISBN 0-520-08755-0
  (pbk. : alk. paper)
    1. American literature—20th century—History and criticism.
2. Pound, Ezra, 1885–1972—Criticism and interpretation.   3.
Joyce, James, 1882–1941—Criticism and interpretation.   4. Stein,
Gertrude, 1874–1946—Criticism and interpretation.   5. Zukofsky,
Louis, 1904–1978—Criticism and interpretation.   6. Reader-
response criticism.   7. Genius.   I. Title.
PS221.P43   1994
810.9'0052—dc20   93-37181
                                                            CIP

Printed in the United States of America
9 8 7 6 5 4 3 2 1

Contents

Acknowledgments

Many of my poetry colleagues have been of great help to me, directly and obliquely, in writing this book. Intending more than the bare formula proclaims, I would like to thank Barrett Watten, Lyn Hejinian, Ron Silliman, Carla Harryman, Steve Benson, Kit Robinson, Michael Davidson, Robert Grenier, David Melnick, Fanny Howe, Rae Armantrout, Charles Bernstein, Laura Moriarty, Norman Fischer, Susan Howe, Bruce Andrews, Abby Child, Ben Friedlander, Jean Day, Michael Palmer, David Bromige, Robert Glück, Bruce Boone, Steve McCaffery, Ted Pearson, Tom Mandel, Geoff Young, Alan Bernheimer, Erica Hunt, Jed Rasula, Alan Davies, Clark Coolidge, James Sherry, Kathleen Fraser, Robert Creeley, Jackson Mac Low, Anselm Hollo, and Donald Hall. I would also like to acknowledge the help of the late Jerry Estrin.

I am grateful to Alex Zwerdling, Michael Bernstein, Martin Jay, David Lloyd, James Breslin, Marjorie Perloff, Peter Quartermain, Alan Golding, Al Filreis, Vicky Mahaffey, Wendy Steiner, Jim English, and Bud Bynack for reading, discussion, information.

I would like to acknowledge the support of the University of Pennsylvania, the University of California, which provided me with a Chancellor's Dissertation Year Fellowship, and the MacDowell Colony.

And since (to paraphrase Gertrude Stein) footnotes are neither literature nor life, thanks to Francie, Max, and Reuben for living through the difficulties of construction with me.

Abbreviations

JJ   Richard Ellmann, *James Joyce* (Oxford: Oxford University Press, 1982)

LJ   *Letters of James Joyce,* ed. Stuart Gilbert (New York: Viking Press, 1952)

PA   *Portrait of the Artist as a Young Man* (New York: Viking Press, 1956)

U   *Ulysses: The Corrected Text,* ed. Hans Walter Gabler (New York: Vintage, 1986)

STEIN

CC   James R. Mellow, *Charmed Circle* (New York: Praeger, 1974)

EA   *Everybody's Autobiography* (New York: Random House, 1937)

FIA   *Four in America* (Freeport: Books for Libraries Press, 1947)

GHOA   *The Geographical History of America or the Relation of Human Nature to the Human Mind* (New York: Vintage, 1973)

GSIP   Richard Bridgman, *Gertrude Stein in Pieces* (New York: Oxford University Press, 1970)

HTW   *How To Write* (West Glover, Vt.: Something Else Press, 1973)

LCA   *Lucy Church Amiably* (Millerton, N.Y.: Something Else Press, 1969)

LIA   *Lectures in America* (Boston: Beacon Press, 1985)

LOP   *Last Operas and Plays* (New York: Vintage, 1975)

MOA   *Making of Americans* (New York: Something Else Press, 1966)

SW   *Selected Writings of Gertrude Stein,* ed. Carl Van Vechten (New York: Vintage, 1962)

WAM   *What Are Masterpieces?* (New York: Pitnam Publishing Corporation, 1970)

YGS   *The Yale Gertrude Stein,* ed. Richard Kostelanetz (New
        Haven: Yale University Press, 1980)

ZUKOFSKY

A   *"A"* (Berkeley: University of California Press, 1978)

B   *Bottom: On Shakespeare* (Austin, Tx.: The Ark Press,
        1963)

CSP   *Collected Short Poetry* (Baltimore: Johns Hopkins
        University Press, 1991)

MAP   *Louis Zukofsky: Man and Poet,* ed. Carroll F. Terrell
        (Orono, Me.: National Poetry Foundation, 1979)

PR   *Prepositions: The Collected Critical Essays of Louis
        Zukofsky,* expanded edition (Berkeley: University of
        California Press, 1981)

PZ   *Pound/Zukofsky: Selected Letters of Ezra Pound and Louis
        Zukofsky,* ed. Barry Ahearn (New York: New Directions,
        1987)

1

News That Stays News

Literary studies exist atop the Arnoldian fault: that is, works of literature are presumed to have social value, but they must be inaccessible to some degree or there would be no need to study them and no need for the structures of authority that study produces. The critical industries that have grown up around Pound, Joyce, Stein, and on a small scale around Zukofsky are poised upon a particularly tense section of this fault: the labor required to make *The Cantos, Ulysses, "A,"* and Stein's writing legible has to be justified, ultimately, by the value that the writing embodies, but that value has most often to be transmitted through hearsay as the writing remains illegible or semilegible for any reader who is not a Poundian, Joycean, Steinian, or—if such a category exists yet—a Zukofskian. Unlike, say, Dickens, where criticism disturbs the consumable clarity of the surface to reveal additional meaning beneath, with these four, unreadability is the raw material that is turned into the finished product of significance, which then gives the works their social importance.[1] But it is striking that such critical mediation has to be made on behalf of writers who often made strong claims for the immediacy of their writing.

The notion of genius in its modernist incarnation is bound up with this strain between presence and obscurity. The modernist genius is not the classic spirit of place, or the producer of universal simplicity, or the Romantic recluse, or the anticipatory figure of national unification. Rather, in a split affirmation of specialization and centrality, an aura of illegible authority surrounds the modernist genius, offering a lure for endless study. But in a critical context, genius is an embarrassment. The kind of remark Goethe made about Beethoven brings criticism back to its Romantic youth most uncomfortably: "To think of teaching him would be an insolence even in one with greater insight than mine, since he has the guiding light of his genius, which frequently illumines his mind like a stroke of lightning while we sit in darkness and scarcely suspect the direction from which daylight will break upon us."[2] Gaping awe and situating oneself in darkness are no longer popular critical stances. When its attributes are stated with such bold drama, the transcendent impetuosity of genius with its lightning flashes seems quite close in spirit to the old ads for Tabu, the "Forbidden Fragrance," where the picture freezes the narrative one frame beyond the Grecian Urn, so to speak: here Truth and Beauty have consummated their affair. The female pianist's back is arched, and her fingers still linger above the keyboard as the male violinist has seized her mouth in a passionate kiss, his violin grasped in one hand. They probably were playing the "Kreutzer."

I'm calling on such a kitschy image because it suggests some of the attributes or effects of genius—freedom, thrill, immediacy, corn. But don't such nonintellectual connotations make genius an odd notion to apply to a fairly heterogeneous group of modernists, each of whom seems emphatically intellectual and non-Romantic? The term does have a more sterilizing philosophical genealogy. Commenting on Kant's definition of genius as that "which gives the rule to nature," Charles Altieri writes that genius is "the mind's elaboration of something fundamental to natural energies. . . . [I]ts role is not to create a capacious personal ethos. . . . [It] cannot be reduced to purposes or subjective interests."[3] But the personal capaciousness of the author is crucial to the writing I will be reading. This may leave me open to accusations of cultural elitism, as well as theoretical naiveté, given that one of the most influential essays of the past few decades, "What Is An Author?" was generated out of Foucault's discomfort at having used the proper names of authors in an unproblematized fashion.[4] Nevertheless, I find genius usefully provocative in focusing on, not the idea of the author, but these particular authors' trajectories, both on the page and through social space. It is central to Stein's self-presentation, Pound's politics, Joyce's and Zukofsky's encyclopedic torsions. Genius is an emblem for the desires that drove all four to conceive of such ambitious writing structures or strategies.

It also is a symptom if not a solution for their improbable demands for social authority. I am not primarily interested in the personal dimension of these demands, but in how they play out on the page and over the writing career. Genius can be a charged compliment, and I would like to avoid empty debate and not praise or blame Pound, Joyce, Stein, and Zukofsky for being or posing as geniuses. They all, one way or another, seem to have been quite aware of the category, however. Pound and Stein did display themselves as geniuses, Joyce perhaps less blatantly, Zukofsky only in a recessed, bitter way. In fact, in one passage in "*A*" he seems expressly to exclude himself from my grouping. Examining a collage made by his young son, he calls it "A realizable desire / Of a genius / In the branch of a tree, / A thought the same as the bough." Then he comments to his wife: "A valentine for our genius / Celia— / No false pride— / Merely our tutelary spirit" (*A*, 241). This invokes the older sense of *genius loci*, where genius is a guardian spirit of a given locale. But in Zukofsky's writing, as we will see, avowal and disavowal are particularly closely linked. In spite of Zukofsky's insistent retreat to a domestic space, reading the totality of his work will situate him in the problematic public territory where genius struggles for authority.

Other modernists who conceivably could be included here—Eliot, Williams, HD, Moore, Stevens—differ primarily in that the limits of form are much more a part of their writing. They produced poems, rather than life-writing. There is a sense of finiteness and social location that is not there in Pound and Stein, certainly. Zukofsky and Joyce were quite conscious of the formal structures of their writing, but this is on the local level; globally, their encyclopedic ambitions were ultimately at odds with this.

Although differing more widely than the blanket term "modernism" would suggest, these works share a common root: *The Cantos, Ulysses*, "*A*," and Stein's books were written to be masterpieces— bibles, permanent maps or X rays of society, blueprints for a new civilization, or demonstrations of the essence of the human mind. However, the social narratives by which these displays of genius were to communicate their values, not only to their often-minute audiences but beyond to society at large, were difficult to follow. Being difficult to follow is central to genius.

Pound's career demonstrates a desire to fuse use value with aesthetic value, but the use that is being imagined doesn't leave much room for other social uses. His justifications for good writing often begin by detailing the clarity of perception and social hygiene that such writing can provide, but as he warms to his subject it turns out that at the higher levels of excellence writing is not a tool of social perception at all, but is itself all that needs to be perceived: "The book shd. be a ball of light in one's hand" (*GK*, 55). *The Cantos* was to be this ball of light that would somehow transform society, but the "somehow" indicates how obscure the transformative process was if the glow of that light was not already perceived.

Initially, Joyce might seem to represent the other extreme: *Ulysses* was not an intervention in society, it was instead a definition of the world. But while in its representational and stylistic mimesis *Ulysses* seems to embrace the world completely, the demands it makes on its readers are so great that it remains separate, a work that requires endless devotion to be read accurately.[5] With *Finnegans Wake,* of course, the demands are intensified. But Joyce was not simply aloof; the numerous remarks on current events woven among the letters of *Finnegans Wake* are symptomatic of Joyce's nostalgia for social location.[6]

These attempts to sublate society into art led to a deeply conflicted sense of audience. On the one hand, an individual was addressed; this reader was imagined variously: often for Pound and Zukofsky as a student; for Stein, as herself or Alice B. Toklas; for Joyce, as the sufferer of an ideal insomnia. But these writers were not just looking to establish a well-defined, congenial audience of experts; they were addressing a larger body as well, "the public," which I put in quotes because in Pound's case this might be a combination of Italy, America, England, Mussolini, and even (for a few months) Roosevelt; for Zukofsky, the poor and Ezra Pound; for Stein, Bennett Cerf, Picasso, and the American army; for Joyce, either Dublin or anywhere but Dublin.[7] But while these positive projections of audience verged on the imaginary, the negative aspect of the public was clear enough: the public occupied the alien territory of mass literacy, where writing became a commodity.[8]

This fallen realm of circulation evoked reactions ranging from condescension to phobia, but beyond this there were more complex evasions and refusals: while the stylistic displacements all four exhibited can be explained as scientistic demonstrations of the writer's craft, they can also be seen as attempts to forestall commodification. The same argument holds for indefinability with respect to genre. If genres are, as Fredric Jameson puts it, "social contracts between a writer and a specific public,"[9] then Pound and the others were not signing any contracts. But to be in circulation, to reach the public, was also an attractive proposition, offering a way out of the marginality to which these writers at times found themselves consigned. Stein's later popular writing actively courts the public, and in light of this, her hermetic work can be read as addressed in a more complex sense to the reporters who mocked her. Near the beginning of his career Zukofsky wrote a manifesto. Pound wrote journalism continually; more than that, *The Cantos* often aspires to be a superior species of journalism while attempting to remain an epic. Many of Pound's heroes, such as Malatesta, Adams, Jefferson, and Mussolini were figures who, to Pound's way of thinking, were immersed in the social world, absorbing and mastering at a glance all information that came at them. Joyce mocked the discourses of mass culture in *Ulysses,* but the book would be very different without them. And the fact that *Ulysses* was banned is evidence of how directly the public felt itself addressed.

One index of these contradictions with regard to audience is the notorious difficulty of these works, which has led to their current status where their principal readers are writers, critics, and captive audiences of graduate students (with some sacrificial undergraduates thrown in). This now seems so obvious a fact that it is easy to feel that originally the public was never considered. But the referential, formal, and syntactic singularities of this writing that now seem riddles so provocatively addressed to specialists can also be read as the conflicted vehicles of polemics, appeals, and pronouncements aimed at, if not exactly addressed to, the writers' contemporaries. Adorno describes modernist works as "windowless monads . . . unconsciously and tacitly polemiciz[ing] against the condition of society at a given time."[10] But Adorno's term carries a ring of self-sufficiency that ignores the tension generated in these works as the authors deal with the social world insistently while with equal insistence they place themselves above it. Their works have become monads through the effects of history as much as by the writers' own choice, have many windows, and their polemics are far from unconscious or tacit. Adorno himself comes much closer to this anti-monadic view while articulating his vision of criticism: "The greatest fetish of cultural criticism is the notion of culture as such. For no authentic work of art and no true philosophy, according to their very meaning, has ever exhausted itself in itself alone, in its being-for-itself. They have always stood in relation to the actual life-process of society from which they have distinguished themselves."[11]

Pound's slogan that "literature is news that STAYS news" (*ABC*, 29) seems more accurate to the condition aspired to, though it's doubtful that he intended the paradox involved. When "news"—information affecting the sphere of exchange where commodification is the key process—"STAYS news," when it stops circulating and is transformed into "eternal" literary value, it can freeze into some remarkable shapes:

CHAPTER XXIV

If men have not changed women and children have.
If men have not changed women and children have.
If men have not changed women and children have.

CHAPTER XXV

If men have not changed women and children have.
Men have not changed women and children have.
Men have not changed women and children have changed.
Simon Therese could and would would would and could could did and would would would and could could did and could would. He would if he were not to be taught to be letting it down and being on it as it is it is it that it is that it is attached.

LCA, 176–77

      ... between the usurer and any man who
   wants to do a good job
     (perenne)
without regard to production—
              a charge
for the use of money or credit.
     "Why do you want to
"—perché si vuol mettere—
    your ideas in order?"
         Date '32

C 87, 583

BEAUFOY

We are considerably out of pocket over this bally pressman johnny, this jackdaw of Rheims, who has not even been to a university.

BLOOM

(indistinctly) University of life. Bad art.

BEAUFOY

(shouts) It's a damnably foul lie, showing the moral rottenness of the man! *(he extends his portfolio)* We have here damning evidence, the *corpus delicti*, my lord, a specimen of my maturer work disfigured by the hallmark of the beast.

A VOICE FROM THE GALLERY

Moses, Moses, king of the jews,
Wiped his arse in the *Daily News*.

U, 15.837–48

---

and the nation's draft my window's: soldiers killed
in small *squirm*ishes (the newspaper's misprint): whose
the hernia of a book: that the devils
not be driven into swine or Jerusalem rabbinate
like the Curia kidnap a little scholar:
the weight of the wait: how many books
can a man read: man unkind womb unkind:
alter ego *jünger* ego: "reality" grammarian added an
ity: philosophize: if I cannot live their lives
for them, to write their costive posies is whose (?) "lie":
fool horse Sophi if these lines were broken
down into such jewelled shorts word for word
they might exceed The Decline and Fall of
the American Poem by six folios,

A 18, 394

Such writing was also, at times, an attempt at public intervention. It might be declared to be the agent of social transformation, as with Pound, and with Zukofsky in the first half of his career. It might be declared the evidence of a society already transformed whether people knew it or not, a position Stein takes at times. For Joyce by the time of *Ulysses*, creating the conscience of his race might only mean creating a guilty conscience in Ireland for rejecting him. The gamut runs from bitterness to a fairly insane optimism, but in all cases the writing was urgently addressed to its contemporaries even though the message was delivered in a form that was "far ahead" of its time. How society was to catch up, aesthetically or politically, to writing that it by and large didn't read and couldn't understand if it did read was a mystery, one that is still there on every page.

In all four cases, narrative is an insoluble crux. *The Cantos* can't end or even progress. Pound's stories of great men setting their marks on history consistently fade into impalpability if not failure; the stories themselves grow more and more compressed, often, finally, into a phrase or single word. The Marxist political narrative that animates the first half of *"A"* collapses with the advent of the Second World War, leaving Zukofsky to assert that the quite disparate writing of the second half of the poem forms a natural, musical "poem of a life." Stein simply dismisses narrative by opposing it to the instantaneous present of genius; nevertheless, once her fame as a genius is established, she continually presents the unnarratable story of her success. *Ulysses* is a narrative, but as the book progresses the relations of the writing styles to that narrative become increasingly vexed. By the end, the cultural references are encyclopedic and the story told, but the one totality clashes with the other.

AESTHETICS AND THE JOB MARKET
FOR GENIUS

While I will be reading the writing of Pound, Joyce, Stein, and Zukofsky as demonstrating the tensions inherent in the social position of the writer, I first want to acknowledge how difficult it is to place their works in any argument that does not ultimately lead back to the works themselves: they are articulated to such a pitch of singularity that attempts to include them in other discourses are doomed to a rather daunting amount of translation. In fact, translation of various kinds dominates the criticism.

Explication has been primary. The writing seems to cry out for handbooks: beyond the massive syntheses they attempt, *The Cantos,* *"A,"* and *Ulysses* bulge with explicability at almost every word—references, repetitions or analogies of various dimensions, hermeneutic paradoxes—and even with the simpler-seeming texture of much of Stein's work, it takes a great deal of space to spell out the minute rhythmic changes and sudden opening-out of semantic vistas that are constantly occurring.

Appreciation often becomes a second kind of translation. Hugh Kenner stands out as particularly adept at turning *The Cantos* and other modernist works into stories of literary value at its peak. But Kenner's work is all translation: in his hands *The Cantos* becomes informative, anecdotal, fun, and even coherent (at least in places).[12] But such translation masks a basic feature of the original: never was literary value less perceptible to most readers. In *The Cantos*, anecdotes are severely truncated, reference is almost always elliptical, often to the point of paranoia, and the guarantee for coherence is finally Pound's consciousness—Kenner's ultimate object of celebration.[13]

A third type of translation uses the works as examples of linguistic processes that are widely representative, if not universal. Lacanian readings where the Joycean subject is dissolved into pure linguistic displacement, or where Pound illustrates the (tragic) impossibility of reaching through the symbolic back to the imaginary, or readings where Stein exemplifies antipatriarchal narrative or description—these are quite free translations in that they universalize their originals, whereas only an extreme need for singularity could have produced anything like *Ulysses*.[14] If Joyce's writing is paradigmatic of the traces left by the linguistic structure of the unconscious, then *Ulysses* (not to mention *Finnegans Wake*) becomes an exemplary instance of language—in other words, an authentic essence of language, an X ray of the real language of men.

Such claims of original, authentic universality extend but do not alter the standard Romantic pattern. For Wordsworth, while authentic language could be heard in the countryside, no one but the poet could write, that is, purposefully wield, the real language of men, and the reader had to put all specialization aside in order to share in the authentic and generalized humanity of the poet, which in fact could only be experienced while reading.[15] A similar dynamic occurs in the writing of these modernists (and it is reinforced by most critics): the language of the writing is universal, but the nonwriter is only a distant follower of the writer's activity. Joyce in *Ulysses* uses the language of "every" segment of society (and in *Finnegans Wake* he uses "every" language), but no one else can actively use that singular code, "Joyce's language." Much of the power of *Ulysses* comes from Joyce's masterful use of "lower" orders of language, but they are redeemed only by their transformation in the hands of the master. Not only is the artist's language beyond ordinary social use, no one can read it without training: to read it accurately is, if not a life's work, at least a full-time job. Of course, it can be argued that this is a job that can supply a synoptic, rather than a specialized, view of the modern world—the Arnoldian position; but, again, this argument only makes sense if one has spent a great deal of time translating these works into their universal content.

I want to suggest that these works be read in the original, without accepting the ancillary coherence supplied by the handbooks. This is not to say that the handbooks should be ignored, but rather that at a certain point it is necessary to forget the soothing coherence they add to the words of *The Cantos* or *Ulysses*. Rather than explicating, evaluating, selecting out thematic coherence, or using the works of these four writers to articulate an argument as to the nature of language, I want to keep strange the strangeness of their verbal surfaces and extreme rhetorical strategies, and at the same time see how this intensely specialized language is continually at the service of the most ambitious attempts at totalization and social authority.

These contradictions arise from attempts by these writers to unite various originary realms—the gods, the human mind, the order of nature—with a fallen or at least a finite historical everydayness. While their writing practices are, in theory, a thaumaturgy powerful enough to accomplish this, at the same time it is important to remember their often-marginal social position. While these works may have been written to express the originary, paradisal space where genius creates value, they do not travel directly to the mind of the ideal reader, the critic who accepts the transcendent claims of these works and the subsequent labor involved. They end up on a published page, in social space, between the author and the bored, cowed, intrigued, illuminated, rejected, plural readers in society. *The Cantos* is a "poem including history," true enough, but history includes *The Cantos* as well.

The polyvocality that critics often have found on their surfaces is traceable not so much to the struggles of various social strata as Bakhtin would have it but to the pressure the writers felt to master all of society, to write masterpieces. It can be said that *Ulysses* is a Bakhtinian carnival, that *The Cantos* displays the permanent open-endedness of language, that *"A"* is a nontotalizible sequence of disparate poetic strategies, and that Stein's works embody a determined effort to avoid closure by continually articulating a radically punctual present. But beyond this, these works display a powerful sense of proprietary control over both language and society. The aim is to abolish the distinction between writing and the world and to fuse social and literary value. The manner in which this fusion is to take place can vary from the complex attempt to duplicate, criticize, and master all of society that *Ulysses* represents to the opposite extreme, where Stein's writing can at times look arbitrary, without systematic reference to rhetorical conventions, as if Stein had boiled the act of writing down to the elemental "*I* [genius] *write* [a transcendent not a social activity] *words* [a masterpiece]." But at either extreme this ambitious fusion easily falls into relativism. For all but devout readers, *Ulysses* and *The Geographical History of America* are highly specialized literature.

The urge to bring the world under the sway of art can seem to put the writing of these four squarely in the category of the avant-garde. There are other similarities as well: Pound, at least when he's involved with *Blast*, looks a bit like Breton; early in her career Stein garnered a notoriety much like that of the Dadaists and Surrealists; and, if avant-garde art is thought to be difficult, a page from Tzara can look rudimentary when compared with most pages from these four. But it is important to distinguish them from the avant-garde. Here, I am using the limited but useful distinction of Peter Bürger, who defines the avant-garde as a series of tendencies that aim at overcoming the separation of art from everyday life.[16] However, this reunion involves an attempt to dismantle the institution of art and the aesthetic as an acknowledged cultural sphere. So, compared with Pound, Tzara *is* rudimentary. His recipe for a Dadaist self-portrait—picking newspaper cuttings out of a hat—while funny, was not ironic: the point was that anyone could produce a Dada work—though "work" is a misnomer in this case. On the other hand, no one but Pound could write *The Cantos*. Of the four, Stein is perhaps the closest to the avant-garde, and the complaints by Lewis, among many others, that her writing was childish prattle are a symptom of this. But as I will show, Stein's work is emphatically predicated on her own genius, and genius does not exist for the avant-garde as Bürger defines it.

While their valuations of the aesthetic were different, both the avant-gardistes and the high modernists faced roughly the same mass of potential readers. Where the avant-garde would call forth shock or scorn, the high modernist text when read naively would be more likely to produce perplexity, discomfort, and shame in the face of the infinite rereading required by Joyce, or the lifetime of research demanded by Pound. Although it could easily be argued that this naive reading would be worthless, it would be more accurate to consider it a constitutive feature of these works. The blankness that they proffer the neophyte needs to be considered as an integral part of their meaning, and not simply to be blamed on inadequate readers, schools, or societies. This is in the spirit of Benjamin's "There is no document of civilization which is not at the same time a document of barbarism,"[17] but I would like to eliminate the pejorative connotations in Benjamin's vocabulary. In the case of difficult modernism there is no document of refined criticism that is not at the same time a chasm of anxious boredom for many readers.

Near the end of *The Cantos*, Pound writes "without ²Mùan ¹bpö / no reality" (C *112*, 798). Having read the studies, I can translate this, and when I do the emphasis falls on "reality": Pound is again pointing to the transcendent essence of the world; he is referring to ceremonies of the Na-khi, an instance of his interest in the East and ritual; the ceremonial stories involve suicide, and the Na-khi have in fact died out: this rhymes with the despair of Pound's old age, his final silence and the broken ending of *The Cantos*. But the coherence this translation provides masks the more obvious significance of the lines, which is only visible on the (illegible) surface: the reader has no direct access to "without ²Mùan ¹bpö / no reality," in other words, no direct access to reality as Pound defines it. The first time Pound mentions "without ²Mùan ¹bpö / no reality," he adds, "There is no substitute for a lifetime" (C *98*, 705). Such valuations of the artist's life and consciousness, no matter how deeply tinged with irony, humor, bitterness they may be, are opposed to the shock and playfulness that the avant-garde used to break down the walls of high culture. Schematically: for Tzara *you* could draw words out of a hat; to read (let alone to write) *The Cantos*, there is no substitute for Pound's lifetime.

While the deep split between reader and writer, or between the social material used by the writer and the forms imposed on it, was similar in the four cases, it did not produce similar results. With generalizations about modernist language still common, it is important to emphasize that there is little formal congruence between the work of any of these four. Stein's stripped-down syntactic geometries are utterly different from the social and literary complexity present in any phrase of *Ulysses,* not to mention the subjective crash courses in the history of Indo-European displayed in the words of *Finnegans Wake.* Joyce and Zukofsky rewrote fanatically, whereas Pound and Stein were committed to spontaneity, Stein reacting to each new bare word, Pound improvising against a midden of books (physically there or not). But this doesn't unite Pound and Stein: nowhere in their literary work do these two sound remotely alike (their public pronouncements are another story however: both could be village explainers). She writes in sentences, often long, anomalous ones, while Pound, as *The Cantos* progresses, uses sentences less and less frequently. Stein uses a simple vocabulary; Pound certainly doesn't—he hardly writes in English for many lines at a time, and when he does it is more often than not eccentric and archaic. For Pound language is all reference; for Stein reference is "not really exciting" (*LIA,* 190–91). A single myth is used in *Ulysses* as a continuous grid, with irony a permanent though variable effect; Pound's eclectic and discontinuous use of myth always marks moments of transcendence; Zukofsky and Stein never use myth. *Ulysses* and *"A"* change styles at discrete intervals, but to very different purposes. Joyce's changes can be read as contributing to an enlarged sense of mimesis—either of quotidian reality or of Homeric myth—and thus as organic; or he can be seen as taking on newspapers, all of English prose, the Church, pulp narratives, and music in an attempt to meet every challenge to the autonomy and centrality of his own writing. On the other hand, the formal shifts in *"A"* are, with some early exceptions, emphatically nonorganic: artificial, arbitrary, and playful.[18] Even Pound and Zukofsky, generally regarded as master and disciple, display senses of poetic language that are finally quite opposed. Pound finds an originary presence in each word, so that his use of syntax becomes minimal as *The Cantos* progresses. Zukofsky, however, refashions English into something of a second language, so that far from registering any primal fullness, each word is often overcoded, belonging simultaneously to the semantic statement on the surface and to a translational, mathematical, or alphabetic game. Pound's exactitude has a theocratic basis: language is to be a reverent trace of state authority and divinity; for Zukofsky accuracy is the result of human labor: one of the ways this shows up in *"A"* is in the hypertrophied syntax.

On the literary-biographical level, there are obvious differences in politics: Pound was a Fascist; Zukofsky a Marxist; Joyce something of a socialist or anarchist—though in all three cases, their conception of the writer as definer and creator of social value left little room for the sense of commitment to any political movement implied by the suffix "ist." Stein's relation to politics was, to reverse the Freudianism, underdetermined: she can be called a feminist if one ignores her early Weininger-inspired misogyny, as well as the sexism of her salon arrangements and her sense of herself as belonging more to the category of genius than of woman. In her last years she displayed a *Saturday Evening Post*–like pro-Americanism. If some of her pronouncements on such subjects as "money" and "negroes" are marshaled together, she could be labeled a patrician.[19] But her views finally extended no further than her own position as a writer who was not a member of a profession, guild, or social group of any kind, but was a singular genius. Pound's allegiances, which were disastrously public, might seem the opposite of this, but his politics, too, were ultimately as imaginary as hers. I say this although I think it can be shown quite clearly that Pound was a Fascist (an eccentric one, though quite committed; he was not just a polite sympathizer like Eliot before the war), that his work never wavered in its support of Mussolini from the late twenties on, and that Fascism (along with anti-Semitism) was not an unfortunate virus, but that his writing, early and late, was founded on the need for the kind of social authority that Fascism seemed to represent. Nevertheless, Pound's politics were finally solipsistic, making sense only when viewed from the center of his writing.

So it is not by virtue of similarities of language or form or political orientation that I am grouping these four together. The disparity that they display can justify charges such as Perry Anderson's that modernism "is the emptiest of all cultural categories."[20] But the grouping I am proposing is useful precisely because of the singularity of the attempts of its members to build a more complete, if not utopian, world in writing. These efforts displayed a hierophantic conception in which writing floated down from a higher world of order that was fully accessible only to the genius-writer and that could be only partially revealed even to the devout reader. This power imbalance can be inverted, however, and looked at from the context of the market for print, where the writer, far from having any power, was an unacknowledged producer inhabiting a precarious market niche. It's not surprising then that these writers claimed such authority for their art and their status as artists while having only problematic social authority for most of their contemporaries. Within the confines of their discipline, they might be considered experts, masters of their craft, geniuses; outside those confines, there were pigeonholes with less complimentary labels: charlatan (Stein); pornographer (Joyce); nonentity (Zukofsky); or madman and traitor (Pound).

What this split embodies is the final flowering, or failure, of the aesthetic solution to the problem of the social position of the artist acutely dramatized by the Romantics. This problem, as it appeared at the end of the eighteenth century, seemed like a central social crux, and both the German aesthetic philosophers and the English Romantics proposed art as the cure for the suddenly all-too-visible displacement, violence, and repression resulting from industrialization and specialization. But there was always a flip side to this analysis, in which the aesthetic solution became the answer not to the problems of society at large but to the career dilemma of the individual artist or intellectual who could not find a place in an industrializing bourgeois society. However beneficial Coleridge's proposal to establish an intellectual clerisy might eventually prove to England as a whole, the most immediate beneficiaries would be intellectuals such as Coleridge.[21] Cynical as this may sound, in Pound's case the self-interest in his calls for educational reform is obvious, given the eccentricity of the proposed curriculum at the Ezruversity.

To repeat an earlier point, these writings were intended as masterpieces, displays of absolute cultural value. But as the productions of private individuals, they can be seen as masterpieces in the older sense: applications for the position of master in a guild. However, it was not the writers' guild Pound and the others wanted to join. Writers for the broad public, figures like Philip Beaufoy in *Ulysses* or middlebrow writers like H. G. Wells, were quite clearly not the company they aspired to keep. They were aiming for admittance to the guild of the genius, and their works were their applications. Once admitted, there were the eternal but intangible benefits to be awarded by the judgment of literary history, and in addition, the theoretical possibility of actual social prestige. Joyce and Stein eventually tasted this worldly success: for Joyce it meant patronage and fame, for Stein a puzzling fame. Pound's wartime radio broadcasts for Mussolini are more comprehensible if looked at from his own point of view, one in which a famous sage is employed to offer advice to a troubled world.

But as Pound's radio broadcasts demonstrate all too glaringly, the nature of the work that this guild performed was problematic: in its excellence and singularity the manufacture of a literary masterpiece was a performance that could not be reproduced. While these four made assertions of mastery that are often repeated (Zukofsky the "poet's poet," Pound having "the finest ear in English since Shakespeare"), can it be said that *"A," The Cantos, Tender Buttons, or Ulysses* give evidence of mastery of any craft other than that of their own production? Writing, for all four, was an inimitable practice. In *The Autobiography of Alice B. Toklas* Stein claims "that in english literature in her time she is the only one. She has always known it and now she says it" (*SW*, 72). There is one living genius per guild.

Olson's lines, "(o Po-ets, you / should getta / job," which make an uneasy and serious joke with lyrics from The Coasters, recognize a situation that had already been experienced by these four.[22] The anecdote of Stein's first meeting with Williams in Paris is illustrative. After small talk about their medical educations—which of course had led to a career for Williams only—Stein showed Williams the mass of her unpublished manuscripts and asked for advice. Williams, who at the time was himself no more published than Stein, said, with characteristic bitterness, to save the best and burn the rest. Stein dismissed this answer—and Doctor Williams—with equal bitterness, saying, "But then writing is not, of course, your métier."[23]

Writing was the métier of Stein and the others. Pound's only stretch of steady employment after World War One was broadcasting for Mussolini. This would have been more evidence of the superiority of Italy: they hired him—that is, they listened to him, at least in theory—while Senator Borah in *The Cantos* sums up his country's failure: "am sure I don't know what a man like you / would find to *do* here" (*C 84,* 551).

If these writers' commitment to the aesthetic solution—one that was growing ever more strained as the market for print diversified—is kept in mind, it can explain both the disparate formal features of their works, which in all cases are most significant when read as social, rhetorical strategies, and the many family resemblances their writing does display. These are far-reaching: all four have a superior relationship to readers and to everyday life; their writing has a tendency to resolve into a record of the writer's mind at work (or play) and hence into a kind of ongoing autobiography (*Work in Progress* is a generic title all of them could have used); and they claim to have obliterated the distinction between literature and society by revealing the ultimately aesthetic order of nature. This explanation will also account for the subsequent fate of their works as objects of study.

THE VICISSITUDES OF PUBLIC ART

Pound embodies the extremes. In everything he said and wrote there is a split between a rarified elitism aimed at selecting out the finest readers (or creating the most obedient ones) and a proselytizing that is wildly universal. This split appears at all levels: his journalistic drumbeating contrasts with the high art for which the drum was beaten; *The Cantos* as a whole contrasts with the radio broadcasts; or within *The Cantos*, the didactic universalism of both the mythology and the economic history is opposed to the abstruse and secretive references; or within a single line, the populist diction of " 'My bikini is worth yr/ raft'. Said Leucothae" (*C* 95, 659) clashes with its referent.

In many curious and often quite imaginary ways Pound was addressing the public, though it was not a public composed of either common or mass readers. The common reader, as posited by writers from Samuel Johnson to Virginia Woolf, is the educated nonspecialist, the consumer of more or less good books, whose tastes represented a market with which the ambitious writer had ultimately to come to terms. This figure, embodying an optimistic appeal to the ultimate aesthetic justice of the marketplace, could stand as an emblem of all that was wrong, for Pound, with the place of the writer in society and, in what is decidedly not a coincidence, with society itself. The common reader was a philistine, the embodiment of the university system, publishing houses, literary magazines, and newspaper reviewers—in other words, the enemy. This enemy lived in the world of money, and his incomprehension was an effect that was deliberately sought in *The Cantos*—sought far more thoroughly than many of his commonsense pronouncements on aesthetics would suggest. In some of Pound's better-known critical work, such as the *ABC of Reading* or *Guide to Kulchur*, it may appear that a figure very much like the common reader is being addressed, but it is not actually a reader (who after all has the autonomy of purchasing power), but a student who is the addressee. As for reaching a mass audience, Pound demonstrated a continual conflicted interest in such a possibility, writing journalism fluently early in his career while attacking the public in *Blast;* retreating from London and then from Paris to Rapallo but ultimately directing his radio broadcasts to the world at large—everyone and no one in particular. Pound wanted the distinction between journalism and literature to be abolished, at least in his own case. In *Jefferson and/or Mussolini* he rewrote his motto "Literature is news that STAYS news" in a way that nearly reverses its point: "literature is journalism that *stays* news" (*JM*, 9).

At first it might seem that Joyce was the least concerned of the four with publicity, or that whatever concern he may have felt about his personal success did not influence his activities as a writer. No journalism (with minor exceptions) or radio, no attempts at manifestos or movements, no attempts to reach the public (if we ignore his leaking of his charts, that is)—he simply wrote his books, which, whether read widely by the public or not, have been accorded the status of masterpieces by academia. The two halves of the picture seem to fit neatly—Nora's remark that Joyce had only Shakespeare to beat can stand as emblem of the striving for atemporal, high-cultural perfection; in *Exiles* the moment of Richard Rowan lighting up a cigarette in bitter celebration at the news of the sale of a thirty-seventh copy of his book shows us an author contemptuously re-signed to the indifference of a philistine public (*E*, 38). The central Joycean masterpiece, *Ulysses*, is often praised for its self-sufficiency. As mimesis it can seem almost more real than its object of imitation: behind Joyce's claim that a destroyed Dublin could be rebuilt from his description of it lies the more than semiserious assumption that *Ulysses* is more durable than the city.[24]

The book contains a complex of intricately nested patterns and symbols, leavened by provocative incommensurability, that is still rich enough, apparently, to last critics a few more decades. A current choice facing interpreters lies between describing the universe of *Ulysses* as closed or open. But these approaches, opposed as they seem, still treat the book as a self-defined high-culture artifact. In either case the surrounding world is lower, a relative chaos in the first instance, or, in the second, a vale of certainty blind to the revolutionary pleasures of jouissance.

But the mass dimensions of *Ulysses* have a more central function than that of merely supplying a Bloom as foil for Odysseus, or using what look like the defective public languages of "Nausicaa" or "Eumaeus" to form exquisite junk sculpture. This is not to say that Joyce wasn't displaying mastery. The shadow of malapropism looms large over Molly and to a lesser extent over Bloom, and there is condescension in the improbable charms Joyce builds into the *pensée sauvage* of Gerty MacDowell: "she wondered why you couldn't eat something poetical like violets or roses" (13.229–30). Nevertheless, Bloom and Molly are given a stature as large and serious as Joyce can conceive, and they are clearly meant to triumph over the crude materials of their construction. The quotidian may be redeemed through art, but beyond this Joyce's art is energized by the thoroughness with which he embraces the discourses of everyday life. If, to conform to the praise of Pound and Eliot, *Ulysses* had simply been composed in Joyce's early style of "scrupulous meanness" with a raft of Homeric correspondences thrown in, it would have been far less remarkable.[25]

The principal public dimension of *Ulysses* is the one over which Joyce displays as little mastery as Leopold Bloom does over Molly or Stephen over literary Dublin: the plot. Beneath its stylistic hurricanes and the higher calculus of its organization, *Ulysses* is a sturdy, unkillable narrative that always reemerges as the focus of attention no matter how vigorously its styles, and ultimately its author, may try to upstage it or expand its scope to the stars. The two components of the narrative, the *Bildungsroman* centered on Stephen and the story of the Blooms' marriage, are always present, even during the relatively few moments when other concerns are more prominent. During the two episodes when Joyce is critiquing the heroic daydreams of Irish nationalism, "Cyclops" and "Eumaeus," Bloom's impotence is foregrounded in the former, and the themes of adultery, returning husbands, and the neglected artist are prominent in the latter. This may be seen as another example of Joyce's coherent composition, but when compared with many other major novels, and certainly with those of similar length, the narrative focus of *Ulysses* is narrow.

This narrowness is masked by the density of detail and the massive stylistic conquests. Because of this, a number of critics have asserted that the story of *Ulysses* doesn't matter. Franco Moretti writes, "Very little happens in the book. . . . [T]he multiplicity of styles . . . focuses [our attention] entirely on the various ways in which events can be seen."[26] I think it would be more accurate, however, to turn this around. When seen from the perspective of society as a whole, "very little happens," but Joyce holds to the two stories he cares most about, marriage and the fate of the artist, with tremendous passion and notices every crumb of discredit that falls on Bloom and Stephen. The imbalances at the center of these stories, Stephen's alienation and Bloom's cuckoldry, while never set right at the narrative level, are the primary fuel for the stylistic explosiveness and the mythic reach of the book. As these narratives move toward their problematic noncompletions, the stylistic and symbolic dimensions of the book expand to compensate.

Stephen is marginalized at school, at the office of the *Freeman's Journal*, and in the library. The three avenues open to the intellectual—education, journalism, and literature—are closed to him. By the end of the book, he is about to have no job, no place to live, and has been snubbed by the second-rate literati of Dublin. It's no surprise that in talking with Deasy in "Nestor" and Bloom in "Eumaeus" he separates himself as much as possible from history, work, and nation.[27] The only way for his *Bildungsroman* to come out right would be for him to write a book as universal as *Ulysses,* one in which history would be sublated into order and myth, and beyond that into art.

A similar split in narrative outcome occurs with Bloom. In addition to his social ostracism, Bloom is of course cuckolded—and not merely that: his wife says (exaggerating, some critics claim) that she has been "fucked yes and damn well fucked too almost to [the] neck nearly not by him 5 or 6 times" (18.1511–12). In terms of a conventional narrative of marriage, this is about as bad as things can get— the phrase even includes Molly's sacred Yes—and it occurs almost at the very end of the story. Joyce hedges the negativity of this by giving many indications of Bloom's centrality to Molly, including her last Yes. But the narrative ends with the imbalance not so much overcome as blended in. Of course, "above" the narrative level, Bloom as Odysseus triumphs as he "slays" the "suitors" and Molly as Penelope loves "only" him. Scare quotes proliferate in this description because the price paid for this happy ending is high. For the suitors to be slain Bloom as a character has to feel his emotions in Joyce's words. It is crucial to the plot that the character Bloom feel "envy, jealousy, abnegation, equanimity," but his experience of these emotions is conveyed, not in the language of his inner monologs, but in Joyce's. At the same time Bloom has to have his integrity as a character thinned out to merge with the physical and temporal extent of the cosmos. Bloom the character has to come to terms with his wife's infidelity; Bloom the transmasculine counter in Joyce's mythic scheme has to touch all the water on earth when he fills the kettle, be dissolved to nothing, merge his name with Stephen, etcetera. And for Penelope to be true, Bloom has to merge with all men in Molly's monolog.

At the level of plot this completion is equivocal. It depends on how convincingly Joyce writes, but criteria for what is convincing float between conventional narrative mimesis and the cosmic overtones of a sacred marriage between Everyman-Odysseus and Gea-Tellus. Are mistakes possible here, or does every additional complexity simply add harmony to harmony? How connect Bloom the exquisite emotionalist of the "envy, jealousy, abnegation, and pity" sequence with the tacky fantasizer of "Flowerville" a few pages back? Wouldn't Bloom at least mind the crumbs of Plumtree's Potted Meat in the bed, especially after he's just bumped his head against the sideboard Boylan moved that afternoon? Perhaps he's a masochist, as is temporarily revealed in "Circe." But would a masochist stand up to the Citizen as Bloom does in "Cyclops"? My point here is not that "even Joyce nods." Rather it is to show what a volatile unity he has posited, how thoroughly narrative the book is, and how the strains that exist on the narrative level are symptoms of a relation between art and the world that makes the story narrated within *Ulysses* impossible and thus calls for the existence of *Ulysses* as a stylistic antinarrative masterpiece.

Joyce's use of Molly as a summation of the multitude of social voices and forces in *Ulysses*, as the "perfectly sane full amoral fertilisable untrustworthy engaging shrewd limited prudent indifferent *Weib*," the flesh that always says yes (*JJ*, 501–2), creates a very strong appeal to closure, suggesting that not only is *Ulysses* completed, but quite possibly all of Western literature as well, now that Woman and Flesh have been given voice (a "womanly," "fleshy" one, of course). Even so cool and competitive a reader as T. S. Eliot felt this for at least one moment, crying out to Virginia Woolf, "How could anyone write again after achieving the immense prodigy of the last chapter?" (*JJ*, 528).[28] To suggest that the structure—not simply the content—of *Ulysses* is contingent is to resist this appeal.

Stein was as serious a writer as Pound or Joyce, but the radical plainness of her vocabulary can obscure this. After years of notoriety for supposedly writing gibberish, she rose to actual fame during which the Olympian and gossipy persona she developed provoked some demand for her writing, as well as making her into something like the first talk-show personality *avant la lettre*. Her popular work was fairly widely read, and she used her success to get Bennett Cerf at Random House to publish her serious work as well. From a Poundian perspective, Stein would hardly count as a "serious artist," especially in this later phase. Perhaps her early work could be assigned to his faintly honorable category of "patient testing of media" (*LE*, 55). But certainly *The Autobiography of Alice B. Toklas* would be damned as mere entertainment. And compared with Pound's and Zukofsky's obsessions with rigorous definition in poetics, economics, and history, Stein's pronouncements about money, history, and art would seem coy at best:

> They read master-pieces, I read what are not master-pieces but which quote pieces of master-pieces in them. And what do I find I find that comparisons and human nature is not what makes master-pieces interesting.
> But money and a word and romanticism.
> They they have nothing of any human nature in them.
> And thank you for not.
> Money and words and romanticism have no time or identity in them, oh please certainly not.
>
> *GHOA*, 168

One can easily imagine the disgust Pound might have felt, and Wyndham Lewis's contempt is on record.[29] Stein is somewhat immune today from such attacks in the name of literature's heroic masculinity. Her work, with its valuation of play, repetition, and meditation, is seen by some feminist critics as a critique of patriarchal narrative and aesthetics, and at many points (though not always) Stein indicates her awareness of the importance of gender and sexuality to her writing. However, to see her simply as a feminist opposed to male modernism, and as a lesbian writer, gives only a partial view of her work. It is important to realize how thoroughly she concerns herself with the same problem that confronted Pound and Zukofsky, that of addressing the public in language more real than it could read.

This is the case in her difficult as well as her popular works. To get a sense of this, one could compare the beginning of *The Autobiography of Alice B. Toklas,* where Toklas tells of having met three geniuses—Picasso, Whitehead, and Stein—with the following lines from "Stanzas in Meditation," a second "autobiography" written more or less simultaneously:

Stanza XIII

.   .   .   .
Which in the midst of can and at bay
Which they could be for it as once in a while
Please can they come there.
This is an autobiography in two instances.

Stanza XIV

.   .   .   .
She knew that she could know
That a genius was a genius
Because just so she could know
She did know three or so
So she says and what she says
No one can deny or try

YGS, 389–90

Granted, this resists paraphrase; Stein's use of painters as models for what she was trying to accomplish always allows for the possibility of a writing from which, at any given point, semantic and syntactic pressure can suddenly disappear. In other words, rather than tortuously resolving "Which in the midst of can and at bay" into an approximation of "having ability but surrounded by enemies," a better approach might be to simply read the line in a "painterly" (or "musical") fashion, as a succession of nine one-syllable words. Nevertheless, at certain points here conventional syntax obtrudes, and it seems crucial for the writer to have the acknowledged power of predication, to be believed when she calls a genius a genius. And in the painting context where Stein situated herself, the issue of how believable a claim to genius might be had a very real effect on the aesthetic, and ultimately the monetary, value of a given painter's work.

Similarly, in *Toklas* the claim put into Toklas's words that Stein was one of only "three first class geniuses" (*SW*, 5) may be seen as bravado, ego, or a display of charming eccentricity, but it is more: it is the premise of the book. The stories told in a way that emphasizes Stein's and Toklas's presence at the events rather than the texture of the events themselves, the hinted-at, suppressed stories ("But what a story that of the real Hem, and one he should tell himself but alas he never will" (*SW*, 204), the assessments of the rankings of painters, and the overall easy carelessness of the narrative sequence—all would fall flat unless Stein could claim complete authority as the equal of Picasso, and the coruler of the Parisian art world. If Stein hints at it, the dirt on Hemingway becomes intriguing, but the identical words in the mouth of a tourist from Muncie? The book, predicated on her genius and causing that claim to be more publicly plausible, thus becomes a nonfictional *Bildungsroman* where the actual author, not the presented narrator, overcomes obstacles to reach a harmonious reconciliation with society in real time. Telling the story of a writer who would never be published by such mainstream magazines as *The Atlantic Monthly*, *Toklas* was in fact first serialized in that magazine. The categories of genius and masterpiece are crucial in solving the problem of the social value of writing for Stein, and in the writing of her job description. However self-defined those categories were for her, they were finally directed outward: a masterpiece was not simply to be submitted silently to the judgment of eternity; the value of a masterpiece was to be impressed on the public. One of Stein's refrains, the performative "Yes you see what I mean," epitomizes this aggressive outreach—although the fact that, according to Stein, genius cannot be narrated contributes to the anxiety of its less frequent echo: "Do you see what I mean?"

Compared with the other three, Zukofsky's relations with the public were slight indeed: his career began with modest notice, became lodged in deep obscurity, and included a bit of specialized acclaim only at the end. He began by imitating Pound's attitude toward the common reader, although the competitive edge he aimed at the educational establishment was even sharper. His scornful fascination with academia shows up in his first poem, "Poem beginning 'The' " (*CSP*, 7–20), a reply to *The Waste Land* with numbered lines and provocative but nevertheless scholarly notes. The prose of his essays, in turns jumpy and scrupulous, demonstrates a similar defensive aggression: he was aiming to write more precisely than any mere professor. He wasn't trying to overthrow the idea of literary standards; witness his parallel to Pound's *ABC of Reading, A Test of Poetry*. While he began his career with an aim of public intervention similar to Pound's, there were major differences. Pound intervened from a position of subjective and to some extent actual power: possessor of vital poetic information, the grandson of a congressman, he felt himself important the moment he set foot in London and in fact quickly made himself (relatively) important. He was already in possession of a significant amount of literary capital when he began to take on the role of public intellectual. On the other hand, Zukofsky was the son of Yiddish-speaking immigrants and had hardly broken into print at the time of his generalship of the "Objectivists" project. For Pound the cultural heritage was there to be identified with and transformed: *The Cantos* begins with that Arnoldian bastion of nature, Homer, and Pound confidently puts his mark on the translation. *"A"* begins in parallel fashion with Bach, an equally natural fact for Zukofsky, except that Bach is exactly what Zukofsky's world can no longer make true.

In his major poems of the 1930s—the seventh and eighth movements of *"A,"* the first half of the ninth movement, and the sestina plus verse-commentary "Mantis" (*CSP*, 65–73)—an intense ambivalence shows up in his address to the public. Once decoded, these poems can be read as anthems to labor and denunciations of capitalism and of the plight of the poor. But as sonnet sequences and sestinas they display tremendous technical ambition; their reference, in *"A"*-8 and *"A"*-9 especially, is hermetic, and their rhetoric is dense and at times "exact" to the point that it is often nearly impossible to decipher them as grammatical, let alone social, speech. In the first half of *"A"*-9, Zukofsky sets words taken from the Everyman edition of *Capital* to the intricate rhyme scheme from Cavalcanti's canzone "Donna Mi Prega."[30] The verbal surface that results from this—and there are other formal procedures operating as well—needs to be decoded a few words at a time, or perhaps contemplated as a pattern in which a deeply complex meaning inheres but from which it does not actually emerge. And yet what is being said is urgently social: capitalism robs workers of the value of their labor. The rhetorical fiction of *"A"*-9 is that things—which should be artifacts but are commodities due to exchange manipulations—are speaking; and the poem, by foregrounding the tremendous labor that went into its making, is to escape the hell of commodification and to achieve the status of redeemed artifact. Here, in as literal a way as can be imagined, Zukofsky is aiming to unite literary and social value. But if the poem is speaking for the workers and speaking as an object of nonexploited labor, it is not speaking *to* anyone. This was true in physical fact—the poem was published privately in an edition of fifty-five mimeographed copies, just enough to establish copyright—but equally true with regard to rhetoric. The cathexis to Pound and Cavalcanti outweighs the gestures toward Marx and social intervention. There was no attempt, in terms of distribution or of the writing itself, to reach the labor movement, to whom the poem's aesthetic strategies of private poetic labor would have seemed utopian at best, if not simply mandarin.

But Zukofsky was also addressing the public urgently; he wasn't joking when he wrote in the introduction to the *"Objectivists" Anthology*, "The 'objectivists' number of *Poetry* appeared in February. Since then there have been March, April, May, June, July and we are now past the middle of August. Don't write, telegraph."[31]

Zukofsky never again brought the problem of the social value of writing to so tortured a conclusion as in *"A"*-9. After the war, while not explicitly recanting his Marxism, he ceased to mention it and turned from Marx to Spinoza, and from politics to his family, with literary sources and minutiae of family life indifferently supplying matter for the continuing intense formality of the writing.[32] But the poet who early on proclaimed his work to arise out of a "desire / for what is objectively perfect / Inextricably the direction of historic and contemporary particulars" (*A*, 24) no longer attempted to be in any sense an agent of history or even a public presence.

Whatever public impact these writers had during their careers, they now share a similar fate in that they have become, to varying degrees, critical touchstones in a post-Arnoldian sense that is not finally all that different from Arnold's own usage: for him a touchstone embodied cultural value; now, it is a critical value that is attributed to these works and/or writers.

I mean the "and/or" to indicate that the distinction between author and text can get blurry at times in the criticism. In fact the death of the author—in the case of Joyce especially—has meant often enough the rebirth of a transcendent authorizer of readerly free play.

But in many cases the value that is asserted to inhere in the reading is only at the service of narratives of critical authority. As burdens of reading the work of these four can force us into situations of permanent debt—a freedom to read that entails submission to endless free play where the playground is an already-written page reconstituted by professional interpretation.

Georg Lukács provides an image of an inverted but not dissimilar situation. Writing of "The Antinomies of Bourgeois Thought," he describes the divorce of method from material, where the "underlying material base is permitted to dwell inviolate and undisturbed in its irrationality ('non-createdness', 'givenness') so that it becomes possible to operate with unproblematic, rational categories in the resulting methodologically purified world."[33] The gap between the precarious totalizations these works attempted and the professionalized use that is now made of them is similar. I do not share Lukács's faith that the trajectory of historical process will necessarily overcome such antinomies. But I am drawn to the work of these four because I see in its often implausible aesthetic claims over society an opportunity to show that writing in all its dimensions is fully social.

2

Pound and the Language of Genius

"—Bosh! Stephen said rudely. A man of genius makes no mistakes. His errors are volitional and are the portals of discovery" (*U*, 9.228–29). Reading this passage from *Ulysses* in context, we can't escape its novelistic ironies: it is a defensive remark made by a fictional would-be author fighting exclusion by the midrange literary lights of Dublin. The irony is substantial as well as dramatic, since we are also meant to consider the statement true: it is at least partially autobiographical, and *Ulysses* courts error successfully.

The existence of such a redemptive literary space surrounding Ezra Pound and *The Cantos* is much more doubtful. While poets, critics, and journalists continue to argue about Pound, one point on which there is widespread consensus is that—to say the least—he made mistakes. But I want to apply Stephen's remarks to Pound because the elements they constellate—rudeness, genius, error, and volition—are central to an understanding of his writing and his career. I will not be inverting Stephen's definition to say that Pound was a genius who made mistakes. Even though he ended up deploring his "errors and wrecks" (*C 116*, 810), Pound stays within Stephen's definition: the notion of the genius who transcends error is central to Pound's career, his language, and the problematic literary status of *The Cantos*.

Another way to open up the paradox of Pound is to take the advice he offers in *Jefferson and/or Mussolini* and apply it to himself rather than to Mussolini: "Jefferson was one genius and Mussolini is another. . . . Any thorough judgment of MUSSOLINI will be in a measure an act of faith, it will depend on what you *believe* the man means. . . . Treat him as *artifex* and all the details fall into place. Take him as anything save the artist and you will get muddled in contradictions" (*JM*, 19, 33–34).

If we are to judge by the historical outcome, Pound himself was deeply muddled. The book, written in 1933 during the weeks after his single, perfunctory meeting with his imagined Boss, Mussolini, displays the frantic claims on the future that so clouded Pound's vision of his own present. But I want to invoke this obsessive, gambling immediacy because I think that it makes an accurate introduction to the whole of his work. Seen through the lens of Pound's faith, Mussolini the *artifex,* the artist of the State, was a genius—a union of utter acuity and irresistible force who perceived multiple perspectives instantly and had only to pronounce his clear and powerful word to create social value, a new language, and a new world. He was not an artist in a separated aesthetic sphere; neither was Pound. Even though for those of us who read him decades later the time for faith in Pound's political/literary future is past, it is important to remember how thoroughly such a model of action and efficacy informed his work.

Of course it also deformed it. The coin of Poundian genius has two sides, and as it circulates in the world the second side is especially visible; authority, speed, and range are inseparable from rage, incoherence, and paranoid obscurity. In other words, Pound's fascination with genius is thoroughly entangled with his Fascist commitments and anti-Semitic obsessions. But analysis cannot strictly confine the problematics of genius to some infected portions of his work: they are present from before World War One through the sixties, although they become more tenuous as they are traced back to his earlier years. Of course the mixed narrative of his career provides gradations: if we want to separate Pound's writing into lodes of literary value and landfills of political dreck, then it's easy enough to say that the early essays and *ABC of Reading* are more benign than *Gold and Work;* the first cantos and *Drafts and Fragments* are more benign than the cantos of the thirties and early forties; *The Cantos* as a whole is more benign than the radio speeches. And even within that dismal bulk some pages are better than others; for instance, in "E. E. Cummings Examined" Pound discusses *Eimi* and *Ulysses* almost exclusively, throwing in an intriguing paragraph on the Jamesian parenthesis as a characteristically American gesture, before veering back to "Dr. Freud's imported stinks," "Jew propaganda," and praise for the writings of Hitler and Mussolini (*RS,* 144).

But reading Pound in terms of passages that are "more benign" is a defensive strategy that will not finally do justice to his work.

Justice is a key concept for Pound, politically, economically, and, through his passion for *le mot juste*, aesthetically, but it is also a traumatic concept for critics who try to assess him and his work: the legal questions raised by his indictment for treason are vexed enough, and the concomitant problems of literary judgment triggered by the Bollingen award are at least as vexed. As a relief from these knots, a literary Pound becomes attractive: it is this figure of the witty, generous, combative producer and entrepreneur of modernism who has inspired some of the best of subsequent American poetry and has engendered a large body of criticism.

Pound was an innovative, often inspired translator and has had a widespread and beneficent influence. He brought a new rhetoric into English in *Cathay,* and "Homage to Sextus Propertius," with its serious, playful aggression toward the classics, demonstrated an oblique but passionate sense of civic-aesthetic responsibility that most readers didn't catch for many decades. As essayist, editor, journalist, letter writer, and instigator he was a crucial figure in the creation and promotion of Anglo-American modernism: Donald Hall's assessment is that "in the history of literature, no writer equals Pound in accuracy of taste, or in energetic magnanimity."[1] I would add that even during the increasingly solipsistic second half of his career his passionate belief in the importance of literature remained unmatched. "Mauberley" and some other early poems fit into anthologies easily, and passages from *The Cantos* can be squeezed in with more difficulty.

But when we come to *The Cantos* we cannot wish away the connections between the ambition and aggression that are positive virtues in his early writing and the rhetorical violence and moral blindness of his later politics. Painful as Pound's Fascism and racism are, and attractive as some of his poetry, literary insights, and pronouncements can be, nevertheless I want to insist on reading him whole. This means reading *The Cantos* as a single project, which in turn, given the nature of its references, involves looking at the rest of his writing and public actions. Pound must be read as *artifex*. This will not mean that "all the details [will] fall into place," either within his literary work or outside it. I will not be attempting to make *The Cantos* cohere, nor will I be claiming that the poem forms a seamless unity with the radio speeches. Pound at various points was writing an epic, saving the Constitution, constructing the Confucian-Fascist blueprint for the Salò Republic, and building "the city of Dioce whose terraces are the colour of stars." In other words, treating Pound as *artifex* will mean that distinctions between the literary and extraliterary become difficult to draw: the supreme social importance of a highly specialized conception of literature is the spur that drives him out into public space. There is a continuous contradictoriness built into Pound's notion of the genius that makes all the details of his writing fall into the charged and problematic place from which they continue to pose crucial questions about politics, aesthetics, and ethics. What gives the best of Pound's writing its power cannot be dissociated from the worst of it.

Another of Pound's descriptions will be instructive: "Apart from the social aspect he was of interest, technically, to serious writers. He never wrote a sentence that has any interest in itself, but he evolved almost a new medium, a sort of expression half way between writing and action" (*SP,* 217). The textual referent here is Lenin, but since Pound knew no Russian, it seems more appropriate to apply his remarks to the generalized Poundian hero, who manifests his genius by manipulating words and—in the central Poundian shortcut—thus changes society without touching it. The contradiction here, that Lenin as writer is hardly a writer and is thus of special interest to serious writers, applies to Pound in a complex manner. Pound's action clearly did not have the efficacy of Lenin's, and many of Pound's sentences remain of interest. But the continual leaps of reference and play of humor, indignation, and aggression that make them interesting are not simply the result of a formal rhetoric: they are situational. Consider both the content and the style of the following Poundian action-writing:

> No british minister, let alone chief bleeder or Chancellor of Exchequer, wd. have the moral courage to pass half an hour in my company discussing, even in parliamentary language, the nature of money, or the infamy of starving the people. . . .
>
> I have no doubt that the reader will think this expression violent, and I shd. think so myself if I had not seen in the flesh a British Colonel . . . shrink from a sheet of paper carrying my 8 Volitionist questions as if it had been an asp or a red-hot iron.
>
> I shoved it into the pocket of his dinner jacket but doubt if he has ever had the moral courage to look at it. "Les hommes ont je ne sais quel peur étrange de la beauté" and that ain't the 'arf ov it dearie.

The kakotropic urge in economics is beyond anything a normal man can believe without long experience. They fear the light as no bed-bug ever feared it.[2]

GK, 250

When writing *Guide to Kulchur* Pound was both encyclopedist and complete outsider, and his eccentric attempts to influence the *res publica* often give his writing the quality of a manifesto shoved into someone's dinner jacket. One could say that Pound means well here—he's disgusted at "the infamy of starving the people"; one could say that his metaphorical connections between beauty and the light of economic truth are inspiring, humorous, and very rapid; and one could say that the last sentence shows a paranoia that is similar in its metaphors to Hitler's writing in *Mein Kampf:* "Was there ever any form of filth or profligacy, particularly in cultural life, without at least one Jew involved in it? If you cut even cautiously into such an abscess, you found, like a maggot in a rotting body, often dazzled by the sudden light, a kike!"[3]

One of Pound's principle contradictions is that he's also deeply involved in—his identity is built around—what Hitler sees as cultural filth. Pound is both Fascist surgeon and linguistic maggot. This tangles the dynamics of his address, even as he continually advocates elemental language. Note the snarl in the last paragraph of the *Kulchur* excerpt: normal man—politically neutral man presumably—cannot believe the kakotropic urge in economics. Who has this urge? "They" do. But how divide "them" from "normal men"? The normal man who can't believe is hard to keep separate from the evil people who fear the light. Presumably a normal man is capable of being enlightened. Perhaps so, but the key educational term, "kakotropic," seems designed to make his normal linguistic status a barrier to understanding. Such a split, greatly exacerbated, will result in Pound's being indicted for treason by the normal people he was ostensibly trying to instruct. The split/fused French and Cockney sentence, "peur étrange . . . and that ain't the 'arf ov it," is funny but it typifies the dynamics of an address that is simultaneously demotic and exclusive.

Attempting to see Pound's work as a whole thus will involve some wide stretches. The worst of Pound's writing is very different politically, morally, and stylistically from Hitler's, but it is very bad nevertheless.[4] It is not easy to consider the following examples as parts of the same whole.

the passage clean-squared in granite:
   descending,
and I through this, and into the earth,
   patet terra,
entered the quiet air
   the new sky,
the light as after a sun-set,
   and by their fountains, the heroes,
Sigismundo, and Malatesta Novello,
   and founders, gazing at the mounts of their cities.
         C 16, 69

 And now I hear New York meat is slaughtered by chewisch butchers, or was a decade ago. Mebbe now there is [more?] of it to slaughter.
Mebbe all American meat is slaughtered by Jewish butchers. Beef as
wuz. Long pig as may be. (Yaaas, long pig is what the cannibals call
it.) . . . the worst of it is that, if you spend your time looking into it, it
will prevent you from filling your mind with the light of the classics.
         RS, 331

The conundrum in this last sentence applies to anyone trying to
come to terms with Pound's work: why spend time looking at such
stupid outpourings when much of his writing would seem to be
much more sane and "light-filled"?

 Throughout his career, Pound used "light" as a shorthand for a
complex set of values that were simultaneously obvious, secret, and
of overwhelming social importance. Later I will be touching on the
senses of sacred sexual initiation and political authority bound up
in Pound's usage.[5] However, there is a generalized referent that can
finesse these problematic areas: inspiration or poetic value. *The Cantos* ends with well-known light images:

  A blown husk that is finished
   but the light sings eternal
  a pale flare over marshes
    where the salt hay whispers to tide's change
        C 115, 808

  Can you enter the great acorn of light?
   But the beauty is not the madness

 . . . .
  A little light, like a rushlight
    to lead back to splendour.
       C 116, 809, 811

Add one of Pound's best-known prose dicta: "Man reading shd. be man intensely alive. The book shd. be a ball of light in one's hand" (*GK*, 55). These lines and phrases have often been cited. This is due to their lyricism and ambition, but also, I think, because they're inoffensive. I imagine I'm not alone in having felt relief when reading passages that did not contain any of Pound's "excesses." Such dynamics will explain the readiness with which Pound's light is accepted as a neutral symbol of value in some generalized literary sense in spite of its frequent political connotations.

To connect the Fascist light of the radio speeches and the wartime prose with the literary light in Canto 16—to read Pound's later politics back into a passage written in the mid-twenties—is seemingly to ignore the narrative of his career. It is a compelling narrative, but we shouldn't let the apologies and agonies of Pound's late years obscure the dynamics of his literary address, which survive steadily.

Narrative will be a particularly touchy subject for the Poundian genius; for now, let me note that reading Canto 16 as if it were governed by Pound's later thematics upsets the compromise by which some purely literary value can be assigned to select parts of his work. This compromise treats Pound somewhat the way Pound claimed that Mussolini acted toward Spain:

> And Muss saved, rem salvavit,
>   in Spain
>   il salvabile.
>   C 105, 760

I am asserting that we cannot really "save the savable" in Pound; we cannot save him from his politics and from Mussolini; we cannot divide his literary light from his Fascist light and his conception of genius.

The purely literary aspect of *The Cantos* is a fragile picture. It is only by keeping our attention focused on the immediate sound and image environment that we can keep the above-quoted passage from Canto 16 free of the elements that so troubled Pound later. Of course the lines from Canto 16 are not Fascist, but they do anticipate Pound's later idolatry of Mussolini. Malatesta is a forerunner of the Boss with all the proper attributes: he has daring, panache, and a passion for construction; he treats artists well and is "a male of the species," as Pound said of Mussolini.[6] In these lines he is posed as *artifex*. The lyricism of the verse is as "clean-squared" as the physical passage it describes, but this does not mean it is not fully involved in Pound's aesthetic-political struggles. The re-entry into the earth here in 16 is accomplished with elemental nouns that receive spondaic and trochaic stress, plus a line of Latin thrown in to heighten the sacramental tinge: this is Pound's typical clean sound. But occurring as it does directly after the narrator has emerged from the excremental, multiplicious horrors of a Medusan hell in the prior two cantos, the passage becomes an odd second descent into the underworld—this time a benign one into a clean, male space. In narrative terms, the passage is sandwiched between hell behind and the trenches of World War One ahead. If this contrast is remembered, then Pound's lyricism becomes more bound up with what it ostensibly escapes.

If we try to deny the shit, slaughter, and madness it is surrounded by, then "entered the quiet air / the new sky, / the light as after a sun-set, / and by their fountains, the heroes" can be read simply as a clean evocation of positive virtues. But we shouldn't let the desire to find a haven of literary innocence in Pound's work disguise the fact that such isolated and innocuous pictures are not all that different in tone and force from a Maxfield Parrish painting: pillars and Nature, god-heroes and nymphs, "light as after a sun-set."

Poundian light is a more disturbing force than that. His furious embrace of politics may well have been fueled by a need to flee the specter of such innocuous decorum. Whatever its roots, this light, while it is used to mark a transcendent dimension, is never free from literary and political engagements:

> To Kung, to avoid their encirclement,
> To the Odes to escape abstract yatter,
>   to Mencius, Dante, and Agassiz
>   for Gestalt seed,
> pity, yes, for the infected,
>   but maintain antisepsis,
>   let the light pour.
>
> C 94, 649

Confucius, Mencius, Dante, and Agassiz are, for Pound, the geniuses of government, art, and science. But his assertion of light as antisepsis evokes the contamination it dreads: encirclement, abstraction, infection.

The most compact demonstration of the binary nature of Poundian light occurs in a nearby passage from Canto 91. The canto begins
with an extended four-page invocation of light, at the end of which
the following lines occur:

> Over harm
> Over hate
>   overflooding, light over light
> And yilden he gon rere
>   (Athelstan before a. D. 940)
> the light flowing, whelming the stars.
>   In the barge of Ra-Set
> On river of crystal
> So hath Sibile a boken isette.
> *Democracies electing their sewage*
> *till there is no clear thought about holiness*
> *a dung flow from 1913*
> *and, in this, their kikery functioned, Marx, Freud*
> *   and the american beaneries*
> *Filth under filth,*
> *   Maritain, Hutchins,*
> *or as Benda remarked: "La trahison"*
>   and damn all
>   I wd/ like to see Verona again
> "ecco il tè"
>
>   C 91, 627–28

The middle lines of this excerpt, italicized by Pound, are probably
the most notorious in the poem. I end this introductory section with
them not to castigate Pound's political judgment (though I am certainly not praising it) but to remind readers that the vast effort he
made to energize poetic language, to live in epic conditions, and to
change the world are as present here as elsewhere in *The Cantos*. Of
course, these lines are not as good as some others, but the point is
that they are not all that distinct in style and theme.

The politics of *"democracies electing their sewage"* are of a piece
with the condemnation of usury and nonauthoritative government
throughout the poem. And as we will see, the nastiness of tone enacts a political mimesis in the same fashion as the spare cleanness
of "Sun up: to work" in Canto 49. The next line, *"till there is no clear
thought about holiness,"* articulates the pervasive concern for the sacred that animates some of the most memorable lines in the poem.
The shift to *"a dung flow from 1913"* is part of a persistent pattern of

elegaic shift in which Pound laments the lack of effect of the sacred upon history:

> Your eyen two wol sleye me sodenly
> I may the beauté of hem nat susteyne

> And for 180 years almost nothing.
>
> *C 81*, 534

The combination of the scatological (*a dung flow*) and a specific moment in history (*from 1913*) occurs throughout: Pound's rage is sparked by the refractory particulars of history. The use of isolated proper names—"*Marx, Freud* . . . Maritain, Hutchins"—to damn or bless is typical Poundian shorthand; compare "Mencius, Dante, and Agassiz." As we will see, the rhetorical pattern of a name followed by a phrase that can be enigmatic—"*or as Benda remarked: 'La trahison' "*—is a characteristic mode of heroic address for the genius. The last three lines are a minor example of the reminiscing that adds such pathos to the *Pisan Cantos*.[7] The fact that the passage as a whole moves without transition from large themes to extremely local details is typically Poundian.

I've left *"kikery"* for last. In it, we can see encapsulated Pound's anti-Semitism, Fascism, and the paranoiac conspiracies that dominate his perception of history. If it were omitted from the lines they would be considerably less offensive—by itself, the bee in Pound's bonnet concerning Freud is almost comic (such resistance is ideal grist for Freud's mill). But I see no way of excluding "kikery" from Pound's work that doesn't mimic his own phobias. Pound's response to what he saw as "kikery" was to call for "the surgeon's knife of Fascism" (*SP*, 300) and to write as if he were one of the heroic few wielding it: are we to respond to all his overt manifestations of Fascism and anti-Semitism by cutting them out of our reading experience with the critic's knife of embarrassed tact? "Kikery," though not funny, is the same type of word as "beaneries," Pound's humorous, aggressive name for universities that encodes impatience with conventional curricula, conflating brains and baked beans, pedagogic prose and farting. The project visible in *ABC of Reading* and *Guide to Kulchur*, the desire to make literature and society yield to instantaneous heroic intention, is behind the word "beaneries"; a similar desire to master history is present in "kikery."

Pound's passion for justice, his humor, his megalomania, his commitment to each word, produced an idiosyncratic language that we learn by reading his work and his sources. As conflicted as it is now for us, the entire language hangs together, somewhat as if it were a holograph; it is as manifest in "kikery" as in "The book shd. be a ball of light in one's hand." The dynamics of Poundian light are equally visible in both places.

Randall Jarrell, in a review of *Rock-Drill*, presents a balanced literary assessment: "Many of Pound's recollections are as engaging as he is; his warmth, delight, disinterestedness, honest indignation help make up for his extraordinary misuse of extraordinary powers." Jarrell's reaction to the *"kikery"* passage is that Pound's "obsessions, at their worst, are a moral and intellectual disaster, and make us ashamed for him," and his conclusion is that "scholars will process [*The Cantos*], anthologies present one or two of its beauties, readers dig through all that blue clay for more than a few diamonds."[8]

Such a response displays empathetic and judicious common sense, but ultimately reads a more pleasant (and more literary) simulacrum of Pound's words and reproduces the structure of diamond and mud that we find Pound himself using. The very metaphor appears in the following passages from *Pisan Cantos*, as Pound pledges allegiance to the eternal regime of Mussolini:[9]

> nor shall diamond die in the avalanche
>   be it torn from its setting
> first must destroy himself ere others destroy him.
> 4 times was the city rebuilded, Hooo Fasa
>   Gassir, Hooo Fasa   dell' Italia tradita
> now in the mind indestructible
>
>   C 74, 444

It also occurs in the Hell Cantos, where Pound castigates "the pusillanimous, raging; / plunging jewels in mud, / and howling to find them unstained" (C 14, 62).

The split in Pound's work that continually produces diamond and mud (Mussolini and Jews; the extraordinary individual and the masses; the genius and the diluting poets) should not be reproduced in critical readings. *The Cantos* is not a repository of beauties set off by error: Pound deserves to be read more closely. Such an approach may not yield as much unproblematic literary value, but the violent dynamics of Pound's writing are worth understanding.

FASCISM AND/OR "FASCISM"

I've picked examples from within and from either side of the Fascist abyss in Pound's career and declared them all to have been written in Poundian genius-language that includes his political allegiance to Fascism and his obsessive catharsis in anti-Semitism. I imagine this could easily be read as an absolute condemnation. But to reemphasize the point I have also been making: Pound's work is compelling, and the intensity of its commitment visible in each word has made him heroic to a number of critics and to some of the best poets who come after him.

His work can be morally dismal if its referents are followed out carefully in certain areas, but the trails that lead to Hitler and the Jews need not be taken: there are other trails from most of Pound's words. For a phrase like "The Unwobbling Pivot," "Mussolini" makes a somewhat more palatable referent than "Hitler," and a more likely one as well; "Kung" [Confucius] or "Adams" make even safer ones, and "the sensibility of Ezra Pound" probably the safest. "Light" can but doesn't have to imply Fascism; *A Visiting Card* begins by affirming that "a thousand candles together blaze with intense brightness. No one candle's light damages another's. So is the liberty of the individual in the ideal and fascist state" (*SP*, 306). But on the next page we read, "the images of the gods, or Byzantine mosaics, move the soul to contemplation of the undivided light." Couldn't religion be read as the more comprehensive frame, enclosing and thus to some extent neutralizing Pound's Fascism?[10] The Fascism would then be a mistake rather than a fundamental pattern of Pound's perception.

Even at his mostly overtly Fascist, Pound continually switches to non-Fascist referents. The dichotomy between synthesis or choice that makes the title *Jefferson and/or Mussolini* almost noncommittal arises on a large scale when we consider Pound's actions. His difficult journey north to serve the Salò Republic in 1943 is proof of an extreme devotion to Mussolini and to Fascist Italy, but his main efforts on behalf of the government, besides his broadcasts, were to get his Italian translations of Confucius published.[11] This can be taken as evidence of his extreme devotion, not to Fascism per se, but to the civic responsibilities of high culture.

Many Poundians have presented him in such a framework. The following remarks by Guy Davenport epitomize the view that Pound represents a level of cultural achievement that calls for elegaic celebration: "Like *The Cantos* [Malatesta's Tempio] is unfinished, is a monument to the skill and sensitivity of its creator, and yet is a realized, useful part of the world: one can go to mass in the Tempio, one can read *The Cantos*."[12]

This veneration—the rhetoric suggests one can go to mass in *The Cantos*, too—mimics Pound's own cultural assertions, though with better manners. Pound's anti-Semitism becomes simply eccentric: "And it was from Pound himself that I first saw how whacky the anti-Semitism was. It made no sense that I could see." Jews aren't the problem for Davenport; nevertheless, he does affirm the Poundian dynamics of cultural rot that underlie Pound's rage: "So the tradition rotted not in but around Pound."[13] "The tradition" is another potentially neutral term; as with my reading of light, I recommend that we read "the tradition" as the product of Pound's genius-language, where tradition and rot are always produced simultaneously. For every incisive, glowing Cavalcanti, there will always be a rotting Milton.

It is difficult to affirm the cultural innocence of Pound after the work of such critics as Bacigalupo, Nicholls, Smith, and especially, Casillo: the evidence is overwhelming.[14] Even if we ignore the radio speeches and the wartime prose, Pound's allegiance to Fascism surfaces in spots throughout *The Cantos* from the thirties on, including the *Pisan Cantos*, which have been considered to mark the occasion of his recantation.[15] While alive, Mussolini was something of a demigod to Pound, uniting, ordering, and purifying society: making it cohere. Although he appears only once in the first half of the poem, it is in a most prominent place, the beginning of Canto 41, the conclusion of the third published section. There, the Boss performs many quasi-miracles, not the least of which is manifesting an instantaneous understanding of the prior *Cantos*. I will be discussing this canto in more detail later; for now, I want to emphasize that it is the fact of Mussolini's rule in Italy that underwrites the next thirty-three cantos up to the war. Thematically, he rhymes with John Adams and the good rulers and sages of Pound's China; he was proof that Pound's ideas about art, government, banking, sexuality, and language could be brought into practice in a social context larger than that of Pound's own writing. But Mussolini's death did not diminish Pound's fervor. The opening lines of the *Pisan Cantos* compare Mussolini to Christ and Dionysus and go on to demonstrate that Pound's faith had acquired a tenacity not to be modified by material circumstance.

Pound's allegiance to Fascism extended beyond Mussolini. A number of collaborators such as Quisling, Laval, and Petain are mentioned sympathetically.[16] Hitler, a lesser figure in Pound's pantheon than Mussolini, is "furious from perception" (*C 104, 755*) and is compared to the good rulers of China, John Adams, and Alexander the Great. But a widespread critical recognition of how central Pound's Fascism is to the latter two-thirds of *The Cantos* has been slow to form. For one thing, the density of the poem's verbal surface is such that almost any particular can be ignored. The comparison of Hitler to Adams occurs in this way: "Providence in which, unfashionable as the faith is, I believe / Schicksal, sagt der Führer [Fate, says the Führer]" (*C 62, 345*)—a single line of German amid eighty pages given over almost exclusively to truncated quotation from Adams's collected papers.[17] Alexander is defined as Hitlerian as follows:

> Pale sea-green, I saw eyes once,
> and Raleigh remarked, on Genova's loans non-productive,
>   that they had only their usury left,
> and there was that Führer of Macedon, dead aetat 38,

> The temple   is holy,
>   because it is not for sale.
>
> > C 97, 690

It could be argued that such idiosyncratic comparisons don't go very far toward making *The Cantos* a Fascist poem—here, the reference to Hitler is followed by an invocation of "the temple." They can simply be ignored as "statistically" insignificant; they can be dismissed as confabulated opinion: if Pound thought Hitler was like John Adams and Alexander the Great, then, the argument might run, "Hitler" becomes a private Poundian usage.[18] "Pound's Fascism" could thus be seen as much less malign than Fascism itself. Similarly with Pound's use of "Jew." Sympathetic critics have attempted to minimize his anti-Semitism by claiming that "Jew" was a metaphor for Pound and by noting that at times he distinguished "Jews" from "usurers." Kenner defends Pound's "kikery" passage as follows: "*kikery:* An opprobrious epithet Pound applies to usurers and financiers—who foster wars and depressions to make money—as well as to intellectuals in universities and the publishing world who appear to support them. Once, when asked how he could say he was not anti-Semitic when he used words such as 'kike' and 'kikery,' he replied with some feeling: 'There are Jew kikes and non-Jew kikes.' . . . The functional words . . . are, 'no clear thought about holiness.' "[19] In Kenner's analysis, the depth of Pound's feeling is seemingly enough to neutralize public consequences of words and to furnish them with happier private meanings. This could justify any use of language. "No clear thought about holiness," on the other hand, is apparently "functional," that is, public language.

As a defense against charges of anti-Semitism, this is of an extremely low order, but it points to a recurring feature in Pound's writing: the swallowing up of historical particulars by his private and ultimately amorphous categories of judgment. Some critics react to this by maintaining a rigorously aesthetic reading. For example, Leon Surette, discussing the religious dimension of Pound's light imagery, dismisses Pound's tendentiousness: "Fortunately it is not part of the task of the present study to convince its readers of the theological or historical verity of Pound's religious views."[20] In a more recent article, Surette separates Pound's aesthetic core from his political follies. Surette has "no palatable explanations" for Pound's political choices, but his desire to "somehow save the poetry from the errors of the man" leads to the conclusion that he "prefer[s] to think of [Pound] as a fool in politics than as mad or morally depraved."[21] In enforcing the divide between man and poet, Surette takes a swipe at the ideology of genius: "Modernism has remained fully committed to the genius theory of artistic creation. On such a theory the valorized artist must be prescient in all areas. Pound certainly subscribed to that theory himself, and claimed to possess superior wisdom in all spheres. . . . If, however, we abandon the naïve notion that an important poet must be a genius, then we have available the explanation that Pound was simply stupid and arrogant on political matters."[22] But Pound's notion of genius sought to overcome just such divisions between poetry and politics.

The division Surette makes is surprisingly similar to that made by Charles Olson, even though Olson's allegiance to a genius theory of a poetic life would seem to be the opposite of Surette's judicial distance. Nevertheless, Olson also split Pound in two, writing soon after visiting Pound in St. Elizabeths, "In Pound I am confronted by the tragic Double of our day. . . . In language and form he is as forward, as much the revolutionist as Lenin. But in social, economic, and political action he is as retrogressive as the Czar."[23] Such a distinction left Olson free to admire "the great man, in his black coat and wide hat, the whole man / wagging, the swag / of Pound."[24] If there's an undercurrent of irony in these lines, it's a modest one.

A similar identification has been made by one of the most astute readers of the mechanics of Pound's textuality, Jean-Michel Rabaté. Extending earlier investigations into the Lacanian paradoxes of Pound's attempts to authorize reality in words, Rabaté's reading displays great finesse.[25] But the following comments reveal that Pound's political pratfalls are all too easily subsumed into the value-free problematics of textuality: "Thus the 'education' towards beauty or light or order will have to follow Pound's own personal progress through cultures, will imitate his readings, his commitments, his agonies and despair—an *imitatio Poundi* which fortunately can be relieved by sudden outbursts of critical negation or by a wry but pervasive sense of humour. 'There is no substitute for a lifetime' must be the conclusion of any serious reading of the *Cantos*."[26]

Such an identification with Pound—no matter how leavened by outbursts of critical negation—will, however, constantly be challenged by Pound's references and his private judgments of public matters. These judgments show up throughout his work, most notably in his choices of targets that can seem at times almost random—"that bitch Mme de Lieven / that bitch Mme de Staël" (C *103*, 747).[27] But while this aspect of Pound is endemic to his abysmal political rages, it is also the key to his ideogrammic method.

The Poundian ideogram can be provisionally defined as a generalization formed by joining particulars in a nonlogical, nonsequential way. The binaries, for Pound, are ideogram versus syllogism, abstraction versus immediate sensuousness:

> Sapor, the flavour,
> pulchritudo

ne divisibilis intellectu
not to be split by syllogization
                    C 105, 762

The ideogram is true for Pound because it is made up of particulars,
which in turn are true because they are not abstract. Such a circular
method grants complete authority to the ideogram's fashioner, who
is backed by the irrefutable singularity of the particulars—the "Luminous Detail" (*SP*, 21), "rain of factual atoms" (*GK*, 98), "gists and
piths" (*ABC*, 92)—at the same time as he gets to assign them a more
comprehensive ethical significance. The well-known Poundian image of the magnet pulling iron filings into the pattern of a rose (*C*
74, 463) grants such ordering the status of a natural occurrence. This
status would seem to guarantee the coherence of the particulars no
matter how far-flung; in practice, however, the results may have
looked natural only to Pound, as when he calls Roosevelt and Churchill Jews. Another image of ideogrammic coherence is of rods in a
bundle—the *fasces*. This symbol also is represented as having natural
authority:

> The Lady Pao Sse brought earthquakes. TCHEOU falleth,
>
> . . . .
>
> Sun darkened, the rivers were frozen. . . .
>
> . . . .
>
> No man was under another
> > 9 Tcheou wd/ not stand together
> > were not rods in a bundle
>
> Sky dark, cloudless and starless
> > at midnight a rain of stars
> > > Wars,
> > > > wars without interest
> boredom of an hundred years' wars.
>
> > > > > C 53, 271–72

The mysterious sympathy here between nature and government,
causing heaven and earth to critique the head of state, is symptomatic of the mystified control that Pound wields over all the heterogeneous material of *The Cantos*. Whatever the ostensible subject,
beneath the scrambled surface display there is an insistent assertion
of natural hierarchy. But how can the assertion be reconciled with
the surface? Pound's truncated presentation habitually makes his
gists and piths close to indecipherable. One can call this an accidental
result of impatience or miscalculation, but it is so constant that it

seems basic if not deliberate. In his digest of the Confucian *Analects* at the beginning of *Guide to Kulchur,* Pound writes: "The dominant element in the sign of learning in the love of learning chapter is a mortar. That is, the knowledge must be ground into fine powder" (*GK*, 21).[28] As *The Cantos* progresses the number of consecutive words devoted to any one item tends to become quite small; Pound grinds the powder fine:

mises ne prises	1272
raised into precedent	25
	1297

Confirmationis
     Chartorum
Cap. vi bitched by Disraeli
de la maletot des leyes
       40 shillings
nous lettres ouverts

C 108, 780

Here the pestle has all the power and the reader has to sift through the resulting powder. Despite the semantic meaning of the last line, these letters are not "open" to any except fluent readers of Poundian shorthand. No extraneous autonomy was permissible within "the new synthesis, the totalitarian" (*GK*, 95), in which Pound's poetry and his politics were to be united. There had to be nothing standing in the way.

But something always did. Though Pound's good rulers, Fascist, Confucian, Roman, American, or Merovingian, all impose the order of nature on their realms and have nature's calm, spare, lyric backing, they always seem to run up against a tide of disorder, immorality, and filth, Pound's shorthand for which was Jews.

It is tempting to say that the reader or the listener was the Jew for Pound: his need to exalt himself above his audience seems closely allied with his anti-Semitism. Or that he himself was the Jew: the insatiability of his hatred suggests projection in a psychological sense, and *The Cantos* can be seen as commenting on the sacred texts and generating a need for endless further commentary, thus becoming a kind of Talmud. But at a more general level, the Jew (or Buddhist, banker, philologist, Churchill, etcetera) was a recurring excrescence arising from a fundamental conflict that existed for Pound every time he used words in whatever social medium. A Confucian slogan he posted in Rapallo illustrates this point clearly: "The un-mixed functions without end, in time and space without end."[29] Se-mantically, this affirms the cleanliness of the sacred words of the poet, but the walls of Rapallo, no matter how socially pure in Pound's perception, do exist in space and time. Pound's words, at whatever point they could be read or heard—the page, the walls of Rapallo, or the airwaves—always faced contamination. They not only had to circulate in society in terms of their potential reception, but on a more basic level, even as he used them they already were inescapably social and circulatory in their semantic and syntactic aspects. The unmixed, in that it was language at all, was incurably mixed. No matter how Pound might try to purify, isolate, and sac-ralize his words by using Chinese ideograms and foreign languages, by drawing pictures and employing musical notation, by drastically truncating syntax, language itself was, as a social medium, impure, rotten, Jewish (that is, social and historical). The only way Pound could protect himself was to form it into ideograms, thus creating instruments of instantaneous, nondiscursive judgment.[30]

Reflecting the process of their own formation, there were finally only two opposing yet interlocked ideograms, the pure and the im-pure: light, health, hierarchy, the phallus, nature, the classics, etcet-era etcetera; and darkness, sickness, swamps, sodomy, Jews, usury, etcetera etcetera. The "etcetera" in these lists is important: while the ostensible object of Pound's celebration was clean language and clear demarcation, these dual ideograms were themselves endlessly agglutinative.[31]

The most comprehensive set of analogs for this pair might be writing and society. To say it is writer and reader would not be quite accurate: for all his megalomania, Pound never identified himself as sun god and all-wise poet. Rather, his position was, as he said of John Heydon, "Secretary of Nature" (C 91, 625); or, in his imagina-tion, it might also be "Secretary to Mussolini." And while groups of readers in his generalized lexicon were smug, provincial, or despi-cable, he courted particular readers as potential converts, as the in-tensity of his responses to his many correspondents makes clear. A similar invitation "to enter arcanum" (C, 817) is issued throughout the poem to any reader who wants to be singled out. Once inside, the troubling distinction between "Fascism" and "the Love that moves the sun and the other stars" would supposedly fade into oblivion.

POUND'S READERS

In the *ABC of Reading,* Pound writes, "Incredible as it now seems, the bad critics of Keats' time found his writing 'obscure', which meant that they couldn't understand WHY Keats wrote" (*ABC*, 64). But even if the "WHY" in Pound's case is understood, it will not banish the obscurity. Not that the surface can't be decoded. One of the founding documents of the Pound industry, Hugh Kenner's *The Poetry of Ezra Pound,* begins by claiming, optimistically as it turned out, that the task would be fairly easy: "[the poem] is difficult as all poetry is difficult, but the hard shell of difficulty is in most places very thin."[32] Such a model of shell and kernel, however, will not be very useful in reading *The Cantos.* The unriddling of the majority of the poem's allusions in Carroll Terrell's *Companion to The Cantos,* while indispensible in learning to read Pound's language, can ultimately be a barrier to a comprehension of the "WHY" of Pound's writing. *The Cantos* is not difficult as all poetry is difficult; its difficulty is specific and ineradicable.

Pound explained his purpose repeatedly, and given its apparent simplicity and the importance he assigned to it, there seems little reason why his writing should not have been straightforward and publicly available. His ambition was to transform poetry from a minor social ornament into an activity of central social importance. Arnold's position that literature is basic to social renewal and the transcending of political fractures was axiomatic for Pound:

> The thought of what America,
> The thought of what America,
> The thought of what America would be like
> If the Classics had a wide circulation
>> Troubles my sleep.
>
> *P,* 183

The citizen-readers longed for here are as imaginary as the doggerel of this early poem is ironic. Pound made an eerily similar call on behalf of the classics during the last days of the Salò Republic, this time without irony: "All scholars isolated in invaded territory as well as in the Republic are invited to reread the Greek and Latin Classics so as to find therein the reason the enemy wants to suppress or diminish the studies of the sources of our culture and our political wisdom."[33]

This wartime plea may ultimately be Arnoldian, but it demonstrates, by its tenuous relation to reality, how extensive and stable a social network Arnoldianism presupposes in order to make any sense. Arnold lived in a society in which the classics were prestigious, and he held a governmental post in education to give his faith some specific prospect for eventual implementation. Pound maintained his commitment to a socially central culture but dropped the utopian or prospective quality of Arnold's position. Arnold urged society to better itself by turning to culture; Pound developed a position in which society already was defined, almost mechanically, by cultural achievement: "Rome rose with the idiom of Caesar, Ovid, and Tacitus, she declined in a welter of rhetoric" (*ABC*, 33). Here, or in his claim that he could read the rate of interest in a given society by looking at its paintings (*GK*, 27), it might seem like Pound simply posits an absolute correlation between base and superstructure. But his investment in the social authority of art was such that he inverted the materialist view: he saw the base as flowing inevitably from the superstructure. He was fond of quoting Flaubert's statement that the Franco-Prussian war wouldn't have happened if the French had read his *Education Sentimentale* (*LE*, 297).

Even though reading is of extreme importance in this model of history, there are few actual readers. Writing acts—more often, the tense is elegaic: writing should have acted—autonomously. In the following from the radio broadcasts the movement from Arnoldian liberalism based on "the best that was thought and said" to this extreme position is quite rapid:

> I thought in 1908 and before then that a nation's literature IS important
> . . . ideas necessary for leading the good life, registered in the best
> books. . . . Waal, the Americans and the English just couldn't believe
> that it made any difference what a man or a nation put inside its head
> via its reading.
>
> Hence I was supposed to exaggerate when I bust out against such
> dung heaps of perfumed pus as the Atlantic Monthly. . . . [I]n London
> I did a *sottisier* [*Blast*], trying to make a few people see why the printed
> matter on sale in that city would finally kill off the inhabitants; witness
> Dunkirk.
>
> *RS*, 91

The final sentence may seem pathologically grandiose, as do many of the assertions in the broadcasts, but such perception of culture and society as a unified field and such passionate commitment to revitalize that field are constants in Pound's writing. However, such generalized grandiosity often flips over into self-absorbed speciali-zation—note that he was trying to make a *few* people see. For Pound, Dunkirk and *Blast* are facts of equal significance if not magnitude; literature is so important that it can substitute for society completely.

In his own poetry, Pound's gestures toward social intervention, relentless though they seem, never hold their social definition. Rather than a streamlined vehicle for economic analysis and political exhortation, the poem will become proof of the poet's uniqueness. A passage may initially seem to make an urgent appeal for economic change, for example by citing the $A + B$ Theorem devised by one of Pound's favorite economic thinkers, Major C. H. Douglas. Sche-matically, this holds that the price of goods is equal to what's paid to workers and stockholders (A) plus what's paid for raw materials and other costs (B), causing a gap in purchasing power at present only made up by borrowing on credit.[34] Or, as Pound put it:

> What it [a factory] pays in wages and dividends
> stays fluid, as power to buy, and this power is less,
> per forza, damn blast your intellex, is less
> than the total payments made by the factory
> (as wages, dividends AND payments for raw material
> bank charges, etcetera)
> and all, that is the whole, that is the total
> of these is added into the total of prices
> caused by that factory, any damn factory
> and there is and must be therefore a clog
> and the power to purchase can never
> (under the present system) catch up with
> prices at large

Not only does this undermine its attempt at straightforward eco-nomic exposition by its aggression and frustrated pleonasm, in the next lines Pound pronounces the failure or the pointlessness of this exposition:

> and the light became so bright and so blindin'
> in this layer of paradise
> that the mind of man was bewildered.
>
> C 38, 190

Even here, in one of most direct passages in *The Cantos,* Pound's didacticism reframes itself as allegory. Rather than crucial economic truths, we are reading a latter-day version of the *Commedia* in which Dante's final anagogic function has withered into irony. The $A + B$ Theorem of Major Douglas has become transcendent in the Poundian light; whatever the degree of irony felt in the tone, the topography is the same: the author is a spokesman for paradisal values, shared by any particular reader who happens to be on Pound's side, while readers in general are damned.

Pound saw literary supremacy and social centrality as a unity in Dante and other writer-heroes. Their literary skill confirmed the value of their economic, religious, and political statements, and the wide range of subject matter confirmed their seriousness as writers. Pound used them to justify documenting economics and history in his poem. But the more he tried to include, the more specialized his work became. Michael Bernstein notes that Pound was the first to quote prose documents in a poem without privileging the verse.[35] On the level of local form, this is true: in Canto 8, Renaissance correspondence appears as prose, without framing, between passages of verse. But the ultimate effect of Pound's documentary method here is to outdo Browning in providing local color. What looks to be a transliterary gesture becomes, in a poem filled with such gestures, intensely literary. Pound's singlemindedness continually splits into two contradictory alternatives that have helped keep *The Cantos* in limbo. For most readers, its economic and historic claims are too "poetic" to take seriously, while the poetry, in its conflicted didacticism, is often "blindin' " if not invisible.

SEEING THE IDEOGRAM VERSUS READING WORDS

Pound's account of the ideogram in the *ABC of Reading* insists on a spare, precise, and automatically legible poetry. "[The Chinaman] is to define red. How can he do it in a picture that isn't painted in red paint?" He solves the problem by putting together pictures of rose, cherry, iron rust, and flamingo. For Pound, this method possesses numerous advantages. It is scientific: "very much the kind of thing a biologist does." It is poetic: "a language written in this way simply HAD TO STAY POETIC." And it is easily perceptible: "the Chinese 'word' or ideogram for red is based on something everyone KNOWS" (*ABC*, 22).

The insistent simplicity of Pound's account is easy to read as advocating a transparent, public language.[36] But naturalness does not lead to commonality, which Pound consistently opposes. The point Pound is making is that poetry is rare, and that "a great deal that you read, you simply need not 'bother about.' " Pound begins by noting that there are too many books: "The weeder is supremely needed if the Garden of the Muses is to persist as a garden" (*ABC*, 87, 17). Nature underwrites the ideogram for Pound and is the opposite of convention; it produces singular flowers and plural weeds.

Pound is not proposing a social model of language; he is certainly not concerned, at this point, with the Chinese reading and writing their own language. Ideograms are not read, but seen, an activity that is proper to the genius: "Gaudier Brzeska, who was accustomed to looking at the real shape of things, could read a certain amount of Chinese writing without ANY STUDY. He said, 'Of course, you can *see* it's a horse' (or a wing or whatever)" (*ABC*, 21; Pound's emphasis). The ideogram is at once more ancient and more experimental than a socially circulating word. It is a poem, a classic, and an act of individual volition and authority: a single "Chinaman" defines red, building an essentialist bridge over the gap between word and thing.

Not everyone can write ideograms. That "a language written in this way simply HAD TO STAY POETIC" (*ABC*, 22) can imply that all anyone has to do is to put common nouns together to produce a kind of populist Imagism, but this is misleading. The quality of the writing and of the writer is crucial. Explaining the ideogram to George Santayana in 1940, Pound emphasized individual gesture, citing the "Chinese saying 'a man's character apparent in every one of his brush strokes.' Early characters were pictures, squared for aesthetic reasons. But I think in a well-brushed ideogram the sun is seen to be rising" (*L*, 333). Having to "STAY POETIC" implies that the naturalness of an ideogram enforces perception. The verbal parallel is to "Literature is news that STAYS news," which Pound amplifies by writing: "I cannot for example, wear out my interest in the *Ta Hio* of Confucius, or in the Homeric poems. . . . [They] are natural phenomena, they serve as measuring-rods, or instruments. For no two people are these 'measures' identical" (*ABC*, 29–30).

That a "measure" would vary from person to person is the paradox at the heart of Pound's method. At times he insists that truth depends on empirical accuracy: A statement's value is only "GOOD if it be ultimately found to correspond to the facts." However, he goes on to qualify this: "BUT no layman can tell at sight whether it is good or bad." Truth does not inhere in the statement but in the utterer: "Even if the general statement of an ignorant man is 'true', it leaves his mouth or pen without any great validity. He doesn't KNOW what he is saying." Whereas "If Marconi says something about ultra-short waves it MEANS something." But this meaning is not public. It "can only be properly estimated by someone who KNOWS" (*ABC*, 25–26). It is the speaker's authority, not the world, that backs up language: "Any general statement is like a cheque drawn on a bank. Its value depends on what is there to meet it."[37] Knowledge is not the issue, finally, but control. In a letter, Pound speaks of his own economic truths as "complex *and* as simple as Marconi's control of electricity" (*L*, 247).

Outside of Pound's China, the ideogram functions not to unite society and nature but to form an elite within society. The account of the ideogram in *ABC* is framed by two anecdotes demonstrating the contradiction between "everyone" and "knowledge." In the first, Pound puts on comparative concerts; he writes, "Everyone present at the two concerts now knows a great more about . . . Debussy and Ravel than they possibly could have found out by reading ALL the criticisms that have ever been written of both" (*ABC*, 23–25). The value of Debussy and Ravel may be as immediately perceptible as red is, but it is not "everyone" who knows this, only "everyone present at the two concerts." And standing in the way of correct evaluation is a mass of criticism, which by implication is as murky as the wordless music is self-evident. This is a central pattern of Pound's thought: immediate perception of the truth is available to a few, while outside the inner sanctum there is a fog of clichés, received ideas, second-hand and second-rate opinions, written darkness.

In the second anecdote, the obstruction to knowledge does not result from secondary diluting descriptions, but is present in language at all levels:

> A post-graduate student equipped with honours and diploma went to Agassiz. . . . The great man offered him a small fish and told him to describe it.

Post-Graduate Student: 'That's only a sunfish.'
Agassiz: 'I know that. Write a description of it.'
After a few minutes the student returned with the description of the Ichthus Heliodiplodokus, or whatever term is used to conceal the common sunfish from vulgar knowledge, family of Heliichtherinkus, etc., as found in textbooks of the subject.
Agassiz again told the student to describe the fish.
The student produced a four-page essay. Agassiz then told him to look at the fish. At the end of three weeks the fish was in an advanced state of decomposition, but the student knew something about it.

ABC, 17–18

This is odd science. There are no scientific institutions, pedagogic procedures, or communicable terminologies. Knowledge is embodied in a laconic master who leads his student to conclude that any mediating term, common ("That's only a sunfish") or highfalutin ("Heliodiplodokus, Heliichtherinkus, etc."), blocks perception. Nor does the student's earnest essay help—it's merely writing. In Pound's China pictures of flamingo and sunrise are unproblematic truth, but here words turn out to be as rotten as the fish finally is. Knowledge resides in the unchanging Agassiz, who is beyond the swamp of linguistic circulation. What looks initially like a commitment to empiricism has led instead to an authoritarian idealism. By the late cantos Agassiz is a Dantescan heavenly figure free of any earthly taint: "Agassiz with the fixed stars, Kung to the crystalline" (*C* 93, 639). The name is merely stated without a verb: knowledge is static, and abbreviated syntax is a ritual of purification. To recall the lines quoted earlier:

> To Kung, to avoid their encirclement,
> To the Odes to escape abstract yatter,
> to Mencius, Dante, and Agassiz
> for Gestalt seed,
> pity, yes, for the infected,
> but maintain antisepsis,
> let the light pour.

C 94, 649

No relation between the individual items is articulated; and the vocabulary is less available than it looks; all the common nouns are bound into specific Poundian ideogrammic webs. Only the few can see (or produce) light or plant seed. Infection is not simply a matter of germs, but like the other nouns, refers to race and systems of money, education, and communication. The meaning of "maintain antisepsis" can be limited to Pound's literary didacticism regarding efficient rhetoric and live curricula only if his many references to bad bankers, writers, and Jews as bacilli are overlooked. "Antisepsis" is also self-referential: Pound's writing here is "clean"; only by approaching the status of sacred signs would the words be pure enough. Agassiz can be named only as an amulet.

The Poundian ideogram, initially promising vivid immediacy, becomes by the latter stages of his career a never-ending gesture of verbal discontinuity designed to evoke masterful artistic distance, of which the Chinese characters strewn throughout the latter half of the poem are, for most Western readers, fitting emblems. Against Pound's claims of the naturalness and social clarity of the ideogram, the remark of a fellow observer of Mussolini, Gramsci, is a useful antidote: "In China there is the phenomenon of the script, an expression of the complete separation between the intellectuals and the people."[38]

THE POET'S JOB: CULT AND CULTURE

Pound began his career by insisting on poetic technique. His self-definition as an expert was clear enough, as was the object of his attack: the amateur status of poetry. In an early essay, "I Gather the Limbs of Osiris," he compares the standard London poetaster to a child who hears Busoni play and immediately arranges to give a concert. Pound complains that "the ordinary piano teacher spends more thought on the art of music than does the average 'poet' on the art of poetry" (*SP*, 31). This insistence on professional literary standards has been crucial for many subsequent poets, but for Pound himself it would lead to the radio broadcasts.

In "Osiris" professionalism is a social bond. Answering the question "How, then, shall the poet in this dreary day attain universality?" Pound sees expertise as the poet's primary claim on an audience: "Every man who does his own job really well has a latent respect for every other man who does *his* own job really well . . . if he be pleased afterwards to talk about it . . . he gets his audience the moment he says something so intimate that it proves him the expert" (*SP*, 32–33).

This makes rhetoric, getting an audience, a primary dimension of poetry, but Pound is far from acknowledging it: "Poetry is . . . an art of pure sound bound in through an art of arbitrary and conventional symbols. In so far as it is an art of pure sound, it is allied with music, painting, sculpture; in so far as it is allied with an art of arbitrary symbols, it is allied to prose. A word exists when two or more people mean the same thing by it" (*SP,* 33–34). Pound begins by including both sound and rhetoric—nature and culture—as components of poetry, but by the second sentence he has eliminated rhetoric, anticipating the distinction he would continue to draw between prose, profane and diagnostic, and poetry, holy and revelatory. (See *LE,* 324, n. 1.)

Syntax is inescapably communal and thus is nonpoetic: "all the qualities which differentiate poetry from prose are things born before syntax." (Following the connotations of the essay's title, "before syntax" would also mean before Osiris was torn apart, before he lost his phallus.) Discussing "the masterly use of words," Pound replaces ordinary syntax with a more arcane poetic syntax, comparing words to "great hollow cones of steel" charged with something more complex than electricity: "This peculiar energy which fills the cones is the power of tradition, of centuries of race consciousness . . . and the control of it is the 'Technique of Content', which nothing short of genius understands" (*SP,* 34).

Such grand pronouncements spring from finite social dilemmas. In the following passage, it is easy to imagine that beneath the impersonal diction Pound is worrying about himself: "How many have I seen . . . produce one book and die of it? . . . [T]he little public that does read new poetry is not twice bored by the same aspirant. . . . But the man who has some standard reasonably high—consider, says Longinus, in what mood Diogenes or Sophocles would have listened to your effusion . . . emerges decently clean after some reasonable purgation, not nearly a master, but licensed, an initiate"(*SP,* 34–35). The young poet may be addressing Sophocles, but he is also addressing the small, easily bored audience for contemporary poetry. He is both "an initiate," one of a select, holy group, and "licensed"—like a pub keeper or plumber. In order to get his license as the latest poet of interest he has to act the initiate and address eternity. The Hell Cantos demonstrate how charged a matter "emerg[ing] decently clean" can be.

The pattern with regard to the dollar value of poetry is similar. While his later tendency to aestheticize all social judgments is well known, the Usura Cantos being the clearest example, this can be traced back to an earlier stage in his career, when he appealed to an image of prevailing social standards for justice in art matters. In a quarrel with Amy Lowell over publicity rights to the term "Imagism," Pound asked her to remove his, Yeats's, and Ford's names from an ad her publishers were running: "I don't suppose any one will sue you for libel; it is too expensive. If your publishers 'of good standing' tried to advertise cement or soap in this manner they would certainly be sued. However, we salute their venality. Blessed are they who have enterprise, for theirs is the magazine public" (*L*, 44).

Pound's irony is thick, but it stems from powerlessness: Lowell had beaten him in a market he cared about. In this early literary struggle he saw business as a fitting analog to literature. By the 1930s, the conflict between wanting money as a sign of professional status and loathing it was acute. His tone is blunt as he demands payment—"The fee is due to *quality*. The stinkingest fourth-rate painter wd. get six times that for work requiring a 25th of the time and acumen" (*L*, 281). But writing for money is also a primal sin. Pound's analogies between art and commerce become incoherent:

> There is one technique for the mattress-maker and one for the builder of linotype machines. A technique of construction applies both to bedsteads and automobiles.
>
> The dirtiest book in our language is a quite astute manual telling people how to earn money by writing. The fact that it advocates the maximum possible intellectual degradation should not blind one to its constructive merits.
>
> Certain parts of the technique of narrative ARE common to Homer, Rudyard Kipling *and* to Mr. Kipling's star disciple, the late Edgar Wallace.
>
> *ABC*, 89

The impulse to connect Kipling and detective stories with the epic world allows Pound to see in the despised manual some of the virtues of order and technique; and yet the manual is also a symbol of the degradation of the modern world: "the dirtiest book in our language," echoing his earlier praise of Golding's Ovid as "the most beautiful book in the language." Pound's desire to dissociate overcame his attempts to unify. By the time of the radio speeches, the

Talmud had become "the dirtiest teaching that any race ever codi-fied" (*RS*, 117).

By this point Pound's vision was absolute, giving evil writing instant power far beyond the aesthetic sphere: the Talmud is also "the one and only begetter of the Bolshevik system" (*RS*, 117). The efficacy of good writing remained dogma, but the evidence was hard to come by. The power of the Talmud could be confirmed by point-ing to a degraded, warring world, but to document the instantane-ous effect of the words of the genius on society, Pound stuck to Mussolini and a few anecdotes: in 1935, he cited Abelard rising up in class, outdebating the tenured pedant in theology, and forcing his retirement (*GK*, 170); in the version Pound used twenty years earlier, five thousand students accompanied Abelard downriver (*SP*, 134). In the subsequent excerpt Pound expands the numbers of those who should follow the artist; it is not just students, but all of society. However, they are kept a safe distance behind: "The artist, the maker is always too far ahead of any revolution, or reaction, or counter-revolution or counter-reaction for his vote to have any immediate result. . . . The party that follows him wins; and the speed with which they set about it, is the measure of their practical capacity and in-telligence. Blessed are they who pick the right artists and makers" (*SP*, 215). The ironic "blessing" hurled at Amy Lowell has become transmuted into the unshakable but hardly followable faith that per-ceived Mussolini as a type of Dionysus, "phallic and ambrosial," and of Confucius.

The stability of Pound's faith ultimately rests on its being untest-able. The increasing pressure of being an initiate made him assert a complete separation between society and the sacred realm of poetry, even as he was saying that society depends on poetry:

> The Duce and Kung fu Tseu equally perceive that their people need poetry; that prose is NOT education but the outer courts of the same. Beyond its doors are the mysteries. Eleusis. Things not to be spoken save in secret.
>
> The mysteries self-defended, the mysteries that *can* not be revealed. Fools can only profane them. . . . Science is hidden. The layman can only attain conic sections by labor. He can only attain the secretum by greater labor, by an attrition of follies. . . . It is quite useless for me to refer men to Provence, or to speculate on Erigena in the market place.
>
> (*GK*, 144–45)

The contradictions here are packed close: poetry is a mystery that is a necessity for "the people," as opposed to "fools," or those in the marketplace, who can't perceive the mysteries and would only sell them if they could see them. In order to receive the benefits of poetry, they need to be rid of their "follies," which would presumably involve making them singular and not "people" at all. In one of his radio speeches, Pound asserts the sacred singularity of the obvious, which only the genius can see: "As to the direct vision, that is the painter's genius, it is the genius of Cummings. Few men could have gone into Russia and not be beaten by ideology" (*RS*, 144). Pound's denial that sacred knowledge can circulate contradicts the stated aim of *Guide to Kulchur*, where he tries to outline a new civilization. The ultimately secret nature of Pound's expertise is enacted by the end of the book, in which he reacts to—but hardly cites—an absent book, the *Nicomachean Ethics*, with a mixture of pedantry and secrecy.[39]

This procedure—producing a mysterious text by reading an absent one—governs the writing of much of *The Cantos*. Pound's source texts are usually absent in a tacit way: he can seem too rushed to reveal them fully. But the clear refusal to communicate that is evident in the paragraph from *Kulchur* quoted above is constitutive of Pound's project of writing *The Cantos*: his information is vital to society, and at the same time, it is vital for his own status that it remain separate.[40]

Before the Second World War, Pound managed to stay afloat between the two sides of this contradiction. "There is no mystery about the Cantos, they are the tale of the tribe." Two sentences later, the focus is on the individual: "The Malatesta cantos . . . are openly volitionist, establishing . . . the effect of the factive personality, Sigismundo" (*GK*, 194). In an article written in the late thirties, Pound praised the "Mediterranean state of mind" for its "*sense of gradations*" and its "exact terminology." But while this precision created a healthy society, it was kept secret from that society. The fall of this "paideuma" occurred when "the cult of terminology lost its grip on general life," and the culprits were the usual mixture of "puritans" and "Hebrews," who Pound refers to as "incult," echoing both "uncultured," and outside of the "cult" (*SP*, 150). Expertise will create a new culture only by remaining outside society and constituting a cult.

This means Pound mentions key facts in the most elliptical manner. In the thirties the town of Wörgl issued stamp scrip—banknotes redeemable only if they had renewable revenue stamps attached. For Pound this was a just monetary system, with the state enforcing the value of money, which thus became a precise measure inside a system, "an exact terminology"; this would make private hoarding and manipulation of currency impossible. But prior to the *Pisan Cantos,* the only mention of Wörgl is in the following:

> Pays to control the Times, for its effect on the market
> "where there is no censorship by the state
> there is a great deal of manipulation..."
> > and news sense?
> Cosimo First guaranteed it.
> To pay 5% on its stock, Monte dei Paschi
> and to lend at 5 and ½
> Overplus of all profit, to relief works
> and the administration on moderate pay..
> > that stood even after Napoleon.
> Said C.H. "To strangle the bankers...?"
> And Woergl in our time?
>
> > > > *C 41,* 205

If one doesn't already know what Pound means by this, reading it won't help much. Key moments in the argument depend on bare naming: the guarantee of Cosimo First, "And Woergl." The analogies between news, money, and natural increase ("stock") are presumed to form an ideogrammic identity; and the contrast between manipulation of money and information by evil forces and emphatic imposition of standards of meaning by a virtuous centralizing power is meant to speak for itself. But one has to be inside Pound's system for his information to seem precise and valuable.

Wörgl is mentioned next in the *Pisan Cantos,* but still remains mostly hidden. The burden of proof is carried by the natural simplicity of the town, supplemented by the clarities of Dante and Henry Ford:

> the state need not borrow
> as was shown by the mayor of Wörgl
> who had a milk route
> and whose wife sold shirts and short breeches
> and on whose book-shelf was the Life of Henry Ford
> and also a copy of the Divina Commedia
>
> . . . .

and when a note of the
small town of Wörgl went over
a counter in Innsbruck
and the banker saw it go over
all the slobs in Europe were terrified

C 74, 455

Pound is like the Wörglians: his utopia lasts only as long as his meaning circulates in its own valley. Together with this paranoiac control of meaning, however, there is also a desire to leave the valley, to terrify all bankers and slobs, the representatives of wider frames of meaning—or at least to be noticed by them. The most intense expression of these conflicted impulses occurs after Pound's arrest by the Americans and before his incarceration at St. Elizabeths. After having risked an indictment for treason in order to save America by the clarity of his ideas, Pound claimed to his examiners that "there was no use to discuss his ideas about monetary theories and and economics because most people . . . would not be able to . . . comprehend them."[41]

The radio broadcasts clearly embody a crisis in Pound's thought, but *The Cantos*, rather than being the sane fraction of his work, embodies the same contradictions. As I said at the beginning of the chapter, the poem needs to be read as existing in the "new medium" that Pound saw uniting literature and action. If one added a sense of specific social location to this notion, then it might seem close to Pierre Bourdieu's sense of "literary field," except that for Pound the field in which the poet's activity was autonomous was the entire extent of society.[42] From inside this field *The Cantos* was to be foundational; if we stand outside it we can see that the turn to epic was a slightly desperate career move on Pound's part. That these perspectives clash does not mean they do not accurately reflect the contradictions of so divided a work. While Pound was writing *The Cantos* he was in conventional terms unemployable: "don't know what a man like you would find to *do* here" (*C 84, 551*) as Senator Borah told him. But at the same time the poem gave him a transcendent line on his résumé, "our job to build light" (*C 98, 698*).

"PRESENTE!": THE POUNDIAN HERO

The ideogrammic method was not a specific poetic technique or rhetorical effect: it was a language speakable only by a hero or genius, and it entailed a vision of a simultaneously natural and hierarchical society—Pound's China or his Italy—where poetry was central and the center was poetic. Only in such poem-societies would ideograms have the meanings claimed for them: language would not be contaminated by abstraction or deadened by cliché; it would be a totalized medium stretching in an ordered and energetic continuum from the state to nature.

The natural side of this spectrum is visible in Canto 49. On the surface, Pound's China is quite different from his Italy. The first line seems to dismiss the centralizing hero: "For the seven lakes, and by no man these verses," and throughout most of the canto there is little mention of the state. Rather than a burst of order and vigor emanating from the Boss's voice, there is a rural emptiness containing little more than the poet's lyric exile: "heavy rain in the twilight / Under the cabin roof was one lantern"; "Sail passed here in April; may return in October." But as Mussolini speaks and creates an ordered, energetic Italy in Canto 41, here the reclusive poet ultimately will turn out to speak the meaning of the invisible but centralizing emperor. Poet and ruler are paired; both are needed for the blend of verbal authority and material aloofness that is the ground and goal of Pound's meaning.

In the first four stanzas, there are shifts of scene, but the scarcity of human figures and the gravity of the verse mute any sense of disruption. Only one line triggers a ripple of historical time, which is quickly folded back into the timeless setting:

> A light moves on the north sky line;
> where the young boys prod stones for shrimp.
> In seventeen hundred came Tsing to these hill lakes.
> A light moves on the south sky line.

The language matches the archaic society: spare, ordered, and static. Everything is in its place and need not circulate, sustained by an ineffable and all-pervasive imperial power that provides an unobtrusive yet authoritative conclusion:

> Sun up; work
> sundown; to rest
> dig well and drink of the water
> dig field; eat of the grain
> Imperial power is? and to us what is it?

The fourth; the dimension of stillness.
And the power over wild beasts.

This passage may look like the speech of a naturally poetic peas-
antry, but it is carefully controlled: it recalls Imagism with its mono-
syllables and the nicely varied rhythms ("Sun up" two words; "sundown" one; "to rest" a relaxation from the stressed "work"; "dig
field; eat" condensing "dig well and drink"). It is tinged with archa-
ism ("eat of the grain"), and it gestures toward two powerful cultural markers, myth and contemporary science: Einstein and relativ-
ity in the penultimate line, Dionysus in the last. But beyond their
rhythmic subtlety and cultural allusion these lines invoke a vision
of society. State power and the peasants' acceptance of it are absolute
and are enacted by the verse. The ruler is beyond verbal embodiment, and while his power is beyond the peasants' understanding,
it is they who assert it: "Imperial power is? and to us what is it?"
Such questions are not rebellious. Obedience is not an issue and
needs no mention; the peasants work all day, beginning after the
words announcing sunrise appear and doing nothing else until sun-
set: "Sun up; work / sundown; to rest."

This authoritarianism has often been read by critics as a calm
celebration of a natural society: "sensibility, which, raised to the *n*th
power, transcends"; "the dispassionate anonymous . . . fused with
. . . immemorial rhythms."[43] One reason for this is that the setting
these lines evoke is, for most readers, exotic. It is also significant that
they occur after a quatrain of capitalized words that turn out to be
a transliteration of a Japanese translation of a Chinese poem. But
point is neither the path of this transmission nor the original meaning; the effect upon almost all readers when they come to

K	E	I	M	E	N	RAN	K E I
K	I	U	M	A	N	MAN	K E I
J I T S U			GETSU			K O	KWA
T	A	N	FUKU			TAN	K A I

resembles the effect of the emperor upon the peasants: "This quatrain is? and to us what is it?" After such semantic closure, the
simplicity of "Sun up; work" might easily evoke readerly relief,
gratitude, and obedience.

Such juxtapositions are, in practice, the stuff of Poundian ideograms. In a closed, ordered world no element would be culturally

distant from another; flamingoes and sunrises should always compose nicely into kaleidoscopic but timeless *natures vivantes.* But Pound was not writing in such a world, however often he might invoke one. Even within this canto, moving back one more stanza will make visible the frangibility of Pound's heroic assertions and the contradictions involved in trying to write an ideogrammic epic:

> State by creating riches shd. thereby get into debt?
> This is infamy; this is Geryon.
> This canal goes still to TenShi
> though the old king built it for pleasure

For a moment we move outside archaic China to glimpse a context in which political authority does not produce natural results. The Poundian ideogram of order—state, ruler, sun, light, grain, natural increase—accounts for only the first half of the first line: the state, not labor, creates wealth.[44] But if such terms are accepted, the next clause is puzzling: what could circumscribe such natural-political power?[45] Debt belongs to a time-ridden, mercantile world; Poundian riches are, like poetry, sacred and timeless, beyond debt. This impossibility rigs the downfall of Pound's historical heroes. In the thirties, it looked to Pound as if Mussolini would avoid this fall, but when dead the Boss fit into Pound's ideograms more firmly than ever. For all Pound's manifest drive to include history in his epic, the ideogrammic method bespeaks a contrary desire, especially if history is conceived as a collective enterprise rather than the tracks of singular heroes, fully legible only to genius. Pound cannot imagine any relationship with history other than mastery. All he can do is judge it—"This is infamy; this is Geryon"—invoking Dantescan categories that he considers timeless.

The end of the quatrain smooths over the jaggedness produced by this brush with history: "This canal goes still to TenShi / though the old king built it for pleasure." The third "this," introducing a new subject, seems a pointed turning away from the problems of history: "This is infamy; this is Geryon. / This canal." We suddenly are back to the world of natural wealth and elided labor: the old king "built" the canal; after this primal act, which was "for pleasure," social use ensues without conflict. Such a vision of the marriage of pleasure and use, which also underlies the invective of the Usura Cantos, has its roots in the aestheticized artisanal projects and projections of Ruskin and Morris, but here there is no hint of collectivism: the use, pleasure, and the will are the king's alone.

Focusing on the sexual overtones in the canal and the old king's pleasure lets us read the canto as a narrative, not an ideogram. The first four stanzas are static, with nature speaking for exiled poet and invisible ruler, but they are disturbed by the mention of historical time near the end. This triggers Pound's judgmental fury, which he pacifies by invoking the king's phallic authority, an uninterpretable absolutism that is embodied in the KEI MEN RAN KEI quatrain. This auratic trace of the old king's pleasure creates the chaste obedience of "Sun up; work."

The narrative of Pound's projections of authority cannot conclude or even progress; it oscillates between paradise and hell. By the end of *The Cantos*, when paradise is to be its sole subject, these shifts are desperately stroboscopic:

> Le Paradis n'est pas artificiel
> > but is jagged,
> For a flash,
> > for an hour.
> Then agony,
> > then an hour,
> > > then agony,
> > > > C 92, 634

Early on, however, it is an attractive procedure for Pound to change context, often with each line and at times with each word. Passages like the following from Canto 4 have been explained in terms of "subject rhyme"—and it is true that Pound weaves together highly truncated references to stories of happy marriages, jealousy, and cannibalism—but such explanations impose a secondary thematic coherence on the writing at the cost of ignoring the more powerful impact of reading the disjunctive clusters of proper names:[46]

> Mount Rokku between the rock and the cedars,
> Polhonac,
> As Gyges on Thracian platter set the feast,
> Cabestan, Tereus,
> > It is Cabestan's heart in the dish,
> Vidal, or Ecbatan, upon the gilded tower in Ecbatan
> Lay the god's bride, lay ever, waiting the golden rain.
> By Garonne. "Saave!"
> The Garonne is thick like paint,

> Procession,—"Et sa'ave, sa'ave, sa'ave Regina!"—
> Moves like a worm, in the crowd.
> Adige, thin film of images
>
> C 4, 16

Such disjunctions, which occur at all levels of the poem, in lines, stanzas, cantos and blocks of cantos, arise directly from Pound's definition of the heroic vocation of the poet. Even the extremely variable left margins, which are apt to strike the first-time reader as the traces of unfathomable expertise, reflect this need for breakthrough. James Laughlin writes that "in the fury of composition, [Pound] couldn't always take the time to go all the way back to the left margin; he would slap the carriage and wherever it stopped that determined the indent."[47]

In the significantly entitled "Praefatio Ad Lectorem Electum" to *The Spirit of Romance* Pound wrote, "The history of an art is the history of masterwork, not of failures, or mediocrity. . . . The study of literature is hero-worship."[48] The master writer or hero is situated not at the apex of a continuum, but is above other writers altogether. The preface continues, "Art or an art is not unlike a river, in that it is perturbed at times by the quality of the river bed, but is in a way independent of that bed." In the just-quoted passage from Canto 4, Pound has further refined this image of aloofness: the water itself is "thick" (always a negative code word for Pound) as opposed to the "film of images" floating above it.[49] The jumps in Canto 4, and throughout *The Cantos*, are an effort to avoid the "thickness," "mediocrity," "failure" that would result from immersion in any one story, context, or tradition.

It is not just context but language that traps the hero, who must invent, like Lenin, "a new medium, something between speech and action that is worth . . . study" (*SP*, 217).[50] In Canto 16, Lenin hardly materializes in language: he is not named and he hardly speaks, but he creates the Russian Revolution with a few laconic phrases:

> There was a man there talking,
> To a thousand, just a short speech, and
> Then move 'em on. And he said:
> Yes, these people, they are all right, they
> Can do everything, everything except act;
> And go an' hear 'em, but when they are through,
> Come to the bolsheviki...
>
> C 16, 74

The hero's speech is a punctual (puncturing) act, not a discourse.[51] The Poundian-Chinese ideogram for truth—man standing beside his word—has been widely admired.[52] But it should be noted that when this man stands beside his word, it is often just that, a single word or phrase—he never stands beside any lengthy discourse. Lenin's speech and the language Pound uses to depict it share a single tone: poet and leader are tacitly united. Their action-speech has such power that the line after it stops, the revolution occurs: "And when it broke . . ." This language contrasts sharply with the dialects of the preceding passages. There has been a long section in slangy but non-colloquial French describing the horrors of trench warfare in rather anaesthetized fashion: "Poo quah? Ma foi on attaquait pour manger"; and then some lines in Poundian dialect: " 'Aint yuh herd? / He vinneh de vore. / De droobs iss released vrom de eastern vront, yess?" As *The Cantos* progresses, accent, especially if "Jewish," will be a sign of moral decay; here, though Pound is not scornful, their overly physical speech identifies the speakers as particles of history, created by it rather than creating it.[53]

Lenin is not using a common medium; he act-speaks, but the resulting word-acts do not circulate; they are "worth study," after the fact. Jefferson's words are also acts; again, rather than circulating, they enforce themselves: "He governed . . . by means of conversation with his more intelligent friends. . . . He canalized American thought by means of his verbal manifestations" (*JM*, 15). Such metaphors are crucial for Pound: the artist, ruler, sage, sun, is superior to and separated from his material, which he controls, sculpts, canalizes, illuminates, renders clean by sharp demarcations. Cutting is holy. For example: the first individual act in *The Cantos* is Odysseus drawing his sword to dig the ritual "ell-square pitkin" soon to be filled with blood. Pound leaves hell in Canto 16 through a "passage clean-squared in granite" (69). "Form is cut in the lute's neck, tone is from the bowl" (*C 109*, 788). In Canto 30, the "complaynt" is that "Nothing is now clean slayne" (147). In his essay on Cavalcanti, Pound laments the loss of "the radiant world where one thought cuts through another with clean edge . . . the matter of Dante's *paradiso*, the glass under water . . . untouched by the two maladies, the Hebrew disease, the Hindoo disease" (*LE*, 154). Pound sees the Chinese ideogram for "sincerity" as "the precise definition of the word, pictorially the sun's lance coming to rest on the precise spot verbally."[54]

As well as creating order, the heroic blade disposes of rot: such is "the surgeon's knife of fascism" or Pound's sense of the function of *Ulysses:* "The sticky, molasses-covered filth of current print, all the fuggs, all the foetors, the whole boil of the European mind, had been lanced" (*GK*, 96).

These senses of surgical exactitude and separation account for two major sources of difficulty in Pound's writing: the foreign words and the elision of quotes. "Good reasons" for both practices can be found in his criticism. The languages embody a specific flavor that can't be translated; the brief quotations and references reflect Pound's desire for efficiency: only the high spots need be narrated.[55] But Pound carries these devices so far that such justifications wear thin. His need for a heroic separation from the reader provides a less contorted explanation.

Pound is considered one of the most literary of authors, but he demonstrates a surprisingly strong distaste for books and writing. His well-known apostrophe to intense reading is followed by something quite opposite: "Man reading shd. be man intensely alive. The book shd. be a ball of light in one's hand. To read and be conscious of the act of reading is for some men (the writer among them) to suffer. I loathe the operation. My eyes are geared for the horizon. Nevertheless I do read for days on end when I have caught the scent of a trail" (*GK*, 55). Pound's loathing of commonality of language extends to the alphabet. Recall the phrase on *Ulysses:* "the sticky, molasses-covered filth of current print," or consider the following: "Until [Eliot] succeeds in detaching the Jewish from the European elements of his peculiar variety of Christianity he will never find the right formula. Not a jot or tittle of the hebraic alphabet can pass into the text without danger of contaminating it" (*SP*, 320). As *The Cantos* progresses, Pound turns to ideograms, musical notation, pictograms, to escape the contamination of common letters.[56]

It will not be surprising that the phallus is the key to heroic action, although the physicality of Pound's conception might surprise a reader used to Lacan's more theoretical entity. The differences are instructive. For Lacan, the nonphysicality of the phallus underlies all other signifiers and the nonempirical nature of fatherhood is the foundation of the symbolic order, leading to a sense of language that is thoroughly social and beyond the control of any individual. Language as the "locus of signifying convention" gives rise to a self that is in a condition of "radical ex-centricity to itself." Language is the site of interpersonal truth (the only kind there is for Lacan): "it is with the appearance of language the dimension of truth appears."[57] Pound on the other hand aspires to a natural language ("from the nature the sign" [C 97, 689]) with the phallus as the icon of congruence: "man's phallic heart is from heaven" (C 99, 711).[58] Lacan sees "phallocentrism" as "entirely conditioned by the intrusion of the signifier in man's psyche"; thus phallocentrism is "strictly impossible to deduce from any pre-established harmony of this psyche with the nature that it expresses."[59]

For Pound the natural, physical phallus is the intimate target of the Jew and the mercantile world he represents: "Shylock wants no mere shinbone or elbow, but wants to end Antonio's natural increase."[60] Circumcision and usury are united for Pound as causes and effects of desensitization. In a chapter from *Kulchur* that, not coincidentally, defends Chaucer from charges of rape, Pound states that "discrimination by the senses is dangerous to avarice. . . . The moneychanger . . . thrives on . . . insensitivity and non-perception. An instant sense of proportion imperils financiers" (281). Desensitization in *The Cantos* refers to sense perception and language, but it governs more elemental areas as well. For the phallus, the instrument of control and cutting, to itself be cut is a nightmare. Pound said to Olson, "It must do something, after all these years and years, where the most sensitive nerves in the body are, rubbing them off, over and over again."[61] To return to Lacanian terms briefly, it seems significant that Pound would also associate Jews and Jehovah with "code worship" (GK, 164), thus segregating off into a hated minority what Lacan saw as a universal phenomenon: the transindividual, systematic nature of language embodied in the ineffable Name-of-the-Father.[62]

The essay where he is most unbuttoned with his ideas in this area, "The Postscript to Remy de Gourmont's *Natural Philosophy of Love*," may strike some readers as an odd attempt at humor. But lighthearted or not, its metaphors will consistently govern Pound's language. He speculates that the brain is "only a sort of great clot of genital fluid held in suspense and reserve." But this remarkable fact does not apply to the species as a whole, it only concerns the genius, "discharging at high pressure." Creation is spermatic: "light is a projection from the luminous fluid"; "the sperm [is] the form-creator, the substance which compels the ovule to evolve in a given pattern." All other causality is overruled: "I believe, and on no better ground than that of a sudden emotion . . . that the species changes as suddenly as a man makes a song or a poem, or as suddenly as he *starts* making them, more suddenly than he can cut a statue in stone" (*PD*, 203, 210, 206, 208).

Phallic creativity commits Pound to impulse and incompletion: he has to believe and create instantaneously. But this creativity is not autonomous since the genius requires incomprehension: this pattern repeats the dependence of paradise on hell throughout *The Cantos*. The "sudden out-spurt" of genius does two things at once: it "creates the answer, and baffles the man counting on the abacus" (*PD*, 208). The creation (not the discovery) of the answer requires the baffled non-genius with the abacus, a more or less Semitic symbol of a mechanical code.

The power dynamics are, not surprisingly, gendered: "There are traces of [the idea of the spermatic brain] in the symbolism of phallic religions, man really the phallus or spermatozoide charging, head-on, the female chaos. . . . Even oneself has felt it, driving any new idea into the great passive vulva of London, a sensation analogous to the male feeling in copulation" (*PD*, 204). Even in this most flagrant statement of will, one can detect the static nature of Pound's project and its roots in his social situation. Only the writer is active: the readers who make up the great vulva remain passive. In order to maintain definition, the phallic hero, or heroic phallus, cannot mix with the world. Lenin's speech may move crowds in a physical sense, but it doesn't change their crowdlike nature. The new idea may be driven into the feminized chaos of readers, but they can never incorporate this idea, become pregnant by it. It remains as aloof as its originator. To ejaculate is to give birth without need for a womb: "Creative thought is . . . like the male cast of the human seed, but given that . . . ejaculation . . . the thought once born . . . does lead an independent life. . . . Gourmont has the phrase 'fecundating a generation of bodies as genius fecundates a generation of minds' " (*PD*, 207). The elision of the feminine and of the recipient of the word in *The Cantos* is articulated in the remarkable line "The production IS the beloved" (*C 104*, 756), which ultimately eliminates the existence of the woman so often gazed upon by Pound's troubadours.[63] Similarly, "You who dare Persephone's threshold, / Be-

loved, do not fall apart in my hands" (C 93, 645) becomes, despite
its lyricism, fit for a horror movie unless we read "Beloved" as the
questing of the poem itself, daring Persephone's threshold.

One could argue that Pound's sense of readership was more re-
ciprocal than this, that he at least intended to communicate with the
elite reader, and that there were many instances when he was speaking for a group of writers or to them. This is true, but it applies
almost exclusively to his criticism and journalism, and as his career
advanced it became less true even there. Eliot's befuddlement with
Pound's attempt to explain the good banking practices of the Monte
dei Paschi demonstrates Pound's need to establish his authority by
means of the reader's incomprehension, as does the opacity of the
explanation of Douglas's $A + B$ Theorem quoted earlier.[64] Lines such
as " 'Every . . . etc . . . / downright corruption' " (C 87, 596; ellipses
in the original) become increasingly common in *The Cantos*. Pound
is referring to one of his central dogmas, a sentence from Adams:
"Every bank of discount is downright corruption" (C 71, 416). The
abbreviation can be justified: Pound had already quoted the sentence
in full. But its importance does not jibe with such presentation,
which makes it incomprehensible to all but the specialist. (The abbreviation does not even take up less space.) Its form—only "downright corruption" is spelled out—follows Pound's habit of associating materialization in language with evil; leaders are often above
embodiment, as with the old king in Canto 49. This pattern appears
even in slight verbal gestures: "Gt. is gt. . Little is little" (C 99, 719).
The hero doesn't appear in language but needs to change it or to
continually distance himself from it each time he speaks. When this
distance is effected, the space fills with the light of paradise; hell is
the smother of any contextualization.

Mussolini is the primary hero: he even "reads" *The Cantos* (at least
he looks at it and demonstrates transverbal seeing, as Gaudier does
with Chinese characters). As a corollary to his superior presence, he
is also supremely active, but while he accomplishes "everything,"
his action typically is instantaneous, and finally does not touch
society:

M A QVESTO,"
    said the Boss, "è divertente."
    catching the point before the aesthetes had got
        there;

Having drained off the muck by Vada
From the marshes, by Circeo, where no one else wd. have
   drained it.
Waited 2000 years, ate grain from the marshes;
Water supply for ten million, another one million *"vani"*
that is rooms for people to live in.
   XI of our era.

                                           C 41, 202

Pound intends a picture of a redeemed society: draining off "the muck" also means revitalizing culture and language. Besides *"grano, bonifica, restauri*, grain, swamp drainage," Pound saw "AN AWAK-ENED INTELLIGENCE in the nation and a new LANGUAGE in the debates in the Chamber" (*JM*, 73). Mussolini is the cause, and yet the effects go no further than himself. Legislators may speak "with clarity and even brevity" but they are either extensions of the Boss's body or they are paper he writes on or discards: "And even here is the hand or eye or ear of the Duce, the Debunker par excellence, for the deputies and ministers know that there is an EDITORIAL eye and ear—precisely—an editor, who will see through their bunkum and for whom they will go to the scrap-basket just as quickly as an incompetent reporter's copy will go to the basket in a live editorial office" (*JM*, 74). As Pound would express it near the end of *The Cantos:* "The whole tribe is from one man's body" (*C* 99, 722).

In Canto 41, the Italy that expresses Mussolini's body is heroic and alive, and the calendar becomes millennial ("XI of our era"), but as the three following ideogrammic moments indicate, the masses on which Mussolini inscribes his heroism remain a swamp. First, the Boss sends bankers into exile; their crime and their race are not spec-ified, but the story is said to be "told by the mezzo-yit" and one financier's speech hints at the castrating "chewisch" dialect Pound employs: "three mill*yum* for my *cut*" (emphases added). Second, a hotel keeper expresses fanatic gratitude: "Noi ci facciam sgannar [scannar] per Mussolini [We would let our throats be cut for Mus-solini]." And third, in a gesture that Pound presents as humorous, a child pronounces sentence: "Populo . . . ignorante!"[65]

Even when the evil moneymen have been magically quarantined by the Boss's voice—"You are all for the *confine*"—the masses remain as passive as the peasants in Canto 49. In a contradiction that is basic to Fascism, a timeless feudalism is, within the freedom from se-quence the ideogram provides, interchangeable with a streamlined modernity.[66] In both cases, the hero is as separate from his materials as quality is from quantity; he embodies form but he also monopolizes it.

As phallus he is the timeless essence of accuracy and specificity, "the unwobbling pivot," but he is also unpredictable, making it new, breaking up clichés and bureaucracies equally. Pound says that Mussolini is "an OPPORTUNIST who is RIGHT, that is who has certain convictions and who drives them through circumstance, or batters and forms circumstance with them" (*JM*, 17–18). On the divine level, such opportunism becomes "hilaritas" (*C 83*, 542; *C 100*, 730), or a Protean omniformity:

> the Divine Mind is abundant
> unceasing
> *improvisatore*
> Omniformis
> unstill
> and that the lice turned from the manifest;
> overlooking the detail
> and their filth now observes mere dynamic;
> That the Pontifex ceased to be holy
> —that was in Caesar's time—
> who was buggar'd
> and the coin ceased to be holy,
>
> *C 92, 634*

In Poundian shorthand coin ceases to be holy when currency doesn't conform immediately to the will and finally the voice of the state and the leader. The contradiction here between authority as improviser and authority as stabilizer of social value is matched by the uncanny similarity between the unstill, dynamic divinity and the filthy dynamism of the amorphous evil ones, whose sexual energy as they bugger Caesar and simultaneously pervert and destabilize the currency seems as powerful as the clean phallicism of Pound's heroes.[67]

Such thinking refuses to come to terms with social structures. Manifest, that is, historical, detail can be kept still in Pound's paradisal or hellish categories only by a dynamic effort of will. As the trajectory of state authority in the above passage demonstrates here, falling from the unceasing Divine Mind to the inexplicably triumphant evil forces, such an effort can never master the world. Gramsci's description of the Crocean hero expresses the contradiction: "It is not possible to think of an organized and permanent passion. Permanent passion is a condition of orgasm and spasm, which means operational incapacity. It excludes parties, and excludes every plan of action worked out in advance."[68] This last phrase is quite accurate to the progress of *The Cantos.*

Another dimension of this contradiction is the dichotomy between voice and code.[69] Mussolini's voice embodies ever-changing "hilaritas": "it differs from town to town. . . . The speech at Forlì was at Forlì and not at Torino" (*JM,* 65). Mussolini promotes the unpredictability of that primary aesthetic quality, play. Twice in *The Cantos* he asks why Pound feels the need to put his ideas in order. And yet this mercurial voice is the source of order for the society. The lira, Pound wrote, "was based on the Duce's word. For me a much more secure basis than other people's gold."[70] Opposed to the authoritative generativeness of voice is the deadness of code on paper—that is, written words:

> Justinian's codes inefficient
> "abbiamo fatto un mucchio . . .
> (a haystack of laws on paper)
> Mus. viva voce:
> "We ask 'em to settle between 'em.
> If they can't, the State intervenes."
> *C 87,* 585

After Mussolini's death, Pound's writing pledged itself to the Fascist state of the Boss's voice. The grammar of the passage destroys the possibility of assigning the quoted voices to specific persons, and yet the quotations represent key statements of the Boss, one of which, paradoxically enough, asserts the necessity for governmental accountability to reside in the name of the leader. The only figures materialized grammatically are the excremental "monopolists" who cause the "merrda" that is assigned to them to overflow with letters:

> "wherein is no responsible person
> having a front name, a hind name and an address"
> "not a right but a duty"
> those words still stand uncancelled,
> "Presente!"
> and merrda for the monopolists
> the bastardly lot of 'em

Put down the slave trade, made the desert to yield
and menaced the loan swine

C 78, 493

These lines themselves have no "address," in the sense of either social location or audience. The diction of the last three lines sways uneasily between a didactic tough-guy tone ("the loan swine") and a biblical religiosity ("made the desert to yield"). By this point, Pound's genius-writing has worn away contextualization so thoroughly nothing is left but the displaced tone of a mind in motion distantly echoing various social origins.

Even when the present of the writing does intrude, as does happen in the *Pisan Cantos* to a greater extent than elsewhere in the poem, it is quickly transmuted to a solipsistic space: in the passage below Pound may be claiming that Fascist Italy was eternally present to him—but the ambiguity of the reference is crucial:

Says the Japanese sentry : Paaak yu djeep over there,
some of the best soldiers we have says the captain
       Dai Nippon Banzai from the Philippines
remembering Kagekiyo : "how stiff the shaft of your neck is."
              and they went off each his own way
"a better fencer than I was," said Kumasaka, a shade,
"I believe in the resurrection of Italy   quia impossibile est
    4 times to the song of Gassir
              now in the mind indestructible

C 74, 456

Though this passage begins in the present, the language of that present is displayed in a degraded register, and Pound quickly escapes to a timeless heroic ideogram: phallic ghosts who are both representatives of Axis Japan and comradely enemies from Noh plays; Fascist Italy; the mythical African city of Wagadu—a melange of imaginary solutions to real narrative and historical cruxes, interchangeable, indestructible, and socially impalpable.

THE PROFESSIONAL EPIC

Pound began *The Cantos* as his career was on the decline, though this may be obscured today by his literary resurrection, problematic as that may be.[71] He himself was quite aware of his position: "*The Dial* has sacked me . . . my communication with America is over";

"My American publishers do not exist. . . . Likewise English" (*L*, 186, 190). The isolation could have been caused by both cultural resistance and flaws in his character; but it can also be seen as arising from the dynamics of his literary ambition: his increasingly absolute pronouncements on all subjects match "his final / Exclusion from the world of letters," as he writes in the only slightly fictitious "Mauberley" (*P*, 202). What was self-mocking there became real over the next twenty-five years as he drove himself to escape those contaminating letters.

The journey that seems so literary at the beginning, "And then went down to the ship," also represented the beginning of an attempt to transform and/or to escape a society that furnished only an ornamental niche for the poet. The "and/or" signals deep conflict in Pound's efforts, as does the fact that the vehicle he used to effect his transformation-escape was the epic, the most prestigious, archaic literary form. Where he arrived was St. Elizabeths and the fractured, quasi-revelatory space of *The Cantos*, which was the message that would have changed the world, if only the world had been different enough to receive it.

The details are tangled, and without a strict chronology; instead there is an interplay between two sets of oppositions: professional writer versus epic poet, and England and France (and ultimately America) versus Italy and China. This second set is not so much geographic as psychic and social. Pound began to write a long poem that was urbane, extremely literary, nostalgic, and addressed to the cultural centers of Western society, first London, then, briefly, Paris. The Hell Cantos mark the shift to a transcendental epic embodying natural truth that was addressed to an abstract audience at the same time as it damned its historical one. But this shift is not purely chronological; it has the binary structure of Pound's ideograms: the writing oscillates between urbanity and absolutism. On a large scale, though, there is a progression: it was only after Pound was launched into his epic that he began to write ideogrammically: such jumps don't occur in his early poems. This process also took over his prose, which grew elliptical to the point that he could barely write any other way.

Pound called "Mauberley" "a farewell to London" (*P*, 185), but, compared with *The Cantos*, it is a polite one with much of its aggression transformed to irony and directed inward toward the poet figure. It is Pound's most complete acceptance of culturally validated verse norms. While the poem enacts Mauberley's banishment, and its publication coincides roughly with Pound's actual departure to Paris, if the door to the cultural drawing room were to reopen it would reveal a most valid poet, capable of impeccable (if "modern") quatrains.

Like "Mauberley," the opening cantos are also a display of aesthetic capital: Homer, Ovid, Henry James, the Troubadours, the Quattrocento, the contemporary art scene (through the mention of Picasso, oddly, rather than Wyndham Lewis), Noh, and Chinese poetry. Pound specifically recalls, via formal echoes, two of his most applauded early literary efforts: "The Seafarer" (in 1), and *Cathay* (in 13). This miscellaneous nature can also be seen in the variety of epic frames: Homer in 1, 2, 4, and 7, Ovid in 2 and 4, Browning in 2, the *Cid* and Camões in 3. Homer and Ovid provide the opportunity for the great set pieces of transformed translation in the first two cantos, but on the whole Pound's attitude toward these would-be predecessors is tinged with regret over their distance from him and some embarrassment at his attempt to revive them:[72]

> Ignez da Castro murdered, and a wall
> Here stripped, here made to stand.
> Drear waste, the pigment flakes from the stone,
> Or plaster flakes, Mantegna painted the wall.
>
> *C 3,* 12

> ELEANOR (she spoiled in a British climate)
>   Ἐλανδρος and Ἑλέπτολις, and
>   poor old Homer blind,
>   blind as a bat,
> Ear, ear for the sea-surge;
>   rattle of old men's voices.
>
> . . . .
>
> Un peu moisi, plancher plus bas que le jardin.
>
> *C 7,* 24

> Hang it all, Robert Browning,
> there can be but the one "Sordello."
> But Sordello, and my Sordello?
> Lo Sordels si fo di Mantovana.
> So-Shu churned in the sea.
>
> *C 2,* 6

Some aggressive confidence can be read in "Hang it all," but the more pervasive sense here is of futility and deadness. In the first excerpt, Ignez da Castro refers to a story in Camões of King Pedro disintering and crowning his murdered mistress. In the early version of *The Cantos* Pound compares his own antiquarian literary interests with this ghoulishness.[73] While the final version cuts out any overt anxiety, it is still visible in the decomposing paint. In the second excerpt, the decrepitude of the classics is obvious, especially when they are transplanted to England; and while the line in French from Flaubert's *Un Coeur simple* is oblique, its musty floor beneath the level of the garden connotes a grave. In the third excerpt, Pound's confident opening is instantly entangled with quasi-identities, "Sordello" (the poem), Sordello (Browning's version of the poet), my Sordello (Pound's version, but existing where?) immediately springing up after the initial assertion of unity. The syntax kicks up more dust with "but the one" echoing oddly in the opposing "But Sordello." The quote from an Italian manuscript about the historical Sordello may be read as a final settlement of the problem, but the shift to So-Shu points to instability, not resolution.

In trying to revive the epic, Pound may have been digging up the dead, or the dead may have been rising from the grave to menace him. The first nontranslated words Pound writes in *The Cantos* are "Lie quiet Divus." In translating Divus's Latin translation of Homer, Pound is a reincarnation of Divus, but possibly just a mask through which the more real Divus—and one step back the even more real Homer—is speaking. The joking abruptness of "Lie quiet Divus" asserts Pound's epic identity, but the semantic import of the words articulates his dread over a possible lack of identity. Divus may not be lying quietly.

Even as late as Canto 46, this anxiety persists. The fact that he read the canto in a broadcast indicates that he considered it accessible to a general audience (*RS*, 34–38). It denounces contemporary social conditions and is as explicit an exposition of Pound's economic beliefs as exists in *The Cantos*, even though it is bisected by a pointedly irrelevant digression spoken in suburban England by an exotic "Abdul Baha" concerning an even more exotic dervish who refuses to talk about religion, answering instead, "I have drunk my milk. I must dance." Throughout the canto there is an odd and insistent play on the word "case." Some of the relevant lines:

> Or the snow fell beside it. Seventeen
> Years on this case, nineteen years, ninety years
>   on this case
>
>   .   .   .   .   .   .
>
> 17 years on this case, and we not the first lot!
>
>   .   .   .   .
>
> The bank makes it [money] *ex nihil*
> Denied by five thousand professors, will any
> Jury convict 'um? This case, and with it
> the first part, draws to a conclusion,
> of the first phase of this opus, Mr Marx, Karl, did not
>   foresee this conclusion
>
>   .   .   .   .
>
> This case is not the last case or the whole case, we ask a
> REVISION, we ask for enlightenment in a case
> moving concurrent, but this case is the first case:
>
>   .   .   .   .
>
> CASE for the prosecution. That is one case, minor case
> in the series/Eunited States of America, a.d. 1935
> England a worse case, France under a foetor of regents.
>
> C 46, 231–35

The rhetorical frame of Pound as prosecutor has its effect, but the insistence on this being the first case (or not the first case) seems odd. The question of primacy would seem to have more to do with Pound's epic status, which he would want to be originary. The worry would be that his poem might be merely "one case, minor case / in the series."

The insertion of Abdul Baha's story of the laconic dervish makes sense if its exoticism is read as emblematic of Pound's strained claims to differential epic status. Abdul Baha is set between originality and derivativeness in a way quite similar to Pound's own situation:

> Thus Abdul Baha
> Third vice-gerent of the First Abdul or whatever Baha,
> the Sage, the Uniter, the founder of a religion,
> in a garden at Uberton, Gubberton, or mebbe it was some
> other damned suburb, but at any rate a suburban suburb
>
> C 46, 232

For an isolate founder of a religion to find himself in an English suburban garden must have been uncomfortably close to trying to create something "*ex nihil,*" and it might also have resembled some of Ezra Pound's experiences as a writer. Turning to a Dantescan epic frame, with its more comprehensive claims to universal, incontrovertible truth, would be one way to leave that suburban garden behind, and to damn it, which Pound did in the Hell Cantos and does elsewhere in the poem.

In moving to Italy and into his epic realm Pound entered a land of sunlit verities, where the Clark Kent–like pedant would reveal absolute powers: "I am a flat-chested highbrow. I can 'cure' the whole trouble simply by criticism of style. Oh, can I? Yes. I have been saying so for some time" (*JM*, 17). But this was written to his imaginary audience, as the flicker from comedy to earnestness indicates; at the same time, a particular member of the Anglo-American literary world would receive staid advice. In 1934 he wrote Mary Barnard "I was certainly right in telling you to work on sapphics," and "Re Gugg.[enheim] make yr. Greek metric plan as *impressive* as possible. Throw in a lot of technical terms: Sapphic, Alcaic, etc. (with the correct spellings, etc.)" (*L*, 261, 259). These same shifts occur in *The Cantos:* Pound writes urbane, even self-deprecatory lines and passages throughout the poem, though absolute moral pronouncements tend to become more frequent.

Pound considered "English free speech, the privilege of Hyde Park oratory," to be "a mark of contempt for thought in *any* form whatsoever" (*JM*, 42). Italy was a Not-England and Not-America, where Pound's word was no longer a Hyde Park vanity, but law: as he wrote in a letter in 1940, "Ez' *Guide to Kulchur*, facilitated by Ez' system of economics, now the program of Ministers Funk and Riccardi. Tho' I don't spose they knew it was mine" (*L*, 347).

The sad naiveté of this matches his description of *The Cantos* in "An Introduction to the Economic Nature of the United States," a pamphlet written in Italian during the war: "For forty years I have schooled myself, not to write an economic history of the U.S. or any other country, but to write an epic poem which begins 'In the Dark Forest' crosses the Purgatory of human error, and ends in the light" (*SP*, 167). Such a homily could only have been written in Italy, where Pound could reveal his student side ("For forty years I have schooled myself"), play teacher to the masses, and watch Mussolini rewrite the world with his help.

Writing to representatives of a literary audience at roughly the same time, Pound treats his epic territory with jaunty irony—"And we agree, je crois, that one can no longer put Mt. Purgatory forty miles high in the midst of Australian sheep land"—and with anxiety: "There *is* at start, descent to the shades, metamorphoses, parallel (Vidal-Actaeon). All of which is mere matter for little ....rs and Harvud instructors *unless* I pull it off as reading matter, singing matter, shouting matter, the tale of the tribe. . . . As to the *form* of *The Cantos:* All I can say or pray is: *wait* till it's there. I mean wait till I get 'em written and then if it don't show, I will start exegesis" (*L,* 190, 294, 323). These anxieties accurately forecast the fate of *The Cantos.*

Like "Mauberley," the Hell Cantos are also a goodbye note to London, but a less ambiguous one; here, the tensions between Pound the professional writer and Pound the epic poet explode.[74] The results were so harsh he was embarrassed to show them to Thomas Hardy, one living literary ancestor he still respected (*L,* 192). While the categories of paradise and, especially, hell were useful in putting London in its place, using these categories meant treating them without any of the irony or regret that tinged Pound's earlier attempts to appropriate epic materials. They had to be real. But to imitate Dante entailed a basic problem: Dante's gradations of sins and virtues formed a syntax that was opposed to the ideogram; to move in an orderly progression from hell to paradise constituted a narrative of submission that contradicted Pound's sense of the genius jumping from context to context.[75] Despite the promise in the poem's title, the only stretches of remotely Dantescan narrative we get occur in the Hell Cantos and in Canto 73, which is written in Italian and uses Dante's model of the dead speaking to the live interlocutor.

Even the Hell Cantos can be seen—with some squinting—as part of the poem's aesthetic display, as a gloss on Dante, an icon whose literary value was equaled only by Homer. Their random position in the sequence of the surrounding cantos—Malatesta; Baldy Bacon; Confucius; Dante; World War One—seems to imply no structural claim as an overall framing device. But this ignores their programmatic violence, which is absolute enough to destroy the possibility of compromise with the contemporary audience.

The hell of Canto 1 is a nonmoral underworld that Odysseus visits for direction and renewal, just as Pound revises Homer via Anglo-Saxon verse to renew his own writing.[76] The piece offers the reader a puzzle that before decoding, and even more afterward, represents an affirmation of a purely literary sphere as it reenacts, via stylistic and referential overlays, the medieval trope of *translatio studii*, the migration of learning from Greece westward through Europe. While Canto 1 deals with life and death thematically, it does not impinge closely on the lives of its contemporaries. The Hell Cantos, on the other hand, though they do contain scattered references to the past, focus on the present: they damn it, as well as simply insulting it. In theory, there is a possibility of literary recoding; these cantos are an equivalent to Dante's hell, which, as the end of 14 tells us, is "without dignity, without tragedy," thus justifying the language used. But only in theory: any critical distance is severely compromised by the visceral impact:

> politicians
> . . . . e and . . . . . n, their wrists bound to
> their ankles,
> Standing bare bum,
> Faces smeared on their rumps,
> wide eye on flat buttock,
> Bush hanging for beard,
> Addressing crowds through their arse-holes,
> Addressing the multitudes in the ooze,
> newts, water-slugs, water-maggots,
> C 14, 61

This is a direct attack, not just on [Lloyd Georg]e and [Woodrow Wilso]n, but on society as a whole, "the multitudes in the ooze"; yet at the same time it is a direct imitation of Dante.[77] Pound damns England to hell because England no longer believes in hell, or in Dante—or in Pound. Here Pound is confronting the marginality of literature while operating rhetorically as if it were divine law. Without Dante's sanction, he is scrawling "The President is full of shit" on a bathroom wall.

The form of the proper names confirms the ambiguity of Pound's position. Is he an epic poet defining society through language and leading the saved out of hell, or is he a professional writer with an obscure share of the literary market, circumscribed by a philistine society whose control extends down to the very material he has to work with? There is a literary reason for the missing letters of the names: Pound writes, "My 'point' being that not even the first but only last letters of their names had resisted corruption" (L, 293). But Pound's rhetoric was also affected by a potent force outside the literary sphere: libel laws, representing the society's power over the poet's language.

This battle of contexts and authority recurs throughout the poem. At times Pound flaunts his powerlessness, insisting on thick bars over lines that would have libeled the Rothschilds in Canto 52.[78] More often with proper names he will demonstrate private control— or it could be read as public self-marginalization—as in the follow- ing abbreviations in the *Pisan Cantos:* "and the only people who did anything of interest with H., M., [Hitler, Mussolini] and Frobenius" (C 74, 450). This conflict over control can be seen behind one of Pound's most frequent stylistic quirks: his increasing inability to use proper names or nouns that refer to social institutions without aggressively distorting them: Roosevelt = Roosenstein, Roosefelt, Jewsfeld; psychiatry = pussy-kike-iatry; American = murkn; and, with less hostility, in *Guide to Kulchur*—note the title of course—even a figure like Aristotle becomes Harry Stotl, or Arry. Could part of the paradisal nimbus around such late lines as "Yet to walk with Mozart, Agassiz and Linneas / 'neath overhanging air under sun- beat" (C 113, 800) be ascribed to the fact that Pound feels temporarily obedient enough to write the proper names properly?

Given the impossible goal of speaking with transcendent epic cer- tainty to a fallen present, it is not surprising that Pound's writing in the Hell Cantos is weak. It is damaged not so much by fury or sca- tology—Pound points out that both are venerable Dantean quali- ties—but by abstraction, so thin as to be allegorical in the received sense that Pound often criticized:

> And Invidia,
> the corruptio, fœtor, fungus,
> liquid animals, melted ossifications,
> slow rot, fœtid combustion,
>> chewed cigar-butts, without dignity, without tragedy,
>> C 14, 63

Technically, Pound would certainly have known better. He had warned neophytes years before in "A Few Don'ts" against writing "dim lands *of peace*" (his emphasis; *LE*, 5), yet the Hell Cantos contain lines like the above or "the great scabrous arse-hole, sh-tting flies, / rumbling *with imperialism*" (my emphasis). While in the *Inferno* Dante the author ranges through history to exemplify precise grades of sin, and Dante the protagonist interacts with and learns from the sinners in a progression that finally includes both hell and heaven in a single dramatic narrative, in Cantos 14 and 15 there is an all-purpose excremental condemnation of the literary, financial, and moral practices of the present. There is no narrative motivation; Pound simply enters hell by quoting a single line from the *Inferno*, and though he takes some forty lines to leave it, the narrative of his exit focuses entirely on his physical contact with, and purification from, materialized evil. By the end of the canto he has "emerged decently clean," to use the language from the "Osiris" essay, but he is not a "licensed initiate," only an unlicensed one, trapped by his literalized allegory. As *The Cantos* progresses, the interplay between clean and dirty, light and mud, hard and rotten, becomes so tight that Pound is never able to leave hell behind, any more than he can escape the mercantile present. Pound is addressing himself as much as he is the reader at the beginning of Canto 46: "you who think you will / get through hell in a hurry."

There is an uncanny similarity between Pound's hell and his paradise. The lines at the end of 14 condemning "monopolists, obstructors of knowledge, / obstructors of distribution" are widely quoted as examples of Pound's moral rage. But in fact if there is one thing not lacking in hell, it is distribution:

> howling, as of a hen-yard in a printing-house,
> the clatter of presses,
> the blowing of dry dust and stray paper,
>
> .   .   .   .
> the air without refuge of silence,
> the drift of lice, teething,
> and above it the mouthing of orators,
>
> .   .   .   .
> mobile earth, a dung hatching obscenities,
> inchoate error,
> boredom born out of boredom,
> british weeklies,
>
> .   .   .   .   .
> a continual bum-belch
> distributing its productions.
>   *C 14, 15,* 61–65

In fact, remembering how Worglian currency—meaning consecrated by the state—circulated correctly only its own valley, we could say that one of Pound's basic fears was of uncontrolled distribution.

From the Hell Cantos on, Pound constantly damns historical figures, with the physicality of his pronouncements compensating for
their lack of narrative and social grounding. "Hell pissed up Met-
ternich" (*C* 50, 248); "and as for Hamilton / we may take it (my
authority, ego scriptor cantilenae) / that he was the Prime snot in
ALL American history" (*C* 62, 350). The shaky authority for such
judgments, coming from Pound's provisional position as an epic
poet, has to be asserted viscerally.

The hellishness of *The Cantos* is where the strain of Pound's social
and literary position shows most glaringly. But it is not just the Dantescan frame that reveals the conflict; the Homeric epic frame functions similarly. Although the narrative goal there should be Penelope and Ithaca, Pound focuses on Circe, who becomes a figure of
hellish enchantment, thus making the Homeric frame Dantescan.

His commitment to a fully redeemed epic life and writing allows
Pound to include a wide range of detail—in fact, in the *Pisan Cantos*
his instantaneous registration of the present can be even quicker than
Williams's. But as fast as the present opens up, it is consistently
veiled with epic authority:

> "all them g.d. m.f. generals c.s. all of 'em fascists"
> "fer a bag o' Dukes"
> > > "the things I saye an' dooo"
> > ac ego in harum
> > so lay men in Circe's swine-sty;
> > > ivi in harum *ego* ac vidi cadaveres animae
> > > > "c'mon small fry" sd/ the little coon to the big black;
> > of the slaver as seen between decks
> > > and all the presidents
> > Washington Adams Monroe Polk Tyler
> > plus Carrol (of Carrolton) Crawford
> > Robbing the public for private individual's gain ΘΕΛΓΕΙΝ
> > > > > > > *C* 74, 450–51

The speed of lines like the first of this passage make them one of the
most influential parts of Pound's work for later poets. But Pound
recontextualizes the present condescendingly: these black prisoners
are pigs, and the historical process that produced them is proclaimed
and denounced by a single epic word: "THELGEIN," to bewitch.

The following passage reveals the limited social base out of which
Pound's epic dimensions unfold:

Among all these twerps and Pulitzer sponges
            no voice for the Constitution,
No objection to the historic blackout.
        "My bikini is worth yr/ raft". Said Leucothae
                                C 95, 659

"The historic blackout" is Pound's term for the conspiracy that suppressed the books crucial for social change. However, while probably not consciously intended, a closer referent is his own lack of literary recognition.

In discussing his concept of the literary field, Bourdieu says that in writing his novels "Flaubert risked the inferior status associated with a minor genre."[79] This is precisely the opposite of Pound's choice. But since his superior status was the product of his own assertion of faith made in and by writing, it would vanish when he stopped. It is no surprise then that Pound couldn't finish *The Cantos*, that he could not "make it cohere" (C 116, 811).

The drama of fragmentation dominates the end of *The Cantos*, but it does not resolve. The following lines from 113 typify the stasis Pound has reached:

            the lifting and folding brightness
                the darkness shattered,
                    the fragment.
                            C 113, 803

There is no single hermeneutic circle to step inside here: has the darkness been shattered into fragments of light? Has the darkness shattered the coherent brightness? Has the brightness shattered the darkness into fragments? (Actually, there is only a single "fragment" mentioned.) The gears of the ideogrammic machinery have been pretty nearly stripped.

The poem could only progress toward the light by endlessly breaking free of its own smothering context; but at the same time it had to be shut tight against the contamination of shared meaning, as its final self-images indicate. It is "arcanum" (C 117 et seq., 817); "the great ball of crystal" (C 116, 809); "That great acorn of light bulging outward" (C 106, 769); "A little light, like a rushlight / to lead back to splendour" (C 116, 811)—phallic displays aimed at, but not addressed to, the public Pound courted and damned.[80]

As single readers we can obediently turn our backs on "imprecise" public language and learn to relive Pound's words, thus escaping his damnation. I've said at the beginning of this chapter that the best of his work cannot be separated from the worst. I'm sure that to some readers it may seem I've focused solely on his worst. In a way, this reflects the deep influence he has had on me: I've learned to read his language and have absorbed his fervor concerning words; I no longer want to savor decontextualized lyricism. Certainly, the vividness of his struggle to make each word both new and true to history has been a powerful influence on poetry in America.[81] Pound's language presents a charged image of speed and lucidity; this charge is valuable for the future of poetry. But I want the full dynamics of Poundian light to be acknowledged; what it illuminates is always accompanied by a phobic shadow.

3

Joyce's Sins:

Ulysses *as a Novel*

With Pound I have used the term "genius," in contradistinction to both Kant and common usage, not as a mark of great endowment or transcendence but to indicate an especially strained literary stance as he claimed a status of absolute meaning and efficacy for his conception of writing; we will see related strains in work of Stein and Zukofsky. I do not mean, certainly, to deny talent to them or achievement and significance to their writing; but I do mean to take away any attribution of transcendence. It is a mystification to say that *The Cantos* embodies the clear light of verbal justice, natural sexuality, and state authority: the poem is a record of the impossibility of writing an epic poem with the scope and authority that Pound required. As we will see, the writings of Zukofsky and Stein also pivot upon their own impossibilities: the fanatically worked-over surfaces of *"A"* may form a utopian musical writing, but the music is anything but natural: Zukofsky is not a nightingale. And if the portraits in *Tender Buttons* reveal a privileged mode of seeing, the objects of that transcendent sight have remained invisible. In each of the three cases, the ambition for totalization, the various formal extremes, and the large-scale difficulties with genre and small-scale difficulties with syntax and reference result from an attempt to make an impossibly valuable and authoritative mark upon the public.

Joyce's work and its reception bear an obvious family resemblance to these cases. However, where the writer as genius had to buy his or her status at a cost high enough that to many readers the written achievement can look like failure, this does not seem true of *Ulysses*. It displays such complexity and interconnection and brings so many writing projects into relation that it is tempting simply to grant Joyce genius in the ordinary sense. But this would be to miss the contradiction that rives the book all the way through its final Yes and even a few words beyond.

After its initial decade of controversy, *Ulysses* has been nearly sanctified, with the particulars of the praise keeping pace with critical fashion.[1] If the critic plays his or her cards right—and the book provides endless cards to play—*Ulysses* can be read in ways that are ordinarily contradictory: it can be a superlative example of naturalism, or symbolism, or of the indeterminate writerly text. Joyce supplies a surfeit of completed generic and rhetorical gestures; the problem becomes choosing between competing readings. One can enjoy the "namby-pamby jammy marmalady drawersy (alto là!)" (*LJ*, 135) display of "Nausicaa" as a satire on *The Lamplighter*, or as a surprising but ultimately shrewd updating of Homer's Nausicaa; one can also appreciate its place in the narrative structure as a counterpart to "Proteus" and as an ironic prelude to the more subtly ironic paean to conception in "Oxen of the Sun"—a chapter that presents an entirely new and very rich set of possible readings depending on whether one emphasizes the stylistic, narrative, thematic, or theological dimension.[2]

This opulence of literary articulation seems opposed to the cases of Pound, Stein, and Zukofsky, where the problem is often one of having to construct a specialized practice in order to generate an initial reading at all.[3] Genius, as I have been using it, is opposed to the socially recognizable categories of genre; the fact that Joyce fulfills so many generic contracts in the chapters of *Ulysses* would seem to place him outside of the group I'm considering. But in the other three cases, genius and narrative are mutually exclusive, and it is on the narrative level that *Ulysses* can usefully be read as displaying the problematics of genius. *Ulysses* is thick with the most subtle explicability; but it is on the basic level of plot that it resists yielding to its readers in the most intricate as well as the most obvious ways.

Before looking at these problems, however, I want to turn briefly to *Finnegans Wake*. If this latter work is seen as the teleological capstone to Joyce's career—an easy assumption to make—then he becomes, in the more conflicted sense I have outlined above, the modernist genius *par excellence*. Written in its highly privatized, "universal" language, *Finnegans Wake* is unreadable in the conventional sense and, for Joyceans, inexhaustibly readable.

While it was being written, it served as an aloof center for a self-designated literary revolution. Joyce didn't bother to sign Eugene Jolas's manifesto, "The Revolution of the Word"—in fact, his status probably would have been lowered a bit if he did sign and thus align himself with those who had particular interests. Nevertheless, Richard Ellmann's observation that "Jolas found in *Finnegans Wake* the principal text for his revolution of the word" (*JJ*, 589) is surely confirmed by the following dicta from the manifesto:

> 6. The literary creator has the right to disintegrate the primal matter of words imposed on him by textbooks and dictionaries. . . .
>
> 7. He has the right to use words of his own fashioning and to disregard existing grammatical and syntactic laws. . . .
>
> 10. Time is a tyranny to be abolished. . . .
>
> 12. The plain reader be damned.
>
> *JJ*, 588

Or as Samuel Beckett put it in *Our Exagmination Round His Factification for Incamination of Work in Progress*, "Here is direct expression—pages and pages of it. And if you don't understand it, Ladies and Gentlemen, it is because you are too decadent to receive it."[4] But this model of an ultravivid language confronting a moribund audience quite predictably did not gather a large revolutionary army.

One of Joyce's many letters to Harriet Weaver about *Work in Progress*, this one written about the same time as the *Exagmination*, is more revealing in its self-mocking megalomania. Joyce finds his own position to be central and magnificent as well as erroneous and imaginary; the greatest locomotive is also, he emphasizes, incapable of motion. Most importantly, he needs to inform Weaver: "I am really one of the greatest engineers, if not the greatest, in the world besides being a musicmaker, philosophist and heaps of other things. All the engines I know are wrong. Simplicity. I am making an engine with only one wheel. No spokes of course. The wheel is a perfect square. You see what I'm driving at, don't you? I am awfully solemn about it, mind you, so you must not think it is a silly story about the mouse and the grapes. No, it's a wheel, I tell the world. *And* it's all square" (*LJ*, 251).

Central though *Finnegans Wake* might be, whatever knowledge the world has of it is mediated by the university. It exists in one of the eccentric spaces modernist works of genius now occupy: within the squared circle of its comprehenders, it has become an object of intense study. The story of the Mookse and the Gripes Joyce mentioned in the letter is framed as a lesson. It is told in a classroom, to "a squad of urchins, snifflynosed, goslingnecked, clothyheaded, tangled in your lacing, tingled in your pants" (*FW*, 152.8–10); at its conclusion, the narrator writes: "As I have now successfully explained to you my own naturalborn rations which are even in excise of my vaultybrain insure me that I am a mouth's more deserving case by genius" (*FW*, 159.24–26). The urchins/genius dyad here is swaddled in layers of flickering identity and irony, but even perceiving those layers reinstates the reader as student-urchin.

As the most difficult and extravagant example of modernist writing, *Finnegans Wake* cements Joyce's transcendent position. Editors of a recent book of essays on Joyce dismiss the possibility of fully comprehending him, writing that he "has withstood the onslaught and has no more been mastered than has Nature."[5] For Kristeva, Joyce provides exemplary and paradoxical articulation of the non-articulable semiotic; she speaks of his work as a "joyous and insane, incestuous plunge summed up in Molly's jouissance or the paternal baby talk in *Finnegans Wake*."[6] On the other hand, for Derrida, the specter of Joyce conjures up, in a gesture more complex than the following excerpt will register, a vision of vast technological power: "a hypermnesic machine, there in advance, decades in advance, to compute you, control you, forbid you the slightest inaugural syllable because you can say nothing that is not programmed on this 1000th generation computer—*Ulysses, Finnegans Wake*—beside which the current technology of our computers and our micro-computerified archives and our translating machines remains a *bricolage* of a prehistoric child's toys."[7]

Such language sufficiently indicates Joyce's transcendent status; as a further index of it, Derrida focuses on only two words from *Finnegans Wake*, "He war." Not that this is a shocking breach of critical decorum. Joyce and to a lesser extent Pound and Zukofsky packed their words tightly, and the brute logistics of trying to come to terms with something of the complexity of *Finnegans Wake* dictates that small samples be studied. But the overall pattern of Derrida's approach is worth schematizing: Joyce, the genius, writes words any of which can be profitably studied more or less endlessly. But at the same time that each of Joyce's words dilates with a quasi-divine fullness of significance, his various writings blur together into a totality. In Derrida's comment, *Ulysses* and *Finnegans Wake* are placed, undifferentiated, into apposition with the hypercomputer.

For Kristeva, both books are examples of Joyce's "incestuous plunge." Similarly, Hélène Cixous focuses not on the later books but on the opening paragraph of the first story of *Dubliners* to articulate Joyce's dissolution of the subject, which she sees "reverberating from book to book . . . for the greater glory of a Word whose power is elevated on the absence or decline of the notion of *a unified* subject. . . . Point which is looking for its departure point, whose invisible pointillage divides up *Finnegans Wake* into explosions and a crazy coalescence of the subject which undoes itself at the very moment when it constitutes itself in the new fragmentation of the word become word-tale or word-book, become one-plural."[8]

The books form a word and each word is a book. Whether Cixous's Joyce is a demiurge or an anti-demiurge, heroically building or undermining the Word, there is something of a divine nimbus playing around him. In a series that can be said to begin with Stephen Dedalus's famous comparison of the artist to God, critics and writers have regularly sacralized Joyce.[9] In a sketch F. Scott Fitzgerald put a halo above a quasi-disembodied Joyce and drew himself kneeling with clasped hands at the master's feet.[10] Hugh Kenner refers to *Ulysses* in cosmic terms: "as the foxes have their holes and the birds their nests, so each speck in this book has its complementary speck, in a cosmos we can trust."[11] In a discussion of "Wandering Rocks," Clive Hart writes that "in order to watch the synchronisms of the action we have to imaginatively raise ourselves to a God's-eye viewpoint . . . in order to apprehend the diachronic motifs we need to become still more God-like and enter the Eternal Now from which we may watch all events at all times happening 'simultaneously.' "[12]

Once Joyce is seen as demiurge, that image can be reenforced by reading his career as a steady progress toward absolute creativity. First the defensive epiphanies of *Stephen Hero,* then the perfect but laconic stories of *Dubliners. Portrait* begins the ironic undercutting of the presented content, and begins to open perspectives of ambivalent expressiveness, with irony and aesthetic assertion both hovering over Stephen. Then follows an interlude of sexually obsessed writing, private, semiprivate, and public: the pornographic letters to Nora, *Giacomo Joyce* and *Exiles.* These sexual concerns, combined with a fabulously increased use of constructive devices, produce the masterpiece *Ulysses.* At this point, amid howls of provincial execration from the New York Society for the Prevention of Vice, Joyce's genius is acclaimed from the literary capital of the world, Paris. Sylvia Beach writes, "He was of medium height, thin, slightly stooped, graceful. One noticed his hands. . . . His eyes, a deep blue, with the light of genius in them, were extremely beautiful. . . . He gave an impression of sensitiveness exceeding any I had ever known."[13] In Paris, Joyce, genius, paterfamilias, and eccentric, repeats the pattern generated by *Ulysses* on a heightened level, gathering an inner sanctum of readers around *Work in Progress,* surrounded by the duller crowd of former readers such as Pound, who had exulted in *Ulysses* but now found the new work offensively incomprehensible.[14]

As teleological as this trajectory seems, I want to set it aside and to concentrate on *Ulysses. Finnegans Wake,* as I have said, might be a fitting example of the specialized results of the attempts of the modernist genius to master the world in and through writing, but my model will be tested in interesting ways by *Ulysses,* with its perverse embrace of public content and narrative. While *Finnegans Wake* may be an example of "omniglossia," it contains no heteroglossia as *Ulysses* does.[15]

Despite the fact that the outlandish surface of *Finnegans Wake* seems to promise endless free play of meaning as the boundaries of words have become porous, the writing there is quite stable in syntax and tone compared to *Ulysses.* There are differing formal dimensions to the chapters in *Finnegans Wake,* but Joyce's night-language is omnipresent and thus, though it is completely elastic in every word, it is also singular and fixed as a whole—in a sense, more fixed than the language of a Dickens novel, where the characters can counteract the narrator. Kenner points out that "if we open *Finnegans Wake* at random it is 'Eumaeus'-like syntax that we are apt to find."[16] It is true that the early corrections to *Finnegans Wake* (now embodied in the text) seem to mock any assertion of stability:

> for "certelleneteutoslavzendlatinsoundscript" read
> "cellelleneteutoslavzendlatinsoundscript."[17]

But the cancellation of syllables suggesting "certain" and their replacement by those suggesting "hellenic" was an authorial fiat; the instruction to "read" the corrected word doesn't promote uncertainty. In *Finnegans Wake* Joyce had reached a stable limit in his attitude toward language: words and sentences were to be packed, under the unitary cover of night, as fully as possible.

Although less experimental than *Finnegans Wake*, *Ulysses* displays a more various set of verbal surfaces and aesthetic strategies: there is no unitary "day-language." Its features—naturalistic detail, the references and symbolic correspondences, the various styles, and the straining away from narrative halfway through, the marriage-plot affirmed and transgressed—when considered together seem intensely centrifugal, and yet, unlike the circular *Finnegans Wake*, *Ulysses* is a novel. I will not be attempting to resolve these antinomies: the *Ulysses* I am proposing results from them.

SWEETS OF SIN

But to concentrate on *Ulysses* as a novel is not easy. It seems to spread out into the rest of Joyce's writing and life, and thus to merge with the genreless "word . . . become word-book" invoked by Cixous. It has roots in Joyce's earlier work: Stephen Dedalus is carried over from *Portrait*, as are other characters from both *Portrait* and *Dubliners*. The two strands of narrative in *Ulysses*, the Blooms' marriage and Stephen's social and artistic struggle, are prefigured in *Exiles*, where Richard is both artist and (possible) cuckold, and his foil, Robert, takes on the roles of Mulligan and Boylan. Joyce's letters, too, figure largely in almost all critical readings of the book. Karen Lawrence, referring to "Oxen of the Sun," writes that "the paragraphs of [Joyce's letter to Budgen (*LJ*, 138–39)] have become almost as sacred a part of the 'text' of *Ulysses* as the paragraphs of the chapter itself."[18] And certainly Joyce's charts and explicatory letters belong in this quasi-sacred category. The titles of the chapters are not printed in the text, yet "there is no Joyce critic writing today who does not regard *Ulysses* as a modern epos divided into eighteen named episodes."[19] But as Leo Bersani points out, it is *only* Joyce critics who regard *Ulysses* this way: "uninformed readers . . . may very well be overcome with embarrassment to discover, upon opening their first work of criticism, that what they had been thinking of quite simply as chapters eight and ten are universally referred to as "Lestrygonians" and "Wandering Rocks."[20]

The distinction between chapter ten and "Wandering Rocks" can be recast as one between a mimetic novel and a mythic machine (or semiotic computer whose "joyceware" we may run endlessly).[21] The initial responses of Pound and Eliot are emblematic of this choice.

Eliot praised Joyce's "mythical method" as "a way of controlling, of ordering, of giving shape to the immense panorama of futility and anarchy which is contemporary history," while Pound saw *Ulysses* as a satire in the vein of Flaubert and Rabelais.[22] Pound did give minimal praise to the mythic parallels, granting that "for the first time since 1321" Joyce has "resurrected the infernal figures." But Pound's assessment contradicted Eliot's: "These correspondences are part of Joyce's mediaevalism and are chiefly his own affair, a scaffold, a means of construction, justified by the result, and justifiable by it only" (*LE*, 406). A decade later, Pound's vision of the book was more directly opposed to Eliot's: where Eliot had seen only form, Pound saw nothing but the grossest matter, hailing Joyce and *Ulysses* as the fulfillment of his early call for a new *uber*satirist:

> In 1912 or eleven I invoked whatever gods may exist, in the quatrain:
>
>> Sweet Christ from hell spew up some Rabelais,
>> To belch and . . . . . and to define today
>> In fitting fashion, and her monument
>> Heap up to her in fadeless excrement.
>
> "Ulysses" I take as my answer.
>
> *GK*, 96

Even before *Ulysses* was published Joyce had begun to train the first of an army of exegetes and to guide them toward an understanding of the enormous cross-referencing of elements in the book, pointing to the mythic dimensions, the stylistic intricacy, the humor, and the characterological subtlety. Following his lead, over a half a century of critical articles have demonstrated, in their aggregate, how partial Pound's and Eliot's readings were, and how thoroughly and elaborately Joyce transcended conventional oppositions. But the complexity of detail in the book tends to be more easily perceived than the overall shape of the plot. Despite the book's many successes— in fact, because of them—the narrative unity of *Ulysses* remains problematic.

Clive Hart's article on "Wandering Rocks" is a good example of critical exegesis of Joyce's fanatic patterning. Hart shows that, in spite of the minimal information provided in the text, it is possible to construct a precise itinerary of each of the characters in the nineteen sections; Hart walked the routes to find that the times give evidence of the characters' moods: "Boylan, who has plenty of time to spare, strolls up Grafton street with a lazy rather than a jaunty walk; O'Molloy, scrounging for money and unsure of himself, hesitates for a few minutes before entering the abbey."[23]

Joyce built numerous highly obscure simultaneities into the chapter. To give two of the many instances Hart provides (which he says are only a fraction of those Joyce created): "While Father Conmee is happily dreaming of the 'joybells . . . ringing in Gay Malahide' . . . the joyless 'Barang!' of the lacquey's bell is heard in Dillon's auction rooms. . . . Lenehan's hands mould 'ample curves of air'. . . while Bloom reads how Raoul's *'hands felt for the opulent curves'* " (194). In keeping with the entrapment the Wandering Rocks represent, there are also many false leads, both for characters—such as when "Artifoni and young Dignam miss their trams" or "an invitation to a boxing match is out of date" (188)—and for readers: outmoded names for landmarks, reference to a secondary Sandymount tramline rather than the more well-known one. Hart details numerous other correspondences: Father Conmee takes the northernmost route of all the characters, thus literalizing the sarcastic pun in the chapter's second word: "The superior, the very reverend Father Conmee." The chapter begins with Conmee and ends with the British viceroy, invoking the Church and the British Empire that oppress Stephen throughout the book. Bloom appears in the central section of the chapter; physically he is in the center of the city, and, as Hart remarks, "at the central point of the novel, he is brought to full awareness of the nub of his psychic and bodily concerns. In the city's sanctum, the undercover porn-shop, *Sweets of Sin* is produced from behind the curtain, like the ark of the tabernacle" (187).

At this point, Hart's reading has shifted into a mode typical of much Joyce criticism. *Ulysses* is no longer simply perfectly mimetic but theologically coherent. Hart's description voices an irony—porn shop as sanctum—that is doubtless implied by Joyce's positing, but irony will not bridge the gap between transcendent coherence and historical contingency. There is an important difference between the scene where Bloom chooses the book and a moment such as the following: "Master Dignam walked along Nassau street, shifted the porksteaks to his other hand. His collar sprang up again and he tugged it down. The blooming stud was too small for the buttonhole of the shirt, blooming end to it. . . . [Pa's] face got all grey instead of being red like it was and there was a fly walking over it up to his eye" (10.1154–62). I have tried to pick a passage that is simply mimetic of the possibilities contained by historical Dublin and that does not become part of Joyce's text-reconnecting machinery. In fact, it is not an easy task. Even here, Joyce manages to reconscript verbal and thematic details. "Blooming" names Bloom, the porksteaks evoke his religion negatively, and the collar springs up again, wittily, in the general salute to the calvacade at the end of the chapter: "Master Patrick Aloysius Dignam, waiting, saw salutes being given to the gent with the topper and raised also his new black cap with fingers greased by porksteak paper. His collar too sprang up" (10.1265–67).

Roland Barthes writes (somewhat suspiciously) of "the reality effect"—a detail standing in synecdoche for a complete representation of the real.[24] I would like to borrow the term and use it to indicate, less suspiciously, details of a writing that recognizes the outside world. There are countless examples in *Ulysses* of what look like such details. But even though *Sweets of Sin* is real in the sense that using such material acknowledges what previously had been untoward for the serious novelist, in fact the scene of Bloom in the porn shop is not real in the same way as the porksteaks are. Ultimately the amount of significance Joyce loads into the porn changes its character; it describes Molly's subsequent actions too accurately.

> He read where his finger opened.
> —*All the dollarbills her husband gave her were spent in the stores on wondrous gowns and costliest frillies. For him! For Raoul!*
> Yes. This. Here. Try.
> —*Her mouth glued on his in a luscious voluptuous kiss while his hands felt for the opulent curves inside her deshabille.*
> Yes. Take this. The end.
>
> 10.607–13

What Bloom reads is a version of the end of *Ulysses*, a fact reinforced by his comment, "The end" and his breathless "Yeses," which prefigure Molly's. Don Gifford points out that "Bloom is inadvertently practicing *sortes Biblicae* (or *Virgilianae* or *Homericae*), divination by the Bible (or Virgil or Homer), in which a passage is selected at random and treated as revelatory or prophetic."[25] It's ironic that Joyce makes soft porn prophetic, but such range, where *Sweets of Sin* is folded into the coherence of *Ulysses*, dulls the reality of the porn, which becomes comic in its degraded repetition of loftier patterns. Joyce reaches outside not simply to make contact with difference, but to enlarge and diversify sameness.

This coherence invites us to practice *sortes Ioyceanae*. The *Sweets of Sin* details reinforce an Eliotic reading: they are bits of "the immense panorama of futility and anarchy" sublated into Joycean order (whether specifically mythic or not). A Poundian reading posits a *Ulysses* full of porksteaks: the stuff of the world, mercilessly depicted, and not redeemed via composition. This reading would be very hard to maintain.

Joyce's remark that a destroyed Dublin could be reconstructed from *Ulysses* has a double edge: does *Ulysses* mime Dublin perfectly or obliterate it by sublating it into art?[26] The many critical assertions of the reality of Joyce's construction often finesse this question by forceful praise. The following assessment by Harold Bloom is hyperbolic (and coy) but not all that atypical: "Poldy is, as Joyce intended, the most *complete* figure in modern fiction, if not indeed in all Western fiction, and so it is appropriate that he have a saint's day in the literary calendar: Bloomsday."[27] David Hayman writes that Joyce "has managed to show the extraordinary as a quality of the ordinary. . . . [He has] written a book that is totally rational and coherent, balanced and harmonious."[28] Richard Ellmann's assessment is similar. Joyce aims are both "mock-heroic . . . and the ennoblement of the mock-heroic" (*JJ*, 360). Commenting on the end of the book, Ellmann writes that "*Ulysses* is an epithalamium; love is the cause of its motion. The spirit is liberated from its bonds through a eucharistic occasion. . . . Though such occasions are as rare as miracles . . . they require no divine intercession. They arise in quintessential purity from the mottled life of everyday" (*JJ*, 379).

The realistic, harmonious, miraculous wisdom such descriptions find is an effect that can only be reconstituted through very highly focused reading, the kind that the book repays so endlessly. However, such reconstructions ignore the primary fact of the immoderate writing of so much of the second half. The plot can seem coherent: Molly's final Yes; the careful balancing of Bloom's and Stephen's actions; their near meetings leading to their thematically rich but "realistically" inconclusive meeting. But these can be seen as resolving the book harmoniously only if the styles of the second-half chapters are translated into much tamer simulacra. Given the extremity of much of the writing, such translation is often a rather violent process.

A. Walton Litz writes that "in the space of three or four years [Joyce] traveled most of the distance from *Dubliners* to *Finnegans*

Wake."[29] But this journey does not traverse a unified space across a harmonious gamut of styles. Litz notes that during this interval of transition Joyce's method of revision underwent a radical reversal from the paring down that produced the earlier work to the accretion that would create *Finnegans Wake.* In revising his early work Joyce had "exercised a rigorous selectivity, discarding the multiple events and elaborate expository passages of the earlier work in favour of a few scenes or 'epiphanies,' " but in the final half of *Ulysses* his revisions "were almost entirely expansive, and the economy Joyce exercised in achieving isolated effects was overshadowed by the incessant elaborations."[30]

The styles present problems if they are read as subservient to the plot. Stanley Sultan asserts that *Ulysses* should be read primarily as a novel, with "its action . . . rising to a climax and proceeding to a resolution."[31] This insistence on a narrative reading is a stance that I find valid; however, it leads him to some contorted interpretation. Here is part of the Bunyanesque paragraph in "Oxen of the Sun" criticizing the students' rowdiness during the ongoing thunderstorm: "Wherein, O wretched company, were ye all deceived for that was the voice of the god that was in a very grievous rage that he would presently lift his arm up and spill their souls for their abuses and their spillings done by them contrariwise to his word which forth to bring brenningly biddeth" (14.470–74).[32] While admitting that this paragraph is "among the funniest passages in the book," Sultan nevertheless affirms that "the author is in complete earnest" (282) in the above sentence and that it reveals a truth crucial for the plot: sins against fertility are the behavioral afflictions that both Bloom and Stephen will need to overcome by following the model of Theodore Purefoy.

But in order to posit such meanings, Sultan has to disregard the satire of the Bunyanesque paragraph, which is so patent in the style and which also exists in the verbal parallel where the students' masturbatory spilling is damned while the spilling of souls is seen as a divine prerogative. He has to read the following encomium to Purefoy as sincere: "Thou sawest thy America, thy lifetask, and didst charge to cover like the transpontine bison" (14.1430–31).

Too strong a desire to read narratively ultimately makes the words of the book quite a bother. Sultan reads the opening of "Oxen" as buttressing his argument, but in order to do so he has to "unscramble" it: he takes the paragraph beginning "Universally that person's acumen is esteemed very little" (14.7–32) and reads it "with the excess verbiage eliminated" as meaning "He is not very wise who is ignorant that the wisest and most worthy men affirm that . . ." (285). After clarifying Joyce's scrambled excess, Sultan asserts the "theme of the chapter is literally that having a family is an exalted thing and man's cardinal responsibility" (286). To read *Ulysses* by ignoring the actual words in order to "literally" find such themes seems to miss the point by a considerable margin, especially in a chapter whose very form can be seen as a blasphemous or at least an envious imitation of gestation and birth.

But there are many points to *Ulysses*. If we hold to the image of Joyce the master stylist, then a phrase such as "excess verbiage" will be a sacrilegious description of his writing (worthy of inclusion in "Eumaeus," where "literally," misused, occurs a number of times). But such an image of mastery and precision belongs more properly to the first years of Joyce's composition of *Ulysses,* before his revisions became inordinately expansive. Take the following passage from "Cyclops": "And after came all saints and martyrs, virgins and confessors: S. Cyr and S. Isidore Arator and S. James the Less and S. Phocas of Sinope and S. Julian Hospitator and S. Felix de Cantalice and S. Simon Stylites and S. Stephen Protomartyr and S. John of God and S. Ferreol and S. Leugarde" and so on for quite awhile without much in the way of extra-ecclesiastical significance or wit to encourage a reader's progress (12.1689–92). Michael Grodin has shown that this list was augmented greatly by last-minute additions: Joyce added saints at six different stages of proofing.[33] Such a passage certainly merits the description "excess verbiage." And as Litz, Grodin, and Ellmann have shown, only the fact that Joyce was determined to have *Ulysses* published on his fortieth birthday prevented the accretion of further verbiage. If one is trying to follow the plot, the words in the second half of the book *do* often get in the way as the coherences Joyce posits become not only more wide-ranging but fight against the plot.

"COMPLETE CARNAL INTERCOURSE"

The new Gabler edition of *Ulysses* gives evidence of a deeply split conception of Joyce. On the one hand, the edition prints line numbers on each page, the physical signs of the settled, classic status of Joyce's words; but Gabler's editorial practice takes account of the frenetic pace of Joyce's final revisions, basing some of the most controversial changes on such hypothetical factors as eyeskips. It is fitting that the major crux would involve the phrase "Word known to all men (9.429–30).[34] *Ulysses* as it now exists in print is turning out to be a book that cannot be "known" completely, but rather one whose words ultimately need to be chosen by every reader. But questions of Gabler's editorial precision aside, this situation registers a key fact about the book. *Ulysses* represents not simply the record of a complex unified act of writing but an accumulation of successive acts of writing by which Joyce continually redefined his position vis-à-vis the book he was producing. The shift in the previous sentence between an "act of writing" and "acts of writing" points toward the basic tension of part and whole that animates *Ulysses*. The succession of new styles can be seen as transgressive acts against the unity of the whole, or, if this is too strong a description, at least they can be seen to overshadow the plot, becoming themselves the major events in the latter half of the book. But at the same time the narration of the day's events continues to unfold, though at unconventional stylistic removes. Certainly, the following passage near the end of "Ithaca," while stylistically far from conventional narration, is crucial to the plot and to any interpretation of the Blooms' marriage:

> What limitations of activity and inhibitions of conjugal rights were perceived by listener and narrator concerning themselves during the course of this intermittent and increasingly more laconic narration?

> By the listener a limitation of fertility inasmuch as marriage had been celebrated 1 calendar month after the 18th anniversary of her birth (8 September 1870), viz. 8 October, and consummated on the same date with female issue born 15 June 1889, having been anticipatorily consummated on the 10 September of the same year and complete carnal intercourse, with ejaculation of semen within the natural female organ, having last taken place 5 weeks previous, viz. 27 November 1893, to the birth on 29 December 1893 of second (and only male) issue, deceased 9 January 1894, aged 11 days, there remained a period of 10 years, 5 months and 18 days during which carnal intercourse had been incomplete, without ejaculation of semen within the natural female organ. By the narrator a limitation of activity, mental and corporal, inasmuch as complete mental intercourse between himself and the listener had not taken place since the consummation of puberty, indicated by catamenic hemorrhage, of the female issue of narrator and

listener, 15 September 1903, there remained a period of 9 months and 1 day during which, in consequence of a preestablished natural comprehension in incomprehension between the consummated females (listener and issue), complete corporal liberty of action had been circumscribed.

17.2271–92

This cessation of conventional sex motivates Molly's taking a lover, and thus it is the key to Bloom's behavior throughout the day as well.[35] But while the reader, as follower of the plot, must be grateful for this information—especially in a book where physical events are often given the barest possible mention or left entirely to inference—there is much here, besides the pedantic phrasing, that the plot follower will find possibly useless, if not destructive of narrative meaning.[36]

The neat rhetorical balance between "complete carnal intercourse" and "complete mental intercourse" might seem meaningful to some, but it's not that easy to imagine Bloom and Molly having complete mental intercourse even in the best of their times, and especially hard to imagine that they communed fully for the first nine years of their sexual estrangement with only the onset of Milly's period breaking the magic spell.[37] There is certainly a grain of plausibility about Milly's maturity causing uneasiness to Bloom (Joyce provides hints of this), but what I find most striking about these phrases is the peremptoriness they display toward the plot, as if Joyce simultaneously clung to and mocked such neat antitheses. (Compare the thematically rich but rhetorically dour conjunction stated by Lynch's cap in "Circe," "Ba! It is because it is. Women's reason. Jewgreek is greekjew. Extremes meet. Death is the highest form of life. Ba!" [15.2097–98]. Clearly the tension between secular and theological culture that underlies the Arnoldian Hellenic/Hebraic contrast resonates throughout every point of *Ulysses*; but when "Jewgreek is greekjew" is spelled out as a "theme"—Bah!)

But if the phrase "complete mental intercourse" produces irony of such intensity as to call into question the narrative meaning the phrase supposedly authorizes, can that irony be prevented from spreading back to undercut "complete carnal intercourse"? Or are we to read the first phrase denotatively while treating the second as a defensive exaggeration or deformation? Quite a bit of the writing in the second half of *Ulysses* can be read as carrying out this pattern of defensiveness. For instance, the following is both a travesty and an accurate description of Joyce's ambitions for the book: "the co-incidence of meeting, discussion, dance, row, old salt of the here today and gone tomorrow type, night loafers, the whole galaxy of events, all went to make up a miniature cameo of the world we live in" (16.1222–25). All of "Eumaeus," from its incessant echoes of late-returning husbands and unfaithful wives to phrases such as "he heroically made light of the mischance" (the loss of a button) and "his own truly miraculous escape" (dodging a sandstrewer) has to be read in the same double way, heroic and mock-heroic (16.38–39, 44–45). In "Cyclops," Bloom's important, stumbling, middling def-inition of love, "Love . . . I mean the opposite of hatred" (12.1485), in addition to being mocked by the mean-spirited denizens of the pub, also provokes this interpolation:

> Love loves to love love. Nurse loves the new chemist. Constable 14A loves Mary Kelly. Gerty MacDowell loves the boy that has the bicycle. M. B. loves a fair gentleman. Li Chi Han lovey up kissy Cha Pu Chow. Jumbo, the elephant, loves Alice, the elephant. Old Mr Ver-schoyle with the ear trumpet loves old Mrs Verschoyle with the turn-edin eye. The man in the brown macintosh loves a lady who is dead. His Majesty the King loves Her Majesty the Queen. Mrs Norman W. Tupper loves officer Taylor. You love a certain person. And this per-son loves that other person because everybody loves somebody but God loves everybody.
>
> 12.1493–1501

Ellmann contextualizes this nicely by pointing out that it parodies not only Bloom but Dante and Aquinas; he says it is "the kind of parody that protects seriousness by immediately going away from intensity. Love cannot be discussed without peril, but Bloom has nobly named it."[38] This explanation is similar to Ellmann's previ-ously quoted summary of the book. The parody is hard to take se-riously, but rather than "going away from intensity" it is rhetorically excessive. While nothing could be kinder or blander on the deno-tative level, "Love loves to love love" seems sadistic in its lack of semantic variation: it is not the stuff of nursery rhymes, it is an as-phyxiation of them. Nurse, Constable 14A, Mary Kelly, Gerty Mac-Dowell, and the boy with the bicycle may twinkle here in a constel-lation of carefree Irish courtship, but the likelihood of these idyllic romances leading to happy marriages is called into question by the mention of Molly (M. B.) and Boylan (or possibly Mulvey)—and cer-tainly Gerty's crush will be shown later to be hopeless. The Irishness of Mary Kelly et al. is mocked by "Li Chi Han lovey up kissy Cha Pu Chow," which ventriloquizes scorn of ethnicity and sexuality. The next sentences deal with marriage, or at least with the joining of sexually differentiated units: elephants, the decaying Verschoyles, Their Majesties. Not much in the way of wedded bliss is promised by these cases, whose immobility is expressed in the ponderous re-petitiveness. But any aspiration toward permanence, however cold, is thwarted by the nicely parallel physical handicaps of the Ver-schoyles and, more emphatically, by the hopeless longing of the man in the macintosh. The last sentences give up on marriage entirely: "Mrs Norman W. Tupper loves"—not Mr Norman W. Tupper—but "officer Taylor." Then follows a singsong merry-go-round of un-matching attractions: you, a certain person, that other person, every-body, somebody, all theoretically resolved by "God loves every-body." It is a bitter resolution after the dead or hopeless outcomes in the preceding sentences; as a final deflation, the rhetorical climax that should fall on the final "everybody" has been spoiled by the word's appearance only six words back.

The tensions that animate both the plot and the writing of *Ulysses* are present here. It is not just that Gerty and Molly appear. Images of marriage, stability, and hierarchy clash with a never-ending metonymy induced by love, and while the denotation supports an orderly universe (God, royalty, everyday humanity, elephants, all concentrically arranged by love and marriage), the idiocy of the tone manifests a loathing of just such hierarchies. Silly as it is, this para-graph provides a version of how plot and significance clash in *Ulysses*.

In the same way, "complete carnal intercourse, with ejaculation of semen within the female organ" at the end of "Ithaca" may be central to the narrative of the book, but as language it scarcely holds a place of honor, echoing, as it does, the dubious voice of Father Conmee, a representative of the Church's constricting authority. In "Wandering Rocks" Conmee thinks: "Who could know the truth? Not the jealous lord Belvedere and not her confessor if she had not committed adultery fully, *eiaculatio seminis inter vas naturale mulieris,* with her husband's brother? . . . Father Conmee thought of that tyr-annous incontinence, needed however for man's race on earth, and of the ways of God which were not our ways" (10.166–73). Conmee's opening question is coy, as all his thoughts are. The Latin in which he distances and safely ogles the sexual act *is* "the truth": a linguistic system from which ambiguity has been banished—a dead language, resurrected as terminology. The purifying authority that such theological language claims over sinful carnality is something that Joyce mimed and undermined repeatedly. His gestures against it were often broad enough to be visible to the outside world: the New York Society for the Prevention of Vice noticed that in "Nausicaa" there was *eiaculatio seminis* quite outside the proper channel, but the following juxtaposition in that chapter was undoubtedly of equal concern to Joyce: "and then Canon O'Hanlon handed the thurible back to Father Conroy and knelt down looking up at the Blessed Sacrament . . . and she just swung her foot in and out in time as the music rose and fell. . . . Three and eleven she paid for those stockings in Sparrows' . . . that was what he was looking at" (13.496–502). Stephen is clearly speaking for his maker when in "Circe" he taps his brow and says, "But in here it is I must kill the priest and king" (15.4436–37).

Numerous narrative gestures reveal Joyce's patent commitment to a writing that fully recognizes the body and all its non-authorized activities: Bloom's shitting (one of the first things we see him do in the book), his imagined masturbation, his musical, anti-patriotic farting, his actual masturbation, the sex scenes in "Circe"—imaginary as they are, they are verbalized forcefully—Molly's menstruating, farting, and the erotic recreations of her soliloquy. These acts or scenes are dramatically situated in the narrative and, more importantly, some affect the writing—effect it one could almost say—intensely. Thus the "factual"—that is, the religiously authoritative—tone of "complete carnal intercourse" implies a closed narrative of conventional marriage that the book tries to overturn, even as the institutional significance of the phrase is crucial to the narrative that *Ulysses* does tell and to the styles it uses.

Such conflict might call for poststructuralist readings. In addition to the readings of Kristeva, Derrida, and Cixous discussed earlier, there have been an increasing number of such critical visions of *Ulysses*. Colin MacCabe, Patrick McGee, Frances Restuccia, Vicky Mahaffey, and Jean-Michel Rabaté have seen the book as, in one way or another, open-ended.[39] MacCabe claims that "Joyce's texts refuse the very category of meta-language. . . . None of the discourses that circulate in *Finnegans Wake* or *Ulysses* can master or make sense of the others." One consequence of this refusal for MacCabe is that there can be no separable "plot" as such. McGee does not go quite this far, claiming only that "the illusion of representation in the initial episodes . . . is [later] exposed as illusion, as a simulacrum, by the monstrous encyclopedia of styles."[40]

These conclusions can be backed up by the many serious, semi-serious, playful, and blasphemous references, parallels, and stylistic echoes and underminings that seem to forestall any unifying resolution. Restuccia points out that the book is constructed typologically: small details are shown by the end to fit into large, complete patterns—just as earthly things fit into a heavenly pattern.[41] However, as Restuccia sees it, Joyce pushes his typology toward parody and a subversive textuality, which "challenges the Father's signature . . . [and] in the end moves *Ulysses* to the status of a Barthesian Text."[42]

But indeterminacy suggests a disinterested openness to possibility that does not register the obsessiveness with which Joyce tells, both faithfully and unfaithfully, his story. By the end of the book, it is not possible to predict what will happen on June 17 (not that critics haven't tried). But this uncertainty differs greatly from randomness: it is the result of intense conflict rather than play. The narrative of *Ulysses,* while most ambivalent in outcome and ultimate meaning, is extremely narrow in focus. It could almost be a sentence in the following set:

ANOTHER WORLD: Sharly promises Grant that she'll end things with the other man in her life. Grant and Anne break their engagement. Josie presses Matt to reconcile with her. Sharly manipulates Emma into leaving town. Sharly delays her plan to ask John for a divorce. Donna's seduction of Jake backfires. Felicia fantasizes that the man in her novel is Lucas. Evan vows to convince Amanda that Sam is dangerous. A spy hired by Lucas photographs Grant with Sharly. Amanda is suspicious of Sam's behavior. Rachel learns that, years ago, Mac slept with the love of Ken's life. When Matt plans to catch Josie's obsessed fan, Reuben urges Josie to tell Matt the truth.[43]

The plots from this synopsis of five days of *Another World* are not utterly distinct from the plot of *Ulysses:* "Molly promises Leopold that she'll end things with the other man in her life; Molly is suspicious of Leopold's behavior." Joyce's styles, parallels, superstructures, overtones, are founded on a plot like the one that the soap opera splinters into endless names and subplots. But though Joyce's writing is excessive—this is where my reading differs from the post-structuralist ones mentioned above—he holds to a single marital story. He does not do this in spite of the stylistic extravagances, but through them.

Molly's body, with what Joyce called its "four cardinal points" (*LJ*, 170)—note the ecclesiastical pun—remains a determinant conclusion to *Ulysses*. The small bit of plot that Joyce contrived for "Penelope" supports this focus: Molly gets her period, and the book ends on an ecstatic memory of complete carnal intercourse. The fact that her last Yes is capitalized seems pregnant with significance. The principal stylistic transgression of "Penelope" is lack of punctuation and capitalization (run-on sentences). Proper nouns, and the words "I" and "O" are capitalized, but nothing else. Thus when Molly's recital quotes Bloom's erotic letter, the capitals stand out: "thinking of him and his mad crazy letters my Precious one everything connected with your glorious Body everything underlined that comes from it is a thing of beauty and of joy for ever something he got out of some nonsensical book" (18.1175–78).

When Molly "writes" her Yes with a similar capital she is embodying Bloom's description. One doesn't have to necessarily see her submitting to Bloom in this word: her memory is of great pleasure and sexually she seems the one in control; her remembered gesture of passing the chewed seedcake into Bloom's mouth (a gesture he remembers as well) suggests a refiguration of conception—she puts seeds into him.[44] Nevertheless, her Yes does affirm, if not the Meaning of her Union with Bloom, then at least her status as Precious Body. And the fact that the affirmation is made in the last three letters of the text gives it, narratively, an emphasis that is all the more dramatic.

Stylistically, "Penelope" presents Molly as nature that is both pre-cultural and postcultural. This is done via her use of the lower case, her frankness, her malapropisms, and—until the very end—her carelessness with specific male identities; if by any chance the reader has missed it, Joyce drives her identity with nature home near the conclusion: "I love flowers Id love to have the whole place swimming in roses God of heaven theres nothing like nature the wild mountains then the sea and the waves rushing then the beautiful country with the fields of oats and wheat" (18.1557–60).

We are used to Joyce deflating sentimental pretensions; when Bloom is struck by the beauty of the Italian he hears spoken outside the cabman's shelter, Stephen informs him that the speakers are arguing about money. (And their Italian is much more obscene than Stephen's laconic translation lets on.) But this doesn't mean Joyce himself finally transcends such subject matter. In the process of writing *Ulysses*, Joyce continually faced a narrative conclusion that, in structural terms, would be hard to differentiate from a sentimental ending. Marriage, achieved or reaffirmed, ends the *Odyssey*, as well as the magazine stories Gerty would have read, and it still hovers spectrally above the thousand and one subplots of contemporary soap opera. Complete carnal intercourse with emission of semen within the natural female organ, and all that can be said to "naturally" attend this act: love, marriage, family relations, fertility, odysseys and novels with happy resolutions, a god who thunders disapproval of adultery—these are central to the world of *Ulysses*.[45] Joyce scorns cheap versions of this centeredness: Deasy's assertion that "all human history moves towards one great goal" (2.380–81), Gerty's language, where summer evenings enfold the world in a sexually repressed "mysterious embrace" (13.1–2). But just as Stephen is disgusted not by Mulligan's blasphemy but by the fact that that blasphemy doesn't take theology seriously enough, Joyce remains deeply involved with the system of value he attacks. As a whole, "Penelope" is not an ironic disavowal of marriage or a display of anything but the most consuming interest in the subject. The last lines of Molly's soliloquy are affirmation, not critique. Its final Yes functions as a dramatic resolution of the book's earlier stylistic and narrative sins.

AN ORDER IN EVERY WAY
APPROPRIATE

To call Joyce's styles sins goes against some deeply received ideas, ideas that are attractive and can be backed up by the authority of *Ulysses*. Consider the following Joyce legend:

> I enquired about *Ulysses*. Was it progressing?
> "I have been working hard on it all day," said Joyce.
> "Does that mean that you have written a great deal?" I said.
> "Two sentences," said Joyce.

I looked sideways but Joyce was not smiling. I thought of Flaubert.
"You have been seeking the *mot juste?"* I said.
"No," said Joyce. "I have the words already. What I am seeking is
the perfect order of words in the sentence. There is an order in every
way appropriate."[46]

It's a moot point whether the author, Budgen, or the actor, Joyce,
should get the primary credit for this perfect vignette. (I am not
implying that Joyce did not work fanatically over *Ulysses,* as he so
clearly did. I am suggesting that he was well aware of the social
narratives that could attend such labors: in addition to writing great
books, he played the great writer.) Budgen's account implies that
the content of *Ulysses* is a given (Joyce "has the words already") and
that through a choice of style—manipulation of the words in the
sentences—he can present the content perfectly. It's not a great
stretch to read the two sentences as *Ulysses* and the "order in every
way appropriate" as the sequence of styles as a whole.

It has been hard for most readers not to say Yes to these implications. Though Joyce's conception of *Ulysses* clearly had changed
enormously by the end, the styles of the latter half are such pleasurable and impressive performances that they are easily read as in-
tentional, masterful elements of the book's significance. This seems
to be the case whether their function is taken as primarily mythic or
novelistic, or whether they are there as lessons in poststructuralism.

The mythic rationales for the styles are some of the hoariest axi-
oms of Joyce criticism, deriving straight from his charts. But the
styles are not so much evocations of anything Homeric as they are
aggressive parody of the *Odyssey.* There are a few Homeric analogs:
"Sirens," "Circe," the interpolations in "Cyclops." Of these, only in
the case of "Circe" can the form be considered an expression (actually an intensification) of Homeric material; the other chapters are
elaborate puns. "Wandering Rocks" is another literary pun, but it
has no parallel in the *Odyssey.* Joyce's rationale for "The Oxen of the
Sun"—that the slaughter of the sacred oxen represents "the crime
against fecundity by sterilising the act of coition"—is very far-
fetched.[47] "Nausicaa" and "Eumaeus" fit the Homeric slots of
Joyce's charts, but the sumptuousness of their bad writing shouldn't
obscure their aggression toward their models. This is even clearer
with the last two chapters. "Ithaca" poses endless linguistic puzzles,
and its dual focus on the human and the trans-human forestalls con-

clusiveness, but if anything is made clear there it is that killing hundreds of suitors is wrong (and is hardly a likely event). "Penelope" contradicts the Homeric Penelope in a more thorough way than the irony of casting a barely literate adulteress as the astute and faithful wife: Joyce emphasizes the precultural givenness of Molly's flesh, whereas when Odysseus regains Penelope it also involves reasserting cultural norms in Ithaca.[48]

The novelistic rationales are also contradictory. If the form of "Circe" is to express the fact that the characters are drunk or hallucinating, this fails to account for one of the most interesting features of the writing: the language in the fantasies mixes citations from the memories of characters with the prose of the narrator's prior descriptions, thus breaking the experiential boundaries of the characters as well as calling the autonomy of the earlier descriptions into question.[49] The rationale of drunkenness also has to ignore the principal narrative burden of the chapter: the fact that Bloom is not drunk and has enough presence of mind to look out for himself as well as Stephen. (The parallel to Homeric *moly* that Joyce finally came up with was "presence of mind" [*LJ*, 147]).[50] The "tired" style of "Eumaeus" has been said to express the emotional state of the characters, but "Ithaca" is an attempt to enlarge their ontological stature, creating a viewpoint from which their emotions are irrelevant.

The most telling argument against such rationales is that they are almost exclusively needed for the writing in the second half of the book. Joyce's naturalism in the first half is a subtle medium and varies considerably in registering the interplay between the moods of the characters and their surroundings, but it is qualitatively different from the later stylistic displacements.[51] It's easy to imagine that such chapters as "Nestor," "Proteus," and especially "Hades" might have presented great opportunities for expressive experiment. The headlines in "Aeolus," the occasional mockery by the narrator in "Scylla and Charybdis" ("Twicreakingly analysis he corantoed off" [9.12]), and the small play near the end of that chapter are stylistic eruptions, to be sure, but they are minor items set in a context of a writing that is committed to narratorial representation and mastery. "Urbane, to comfort them, the quaker librarian purred"; "A noiseless attendant setting open the door but slightly made him a noiseless beck" (9.1, 7–8)—such descriptive language and the dramatic registration of Stephen's thinking make up most of the chapter. Except for the headings, added later, the writing in "Aeolus" is representational.

But if the styles do not serve the narrative, they do not transcend it, either. "The exercises of style are not extrinsic to a central meaning; rather, they create the meanings in the book," writes Karen Lawrence. This seems close to the conclusion I want to draw. But just prior to this she writes that "Joyce reveals how style is always an interpretation of reality, a choice among many possibilities . . . from the breakdown of narrative, to the borrowing of styles, to the new mode beyond parody that he created in 'Ithaca,' Joyce signaled the end and the reconstruction of the form of the novel."[52] As is the case with much current Joyce criticism, this sees *Ulysses* as a controlled demonstration, this time not of naturalistic accuracy or of the mythic dimensions of modern life but of a primal version of poststructuralism. Joyce is placed in a position above his styles, from which he chooses one of many possibilities and thus reveals the contingency of style in general. Franco Moretti makes the point in a less complimentary way, writing that Joyce "aims completely at showing that every style is arbitrary and therefore irrelevant."[53]

But such contingency or irrelevance is simply not accurate to the book. This can be seen if we conduct a thought-experiment with Joyce's styles. Could "Penelope" be written in the style(s) of "Cyclops" or "Oxen of the Sun"? How about using "Nausicaa"? Imagine the book ending with Molly remembering how Bloom "had embraced her gently, like a real man, crushing her soft body to him, and loved her, his ownest girlie, for herself alone" (13.439–41, modified). How about rewriting "Circe" in the style of "Eumaeus"? I don't think I need to go through more proposed switches—though the possibilities are amusing. The point, which I think is central to the book, is that Joyce's styles are not separable from the material they treat.

The precise prose of the first half and the wonderful performances of the second have reinforced the sense of Joyce as an omnipotent writer: in the terms of Budgen's vignette, he could arrange his words in any order. But the prose of the first half, while easily registering motion, conversation, thought, and disposition of physical objects, would have a hard time with certain phenomena. Imagine the first half of "Nausicaa" written in the early style, each minute augmentation of Gerty's provoking posture noted with economical accuracy. It's doubtful that much sexual excitement could have been registered. It is not the underwear *per se*, but the style, so primly simpering at first, then gradually revealing a well-nigh total but excitingly unacknowledged fascination with sex, that stimulates Bloom—at least as we recreate that stimulation in our reading experience, since the style furnishes us with a peepshow into Gerty's and Bloom's feelings that is something like the physical one Gerty provides Bloom.[54] It is both Gerty's posture and her prose that Bloom masturbates over.

Bloom can't be reading her prose, can he? Of course it is wrong to say he is: such a statement signals an elementary confusion between medium and representation that is one of the banes of English professors. But the second half of *Ulysses* forces us into such confusion, especially "Circe," which reads the previous chapters of the book as well as reading itself:[55]

BLOOM

(*dejected*) Yes. *Peccavi!* I have paid homage on that living altar where the back changes name. (*with sudden fervour*) For why should the dainty scented jewelled hand, the hand that rules?...

(*Figures wind serpenting in slow woodland pattern around the treestems, cooeeing.*)

THE VOICE OF KITTY

(*in the thicket*) Show us one of them cushions.

THE VOICE OF FLORRY

Here.

(*A grouse wings clumsily through the underwood.*)

THE VOICE OF LYNCH

(*in the thicket*) Whew! Piping hot!

THE VOICE OF ZOE

(*in the thicket*) Came from a hot place.

THE VOICE OF VIRAG

(*a birdchief, bluestreaked and feathered in war panoply with his assegai, striding through a crackling canebrake over beechmast and acorns*) Hot! Hot! Ware Sitting Bull!

BLOOM

It overpowers me. The warm impress of her warm form. Even to sit where a woman has sat, especially with divaricated thighs, as though

to grant the last favours, most especially with previously well uplifted
white sateen coatpans. So womanly, full. It fills me full.

THE WATERFALL

Phillaphulla Poulaphouca
Poulaphouca Poulaphouca.

15.3405–30

The reader keeping track of the physical action can note that Kitty,
Florry, Lynch, and Zoe speak, and that Florry tosses a cushion she
had been sitting on (Lynch seems to intercept it). The women's
speech is convincing: we shouldn't forget Robert McAlmon's sly remark that "Circe" demonstrated the great author was not unfamiliar
with whorehouses. The reader keeping track of the symbolic coherences can connect the beechmast and acorns that Virag strides over,
Bloom's *"Peccavi!"* and his nearby remark "O I have been a perfect
pig" (3397) to reconfirm that we're in the territory of Circe's pigsty.
But there are narrative problems here. Most obvious is the impossibility of what is represented: the cushion-grouse, the waterfall that
echoes (with watery obscenity) Bloom's speech, and Virag, who is
twice or thrice impossible already: a most surreal being, he was dead
when he first appeared to Bloom; then he "died" again, or at least
unscrewed his head and stalked out of the printed action.

Such impossibilities are acceptable, however, because the prose
of "Circe" presents them very forcefully, in complete sentences that
almost always employ standard diction.[56] (We could almost say that
Joyce invented what Pound kept calling for: "a new medium, a sort
of expression half-way between writing and action," except that here
the action is the represented plot, not the Russian Revolution or
Italian Fascism.) But in the overall narrative of *Ulysses,* Bloom's self-
defined sin of "pay[ing] homage on that living altar where the back
changes name" cannot be read as a swerve into swinishness that will
be set to rights by the conclusion. In fact, one of the last things we
see Bloom do is kiss "the plump mellow yellow smellow melons of
her rump, on each plump melonous hemisphere, in their mellow
yellow furrow, with obscure prolonged provocative melonsmellon-
ous osculation" (17.2241–43). In both cases, the writing mixes erot-
icism and lyricism: first case is almost Keatsian, the living altar suggesting the "living trellis of a working brain"; in the second case,
the luscious obsessiveness of the rhyme is thoroughly mimetic of

Bloom's pleasure in sight, touch, smell, and taste, while at the same time the diction of "hemisphere," "provocative," and "osculation" includes the pedantic narrator in the perverse kiss. In both writing and plot, Joyce keeps resisting, almost to the end, a proper conclusion to *Ulysses*, where in Molly's memory Bloom will finally kiss her "correctly."

This interaction between the style and the action makes narrative a very tricky business in the second half of the book, but does not liberate the book from either its conventional plot or from the companion narrative of its successive styles: the writing becomes a dramatic reaction to the plot. But while the stylistic and the external narrative are at odds in the late chapters, in "Penelope" they are crucially united again. If Joyce's styles are seen simply as open possibility, then "Penelope" is a regression. For instance, Lawrence, who reads "Ithaca" as the capstone of Joyce's stylistic odyssey, has to place "Penelope" outside the narrative: "It is not the single voice and 'nonliterariness' of 'Penelope' that provided Joyce's fiction with a new direction; it is, instead, the artifice and the curious blend of dream, culture, myth, and nursery rhyme at the end of 'Ithaca' that was to be the most open-ended for Joyce—both in terms of *Ulysses* and *Finnegans Wake*. However beautifully and powerfully Joyce presented the return to a single voice in 'Penelope,' he gives us a kind of closure that the rest of the book seems to subvert."[57] Lawrence's judgment, positing open-ended indeterminacy as primary and the single voice of "Penelope" as ancillary, needs to be reversed. The stylistic display of the preceding chapters is better read as postponing the necessity of finally writing "Penelope"—of coming to a conclusion, or at least facing the problem. In one sense, to have to insist that the final chapter is the end of the book is a very odd thing, but it is fairly common for critics to see "Ithaca" as the conclusion. Fredric Jameson finds "the vitalist ideology of Molly's . . . final affirmation" less valuable than the invocation of history and labor that he reads in the description of the Dublin reservoir system.[58] Joyce himself felt a similar discomfort with "Penelope," writing that "The *Ithaca* episode . . . is in reality the end as *Penelope* has no beginning, middle or end" (*LJ*, 172), and in his charts he placed Molly's soliloquy outside of the time scheme of the novel. But his charts are part of the symbolic overview of the writing, not the writing itself.

WRITING AND INFIDELITY

As is the case elsewhere in Joyce's work, in *Ulysses* there is a strong connection between being a cuckold and being a potent writer, though the pattern is complex, spread out among more than one character, and existing on narrative, thematic, and stylistic levels.[59] Bloom and Molly act it out primarily on the narrative level, Stephen enunciates it as a literary-philosophical construct, and finally Joyce demonstrates, by his stylistic choices, its importance to him as well.[60]

While cuckoldry constitutes the primary narrative obstacle to be overcome by Bloom, he also can be seen to court and relish the condition. In addition to the very powerful but narratively inconclusive evidence that "Circe" provides of his pleasure in watching Molly and Boylan make love, there are more trustworthy confirmations in the plot of the fact that he wants to be cuckolded. Molly thinks that he does: "because he has an idea about him and me hes not such a fool. . . . now with Milly away such an idea for him to send the girl down there . . . only hed do a thing like that all the same on account of me and Boylan thats why he did it Im certain the way he plots and plans everything out" (18.81, 1004–09). Cuckoldry does not make him a great writer, the way Stephen says it does for Shakespeare, but in the mock-heroic register he fits the part surprisingly well.

The sexual lives of both Bloom and Molly have a well-defined epistolary and literary dimension. We first see Molly in bed, reading *Ruby: The Pride of the Ring*. Her incipient affair is announced by the "Bold hand" of Boylan's letter, which precedes its writer into her bed (4.308–11). In the outhouse, Bloom reads a piece of newspaper fiction that Joyce carefully ironizes by equating it to Bloom's turd and then having Bloom wipe himself with it;[61] nevertheless, in the symbolic machinery of the book the phrase *"Matcham often thinks of the masterstroke by which he won the laughing witch who now"* shows us Molly as Calypso and hints at Bloom's eventual victory that will turn her into Penelope.

While Bloom's affair stays on the written level the epistolary side of extramarital sex is finally disappointing to Molly and Bloom in equal measure. In replying to Martha's letter in "Sirens," Bloom feels bored even as he writes of his excitement: "Bloom dipped, Bloo mur: dear sir. Dear Henry wrote: dear Mady. Got your lett and flow. Hell did I put? Some pock or oth. It is utterl imposs. Underline *imposs.*

To write today. Bore this. Bored Bloom tambourined gently with I am just reflecting fingers on flat pad Pat brought" (11.860–64). After masturbating on the beach, all he can write are the words "I AM A," underlining his literary impotence with respect to women other than Molly. As part of the narrative these words are nugatory, but they can be read as hinting at much grander significance: "I am alpha," from Revelation.[62] (The tension animating Zukofsky's *"A"* arises out of a conflict between two similar frames.) As for Molly, while she has been satisfied with Boylan's physical performance, she finds his literary abilities lacking: "I hope hell write me a longer letter the next time if its a thing he really likes me O thanks be to the great God I got somebody to give me what I badly wanted I wish somebody would write me a loveletter his wasnt much" (18.731–37). Bloom's great capacity for sympathy and his endearing oddities finally incline Molly toward him, but primary in the constellation of Bloom's victorious traits is his prowess as a writer. Molly finds his "mad crazy letters" very exciting: "he had me always at myself 4 and 5 times a day" (18.1176–79). As is the case with "he plots and plans everything out," "he" implicates Joyce as well.

But writers do not experience contemporary success within the plot of *Ulysses*. Stephen ends up without a job or a place to stay; his parables and literary analysis have been received with incomprehension or tepid approval. He is knocked unconscious. It is prophesied within the text that he will write *Ulysses*, but as a writer he does little; he ruminates on the beach and scribbles a few lines, but as in *Portrait*, he writes only during windows of erotic-aesthetic contemplation.[63] When he garlands himself in "Oxen of the Sun," Vincent chides: "those leaves . . . will adorn you more fitly when something more, and greatly more, than a capful of light odes can call your genius father" (14.1117–19). The puns on condom in "capful" and whore in "light" fit in well with the thematics of writing and masturbation in "Scylla and Charybdis" that I will discuss in a moment.

While Stephen's meeting Bloom has been seen as crucial to developing the broad perspective necessary to write *Ulysses*, the positive features of that union for the most part depend on Joyce's verbal emphases. Stephen and Bloom are united in the image of Shakespeare's face; he allows Bloom to take his arm, they have cocoa, they sing. But the joining of their faces in Shakespeare's takes place only in the words of "Circe." In the external narrative, Stephen accepts Bloom's kindness to a limited extent and keeps his distance. The last bit of "writing" he produces is the parable of The Queen's Hotel (17.612–17). It serves Joyce's patterning that Stephen picks the site of Bloom's father's suicide, but the parable is a work of paralyzed isolation, obsessively naming what is not the mother's home, but only a hotel. From such a site, exile and longing seem likely sequels. Stephen exits hearing the psalm from "Telemachus"; he is still imagining dead mothers and ecclesiastical virgins.

As his discussion of Shakespeare indicates, it is not simply marriage that is lacking to make Stephen a writer, but cuckoldry. Stephen's Shakespeare becomes an omnipotent writer through cuckoldry, which is the same means that Richard Rowan in *Exiles* is enabled to "write all the night." And, as I have been suggesting, Molly's infidelity to Bloom is a key instigation to Joyce's own writerly infidelities with regard to the plot of *Ulysses:* "The tusk of the boar has wounded him there where love lies ableeding. . . . There is, I feel in the words, some goad of the flesh driving him into a new passion" (9.459–62). This sexual wound gives power. Shakespeare was more than "a lord of language" (9.454); he becomes, at the end of the following passage, godlike: "He is a ghost, a shadow now, the wind by Elsinore's rocks or what you will, the sea's voice, a voice heard only in the heart of him who is the substance of his shadow, the son consubstantial with the father" (9.478–81).

In the beginning of the sentence, though, he is a ghost. In addition to the reference to the Trinity—god, son, and ghost—there is a duality in this description: Shakespeare is both all-powerful and nonexistent. In this, he is consonant with Joyce's conception of Odysseus as "a combination of *Outis*—nobody, and *Zeus*—god" (*JJ*, 361) and his description of Bloom as "Everyman or Noman" (17.2008). It is not an inaccurate stretch to see Joyce writing himself into the book in these terms. As stand-ins for Joyce, Stephen the artist and Bloom the husband are, in narrative terms, often Noman. But Joyce also wrote himself into the book as Everyauthor, the quasi-divine figure who not only wrote and capitalized Molly's last Yes, but beyond it, gave himself the last words:

Trieste-Zurich-Paris
1914–1921

These words constitute Joyce's odyssey while writing *Ulysses*. It ends with him both remaining in exile, Noman undone by an unfaithful Ireland, and triumphantly arriving home at the art capital of the world as the universal author.

If the artist's power arises through the wound administered by unfaithful woman, Stephen's rapt description of Shakespeare is soon taken up by Buck Mulligan, who recasts the male creativity of the artist in the crudest way: "Himself his own father, Sonmulligan told himself. Wait. I am big with child. I have an unborn child in my brain. Pallas Athena! A play! The play's the thing! Let me parturiate!" (9.875–77). Pages later, Mulligan's parodic twins issue forth: a poem,

> *I hardly hear the purlieu cry*
> *Or a Tommy talk as I pass one by*
> *Before my thoughts begin to run*
> *On F. M'Curdy Atkinson*
>
> . . . .
>
> *Being afraid to marry on earth*
> *They masturbated for all they were worth.*

and a play entitled "Everyman His Own Wife or A Honeymoon in the Hand" (9.1143–73).

The last two lines of the Yeats poem "Baile and Aillinn" that Mulligan and Joyce mock are "Being forbid to marry on earth / They blossomed to immortal mirth."[64] Among its many other targets, *Ulysses* is devoted to attacking just such etherealization of love. But the blades of irony continue to slice. Mulligan goes on: "—Longworth is awfully sick . . . after what you wrote about that old hake Gregory. O you inquisitional drunken jewjesuit! She gets you a job on the paper and then you go and slate her drivel to Jaysus. Couldn't you do the Yeats touch? . . . The most beautiful book that has come out of our country in my time. One thinks of Homer" (9.1158–66). It is hard not to read these last sentences as Joyce's assessment of the book he is writing, an assessment put into the mouth of his mocking rival who is skewering the sycophancy of Yeats, the poet whose lines define love for Stephen as well as anything else throughout the day.[65]

In the midst of the larger Shakespearean, Homeric, Aquinian traceries of the chapter, it is important to remember that in the plot Stephen is fighting a local battle for rank in the small male world of

1904 literary Dublin. At the mention of Russell's anthology of younger poets, which excludes him, he thinks: "See this. Remember" (9.294)—advice that Joyce clearly followed. At such a moment, the line between Joyce and Stephen is thin, as it is in the parody of Yeats. The lineage that both Stephen and Joyce strive to enter and then to ascend is male, from Shakespeare all the way down to F. M'Curdy Atkinson, although Shakespeare's all-inclusive creativity tends to usurp most places in the chain:

> Judge Eglington summed up.
> —The truth is midway, he affirmed. He is the ghost and the prince. He is all in all.
> —He is, Stephen said. The boy of act one is the mature man of act five. All in all. In *Cymbeline,* in *Othello* he is bawd and cuckold. . . . His unremitting intellect is the hornmad Iago ceaselessly willing that the moor in him shall suffer.
> —Cuckoo! Cuckoo! Cuck Mulligan clucked lewdly. O word of fear! . . . .
> —And what a character is Iago! undaunted John Eglington exclaimed. When all is said Dumas *fils* (or is it Dumas *père?*) is right. After God Shakespeare has created most.
>
> 9.1017–29

The stable wisdom of Eglington can look like the truth here. (And it is quite like Ellmann's moderate readings.) But Mulligan's intrusion punctures this by reminding us that the writing of *Ulysses* is not so seemly and moderate. His interruption also may remind us that "All in all"—ghost, prince, boy, man, bawd, and cuckold—barely includes women. "All" writers, such as Dumas *père et fils* here, usurp the role of mothers, a pattern close to Pound's fantasies of autonomous spermatic creativity. Stephen will be shown in one of the climactic moments of "Circe" that such elision of the mother creates a terrifying presence when the repression is suddenly lifted. His dead mother appears, not coincidentally, soon after he and Bloom are united in the cuckolded visage of Shakespeare. But the lessons taught in "Circe" are not visible to their students, and the chapter ends with another male birth: the apparition of Rudy.

At the end of "Scylla and Charybdis" it is possible to see, in Joyce's symbolic machinery, hints that Bloom is to lead Stephen away from such an a-feminine *cul-de-sac.* Stephen's decision to end his relationship to Mulligan is punctuated, a bit heavily by Joyce's standards, with a number of narrative and thematic markers:

Part. The moment is now. . . .
My will: his will that fronts me. Seas between.
A man passed out between them, bowing, greeting. . . .
. . . Last night I flew. Easily flew. Men wondered. Street of harlots
after. A creamfruit melon he held to me. In. You will see.
—The wandering jew, Buck Mulligan whispered with clown's awe.
Did you see his eye? He looked upon you to lust after you. I fear thee,
ancient mariner.

9.1199–1211

Bloom is here "the ancient mariner," Odysseus, passing between the Scylla and Charybdis of Stephen and Mulligan. Bloom's safe passage triggers Stephen's recall of a dream of flying (that is, of fulfilling his name's destiny and becoming an artist). This dream also prophesies his adventures in "Circe" ("Street of harlots after"), "Eumaeus" ("A creamfruit melon he held to me"—Bloom holds out the photograph depicting Molly's "liberal display of bosom" [16.1430]), and "Ithaca" ("In. You will see."). But this symbolic consonance exists at the level of the word only.

Mulligan's mockery is not so easily disposed of. His crude parodies involving male masturbation and parturition do not fade out of the book by any means: both are dominant motifs in "Nausicaa," "Oxen of the Sun," and "Circe." The space in which Joyce's stylistic displacements occur is bounded on one side by Shakespeare's male fecundity and on the other by Molly's body and soliloquy.

The styles of "The Oxen of the Sun" enact Mulligan's fantasy of male birth in their phylogeny of styles, while they narrate, through their stylistic veils, a male discussion of masturbation and birth in ironic counterpoint to the actual feminine labor offstage. Joyce is having an aesthetic child—a male as we are informed at the second word: "Hoopsa, boyaboy, hoopsa!," and as Restuccia points out, "no women writers are imitated": women are banished from the process of literary gestation.[66] This in itself is odd as it compromises Joyce's stated aim of parodying the history of English prose: wouldn't Austen, the Brontës, and George Eliot be likely to figure in many histories? But more significant is the fact that as the chapter approaches "the present," the writing changes from parody to what Joyce intended as chaos: "a frightful jumble of pidgin English, nigger English, Cockney, Irish, Bowery slang and broken doggerel" (*LJ*, 139). It might have been beyond expectation for Joyce to have used his own naturalist style from the first half of *Ulysses* as a final foil in the sequence of parody styles, though in the narrative of literary history his scrupulously mean style does emerge as a reaction, among other things, to Newman, Pater, Ruskin, and Carlyle. But the explosion of slang that he does give us, besides not belonging in a parody survey of high literary models, destroys any link between the prior sequences and the writing in the first half of *Ulysses*. As Joyce presents it in "Oxen," the history of literature has marched off a cliff, and *Ulysses* is somehow on the other side of the chasm.

A novelistic rationale exists for these final paragraphs. One critic reads them as "a literary equivalent of drunkenness. . . . [T]he effect . . . is precisely what Joyce intended. 'Significant form' can be taken no further."[67] Again we have a reading in which whatever is, in *Ulysses*, is right. But if the form at the end of "Oxen" is significant, then that of all the earlier paragraphs would have to be anti-significant unless the moments immediately prior to total drunkenness were Paterean-aesthetic, Carlylean-heroic, etcetera. Rather, the final pages seem more significant as a reaction against the thickly ironic paean to the hopelessly fertile, institutionally correct sexuality of the Purefoys that is concluded in the paragraph immediately preceding: "To her, old patriarch! Pap! *Per deam Partulam et Pertundam nunc est bibendum!* [By the goddesses Partula and Pertunda now we must drink]" (14.1438–39).

It seems unlikely that it was the prospect of dealing with the present that derailed the march of the parodies; in the first half the book Joyce had written down contemporary life with precision. Rather, the stylistic progression explodes when it nears a present articulated in Latin and presided over by the goddesses of childbirth (Partula) and penetration (Pertunda)—an enthusiastic secular version of Father Conmee's detached musings concerning *eiaculatio seminis inter vas naturale mulieris*. Joyce could conceive of but not bear a conventional tale of marriage where, presided over by Latinate fathers, man and woman produce child. But a male parody-chronicle of birth could not be carried to term either. The conflict raised by narrative of styles in "Oxen" is all the more interesting in that the chapter mimes *Ulysses* as a whole: the sequence of styles in "Oxen" mirrors the larger shifts in the book; and, dramatically, "Oxen" is focused on a woman who is kept offstage (in a bed). This is very much the position of Molly: we never see her out of bed, and she functions for almost all of the book as the absent goal of the narrative.[68] The key difference of course is that Mrs. Purefoy is the patriarchal wife *par excellence,* while Molly is a more conflicted creation.

"HIS TRUE PENELOPE WAS FLAUBERT"

The narrative outcome of the marriage of Bloom and Molly is notoriously difficult to decide. There is a general consensus that Molly finally chooses Bloom over Boylan in some sense, or that she loves Bloom and not Boylan, but what this means is far from clear. To revert to soap-opera thinking for a second: are we to think that she will stop seeing Boylan and that Bloom will regain his potency in the proper Father Conmee sense of the word? Or is Molly simply waxing sentimental over a past-tense Bloom at three in the morning? Crude questions, but they occur because Molly's infidelity has been the dramatic focus throughout the book, and is the largest departure from the Homeric narrative. In making Molly unfaithful, Joyce strayed further from the *Odyssey* than he did by making Bloom ordinary, since Bloom is still granted heroic qualities in the midst of his mock-heroic treatment. Molly is given similar heroic/mock-heroic qualities, but it is her malapropism and her overall lack of education that contribute to her comic side, not her infidelity, which is an anti-Homeric gesture on the narrative level. The equivalent in Bloom's case would be not coming home. In his shifts in style, Joyce comes close (but only close) to such a departure from the original.

Critics have posited resolutions of the Blooms' marriage either in subtle characterological shifts or even subtler verbal-symbolic clues. Stanley Sultan sees Bloom winning Molly back by piquing her interest in Stephen in order to shatter her infatuation with Boylan.[69] Father Robert Boyle couches Bloom's eventual triumph in such terms as these:

> In the eight sentences in ["Penelope"], I suspect that Joyce is using the shape and the structure of the figure 8, so frequently repeated, for sexual symbolism. . . . Since, as I see it, the black dot at the end of the 'Ithaca' chapter signifies not only darkness but Molly's anus as well, Bloom is at present allowed to approach only the bottom half of the total eight which represents Molly's mesial groove. He does not now have the proper husband's control over Molly's vagina, the upper half of the eight. But . . . Bloom aims, at this point in the book, toward total husbandly control, as his demand for breakfast eggs discloses.[70]

Perhaps all of Boyle's suspicions as to Joyce's symbolism are well founded, but if so, such symbolism concludes the narrative in an extremely tenuous fashion, functioning on the level of individual words and almost invisible motifs.

To a non-Joycean such critical constructions may seem like the subtlest raving, but they are not false to Joyce's work.[71] They result from attempts to make *Ulysses* fully coherent apart from its narrative; Joyce engaged in these more than the most fanatic critic. But some of the most powerful moments in *Ulysses* occur when Joyce's stylistic shifts allow him to reach outside his narrative commitments. Earlier I used *Sweets of Sin* and porksteaks to exemplify the dichotomy between a fully coherent *Ulysses* that engulfs a redeemed world and a *Ulysses* that makes contact with an outside world beyond the resurrecting touch of art. Passages like the following near the end of "Circe" make a stronger case for the value of such open-ended art:

STEPHEN

The harlot's cry from street to street
Shall weave Old Ireland's windingsheet.

PRIVATE CARR

(*loosening his belt, shouts*) I'll wring the neck of any fucking bastard says a word against my bleeding fucking king.

BLOOM

(*shakes Cissy Caffrey's shoulders*) Speak, you! Are you struck dumb? You are the link between nations and generations. Speak, woman, sacred lifegiver!

CISSY CAFFREY

(*alarmed, seizes Private Carr's sleeve*) Amn't I with you? Amn't I your girl? Cissy's your girl. (*she cries*) Police!

STEPHEN

(*ecstatically, to Cissy Caffrey*)

White thy fambles, red thy gan
And thy quarrons dainty is.

15.4640–56

The larger passage this is taken from, with its political, literary, and religious allusions, is very powerful. Here, the speeches of Bloom and Carr contrast strongly, both with each other and with the poetry Stephen quotes. In Carr's words, history shouts out, non-symbolic, incoherent, raw. As is always the case with Joyce, this sentence is addressed to the intelligence, as it invites us to notice the rage against the father that is built into blind, patriotic obedience. But we shouldn't ignore the obvious: that the sentence is violent, more so than Pound's Hell Cantos, where Pound shields himself behind Dante in order to swear at authority. This is ordinary, unfocused rage: "I'll wring the neck of any fucking bastard says a word against my bleeding fucking king." A voice contemporary with the writing of *Ulysses* speaks in the book, without resolution within the narrative.

Bloom reacts to Carr by appealing to the narrative conclusion of *Ulysses*. Woman, sacred lifegiver, is to transcend divisiveness on the personal and the national level. Joyce carefully qualifies these speeches: "the sacred lifegiver" is also, by her own report, "only a shilling whore" (4383), yet Bloom as hero and as enunciator of the narrative resolution is not undercut.

The chapter's breaking of the physical and psychological bonds of the characters allows Joyce tremendous freedom, which he focuses on the area of gender. Bloom is made "womanly" many times over in "Circe." He chats with Mrs. Breen in an exaggeratedly feminine register: "Because it didn't suit you one quarter as well as the other ducky little tammy toque with the bird of paradise wing in it that I admired on you and you honestly looked just too fetching in it though it was a pity to kill it, you cruel naughty creature" (15.556–59). In attempting to identify himself to the watch, he doubles his gender: "I am a respectable married man. . . . My wife, I am the daughter of a most distinguished commander" (776–78); he is nearly flagellated by a trio of society amazons (1014–1121); he has eight babies (1810–32). Most notable is the long sequence in which he succumbs to Bello's sadism: he is trod upon, ridden, farted on, invaginated, burned with a cigar, killed. There are many moments in this sequence in which Bloom's masochistic impulses are on display: "BLOOM (*bends his blushing face into his armpit and simpers with forefinger in mouth*) O, I know what you're hinting at now!" (3124–26). But the brutality with which s/he is treated goes far beyond psychological role playing and physical possibility:

BELLO

. . . Trained by owner to fetch and carry, basket in mouth. (*he bares his arm and plunges it elbowdeep in Bloom's vulva*) There's fine depth for you! What, boys? That give you a hardon? (*he shoves his arm in a bid-der's face*) Here wet the deck and wipe it round!

3088–91

But the larger gender narrative of *Ulysses* exerts an overwhelming pull on such material. Bloom reasserts himself, besting the prim Nymph, harshly spurning Bella's domination, getting his potato talisman back from Zoe, saving Stephen from Bella's financial clutches, seconding him compassionately and intelligently in the quarrel with the soldiers, and taking care of him afterward. Bloom does not represent masculinity in a conventional sense, but he does become so vigorously heroic that a number of his actual speeches verge on being unconvincing.[72] This is an odd assertion to make about anything in "Circe," since character is so malleable during the fantasy sequences. But these fantasies, while unrealistic in content, are quite realistic in tone. The immense excitement that "Circe" generates depends on the accuracy of Joyce's misplacements and exaggerations. Cheryl Herr makes the point that the tones and materials of "Circe" derive to a large extent from music-hall culture: "Joyce used theatrical form to demonstrate the cultural scripting of the 'inner.' " She sees the exteriorization of these inner scripts as, ultimately, part of a deconstructive gesture: "Joyce's steady and various undermining of the absolute opposition of those binarisms (male/female, saved/damned, upper class/lower class, and good/evil) on which Western cultural mores are built engineers in his text what we might call a liberating vision of culture."[73] But Joyce reconstructs these binaries in Bloom's climactic speeches, such as the one quoted above, or when Bloom, dashing out of the brothel, cries "I need mountain air" (4313). The soldier's shout reverberates from the outside, but Bloom's speeches feel like programmed statements about heroism, gender, and the ultimate narrative destination of marriage, statements that are all the more glaring in their phantasmagoric surroundings.

"Circe" is such a massively powerful performance that it is not surprising that there would be signs of strain as Joyce tries to conclude it and yoke it back into the overall narrative of the book. The theatrics of "Circe" show the transgressive territory beyond conventionally gendered social roles—let these be exemplified by Bloom's "Nes. Yo." (2766) as he becomes "woman." But within the chapter conventional roles are reaffirmed, and *Ulysses* as a whole rebels against but finally concludes with a narrative Yes. It separates the genders back into man, the artist and hero who needs mountain air—the air on Howth for instance, while he's making love to Molly—and woman, who may be the sacred lifegiver but who remains a rival to, and finally an object of, the artist's creativity.

Although Molly challenges men at an important point in her soliloquy—"nature it is as for them saying theres no God I wouldnt give a snap of my two fingers for all their learning why dont they go and create something" (18.1563–65)—this challenge can be reversed: men can't create children, but can (Joycean) women create art? The answer in *Ulysses* seems to be no. Molly is not particularly literate, and Gerty's brush with literacy is one of her larger blemishes.

The final three chapters complete, in Joyce's resistant fashion, the narrative that separates man from woman and unites them in marriage. The styles of "Eumaeus" and "Ithaca" both display intense resistance to the narrative denouement. "Eumaeus" demonstrates a passive-aggressive debility and obtuseness toward its burden in the plot's trajectory. With the problem of the resolution of the Blooms' marriage approaching, we are given, as the last of the chapter's many duplicities, three horse turds and a cloudy hint about a marriage of Stephen and Bloom, "The driver . . . watched the two figures, *as he sat on his lowbacked car,* both black, one full, one lean, walk towards the railway bridge, *to be married by Father Maher*" (1874–78, 1885–87). On the micro level, endings are also made problematic. The chapter's style has often been called tired or boring, but its individual sentences display as much energy as any in *Ulysses* as they conclude in wonderful grammatical tangles. They are far beyond the obsessive copying of cliché that animates the plot and sentences of *Bouvard and Pecuchet.*

"Ithaca" stalls the narrative in a different way, breaking the flow of events into freestanding "facts," the trivial and the profound promiscuously mixed, each separate and timeless as an epiphany. "Ithaca" begins with scientistic descriptions of walking routes and ends with obsessively elaborated nursery rhymes—a backward motion if anything: even though we can follow the narrative moving forward, formally the writing in "Ithaca" is non-narrative.

The overall narrative is not abandoned, though. It is important that Bloom and Stephen meet; we learn key facts about Molly and

Bloom. But most puzzling for a reader trying to construct the significance of the conventional narrative, there are events that are simultaneously portentous and random, like the shooting star that Bloom and Stephen see while urinating (1210–14). One can grant it cosmic significance, and one can do the same with the "brief sharp unforeseen heard loud lone crack emitted by the insentient material of a strainveined timber table" (2061–62), reading it as a sign of divine approval: "Bloom's 'prayerful' review of his day is rewarded by a clap of thunder out of a cloudless sky, as Odysseus is rewarded in *The Odyssey* when he strings the bow . . . and prepares to kill [the suitors]."[74] Such readings are not wrong, but they are also contradicted by the grosser external narrative, which obviously does not support such a happy ending. Unlike Telemachus, Stephen has left—after singing an anti-Semitic song—and of course Molly has been faithful to Bloom only if the physical narrative is ignored. There are even more insidious oppositions to a full symbolic recovery of significance: those places where Joyce teases the seeker of such meaning with touches such as the clown calling Bloom father, and the marked coin not returning. In these infidelities, Joyce is treating the reader like Molly treats Bloom.

But as Molly's Yes reaffirms the meaning of marriage, her chapter as a whole represents an utterly faithful return to narration: "Penelope" is only timeless in Joyce's ideological labeling in his charts. Nowhere else in *Ulysses* do we get such pure narration: we are to assume a woman who thinks each one of the phrases we read in the precise order we read them. Nothing else intervenes; there are no significant elisions in the reportage.

But if in this sense Joyce ends *Ulysses* with total submission to narrative, we shouldn't forget that he has been most aggressive toward the marriage story he inherited from Homer, violating it throughout and fulfilling it only in tenuous, symbolic ways. Even the conclusiveness of Molly's final Yes is qualified by having her conflate Mulvey and Bloom—"yes and how he kissed me under the Moorish wall and I thought well as well him as another" (18.1603–05)—a refusal to individuate the objects of her passion that makes her all the more comprehensively natural. The thoroughness of these violations on the stylistic level and the impalpable subtlety of the fulfillments on the narrative level make the most likely outcome on June 17, 1904, a book like *Finnegans Wake*: layerings of marriage, infidelity, Oedipal skirmishes, incest, all dissolving into multiple males and omnipresent female.

As Nature, Molly is to transcend contradiction: she is the "sacred lifegiver" at the same time as she is "always at herself 4 and 5 times a day"; she is both Bloom's mountain flower and his unfaithful wife. Some critics have balked at accepting her, though paeans to her naturalness are a staple of the older criticism.[75] This extreme instability at the site where the narrative of *Ulysses* is to be firmly anchored is emblematic of the problematics of genius.

In her bodily transcendence of social codings Molly is, surprisingly, not that far from a representation of the pure Kantian genius: nature, not governable by rules, speaking to culture. But genius—Stein asserts this programmatically—is beyond narrative. The main contradiction with regard to Molly, then, is not the inconsistency of her character (though there are grounds for such an assertion), but that formally she is presented as pure narrative at the same time that she has to be timeless nature, both the power behind and the goal of Joyce's pen. Thus all she can do when on the page in the novel is to remember or plan. Joyce makes a great effort to have her remember enough so that she will become nearly as complete a character as Bloom. But unlike him she cannot act in the present or even be situated in social space. She has been excluded from the bulk of the book, not just for drama, as has usually been assumed, but because, as the genius of Flesh, she cannot be narrated in social terms.

It could be argued that this is not strictly true, as she has appeared in "Calypso." But, again, one can imagine a thought-experiment using the style of "Calypso": could a conventionally depicted Molly speak with Bloom at the end of the book? *Ulysses* would end as a soap opera. The Molly of "Calypso" is not the narrator of the final chapter.

Character and plot are categories of intense conflict in *Ulysses,* but they are not done away with. The final Yes is the site of a precarious stylistic and narrative conclusiveness. It is easy to project a utopic fullness into the word, but a dream Joyce had after the publication of the book seems truer to the impasse the ending represented. In the dream, Molly broke with Bloom, throwing a child's coffin at him, while Ezra Pound, an "American journalist," looked on and laughed. Indignant, Joyce passionately explained the last chapter to Molly: "I . . . delivered the one speech on my life . . . [ending] on an astronomical climax." She smiled, threw a small coffin-shaped snuff-box at Joyce, saying, "And I have done with you, too, Mr. Joyce" (*JJ*, 549). Since that point, critics have picked up Joyce's passion for explanation in the face of a foreclosed but endless alluring narrative possibility. Joyce himself moved on to *Finnegans Wake*. Its circularity, along with "the great ball of crystal" Pound wanted *The Cantos* to be, the circle of "Rose is a rose is a rose is a rose," and the musical "recurrence" we will see Zukofsky posit as the meaning of "*A*," demonstrate the antipathy of modernist genius to linear, social plot.

4

Seeing What Gertrude Stein Means

If Molly makes a surprising genius, for many readers Gertrude Stein has seemed an even less likely candidate. The premise underlying this chapter is that Stein belongs in the company of Joyce, Pound, and Zukofsky: a defensible proposition, but one that involves a certain amount of defensiveness, too. Stein is unavoidably part of most literary histories, and conventional literary-historical reasons can be found as justification. Like her male counterparts, she is the author of a diverse, complex body of writing. In *Q.E.D.* her narration of lesbian relationships was remarkably calm, especially for a pioneering effort. *Three Lives* has been read as having extended the stylistic possibilities of naturalism or as having gone beyond naturalism into a nonrepresentational, linguistic writing.[1] If *Three Lives* didn't take this latter step, *The Making of Americans* certainly did. In *Tender Buttons* and the early word portraits Stein experimented with the basic mechanisms of verbal representation, inventing, according to some views, a kind of written Cubism, and according to others, rethinking the writer's relation to patriarchy.[2] In the twenties, she developed the nonnarrative play, and her interest in this form continued through to the development of quasidramatic, evocative plays and operas such as *Dr. Faustus Lights the Lights* and *The Mother of Us All*. Her autobiographies explore the mechanisms of voice and narrative time; her novel *Ida* plays with the interrelation of narrative and gender.[3] Her lectures on her own work are sensible and funny and have been recognized by some as important poetic theory; Lyn Hejinian sees her work as a crucial antecedent of language writing.[4] Her more hermetic explanatory or philosophical works, such as *How To Write, The Geographical History of America,* and *Four In America,* are also valued as a merging of practice with theory.[5] *Stanzas in Meditation* is an extended display of verbal abstraction that was not equaled for decades. Her wartime narratives have been praised for their literary sophistication and the quality of their human witness.

But such a defensive list of achievements does not finally catch what makes Stein's writing so provocative. The list is heterogeneous and displays more or less conventional genres and recognizable functions: portraits, plays, theory, new ways of representation, but Stein's lifelong commitment to the present moment of writing makes such a generic panoply secondary if not false. What John Ashbery writes of *Stanzas* can be extended to her work as a whole: "And if, on laying the book aside, we feel that it is still impossible to accomplish the impossible, we are also left with the conviction that it is the only thing worth trying to do."[6]

Stein was a sophisticated innovator—all the more remarkable considering how isolated she was in the first decades of her career—and an accomplished writer, but the innovation and the accomplishment are in uneven relation to one another. There are thousands of pages of her work where she is not innovating, or apparently trying to accomplish anything; notions of craft and inspiration do not seem to apply. Her imperturbable commitment to her daily practice of writing rather than to the quality of any particular bit of the product is the primary fact. There is a literalism and self-assertion to her work that is not easy to assimilate to aesthetic or literary-historical categories of judgment. "I cannot tell you how often like and alike are not alike" (*FIA*, 72) is something *Stein* is telling *me:* there is no literary distance involved. The linguistic—one could really say the proto-poststructuralist—wit of the play between "like" and "alike" and between the distinct instances of "alike" (the first an instance of itself, the second an adjective) remains live; but the "often" points to Stein's practice: "like and alike are not alike" very often and Stein tells me so very often. I've quoted one sentence from an eighty-page piece from a two-hundred-page book, from the eight thousand or so pages she wrote. And the "I" embodies the problematics of Stein's career: her seemingly endless output was not selfless meditation: she insisted on its value as masterpiece and her own value as genius.

And yet Stein's writing attacks the notion of literary quality in telling ways. Her continuous celebration of a merged self and writing and the simplicity of her defiance of conventional aesthetic evaluation made her the subject of mockery by reporters and of scorn by male modernists. Her lesbianism may have been one cause of fear, but something at a more elemental level provoked reactions such as this of Wyndham Lewis, who wrote that her "prose-song is a cold, black suet-pudding . . . of fabulously reptilian length.'"[7] I find this dismissal slightly comic in its blindness to its own metaphors. One does not have to share such phobias, or those of the critic B. L. Reid, who in the fifties wanted to "decapitate" Stein,[8] to find Stein's own claims for the status of her writing problematic: "A thing you all know is that in the three novels written in this generation that are the important things written in this generation, there is, in none of them a story. There is none in Proust in The Making of Americans or in Ulysses" (*LIA*, 184). This is written in Stein's public style, but even here the primal assumption of critical and literary discourse— that to articulate language is difficult and valuable—is disturbed in small ways that I will discuss in a moment. Certainly most of Stein's writing is quite a bit more disturbing than this. Such is not the case with Pound and Zukofsky: no matter how odd the results, their writing is governed, in theory at least, by assumptions of exact uses of language, referential or formal. What exactitude might possibly mean in a literary context is endlessly discussible, of course. Here, I am simply pointing to the mentions of exactitude that are so common in the rhetoric of Pound, Zukofsky, and their critics. Similar assumptions govern Joyce's work; even in *Finnegans Wake*, so commonly thought of as playful, the play is precise. Many specific meanings are explosively packed into the words: a phrase may implicate seven meanings, but these can be explicated.[9] The expertise needed to read Joyce, Pound, and Zukofsky is readily subsumed under the category of "higher learning." One does not need such expertise to read Stein.[10]

While she aspired to more than a simple fame as an iconoclast and wanted to succeed in the same arena with Joyce and Proust, it needs to be remembered how opposed to, or indifferent to, general ideas of exactitude, efficiency, and "good writing" her own writing is. Whether this condition is ascribed to her genius, her courage, her need, or to her lack of ability, it is ubiquitous.[11] Even in the excerpt quoted above there are features that could be labeled errors or weaknesses, or else praised as challenges to conventional notions of good and bad. The bifurcation is there almost in every word. Should we call the diction of "A thing" elemental or childish? Does "the three novels written in this generation that are the important things written in this generation" embody insistent repetition or prolixity? "A thing you all know is"—directness or bullying? The assertion that

The Making of Americans, Ulysses, and *Remembrance of Things Past* are not narratives—subtle criticism or simple error? Does the comparison of the three novels reflect confidence or anxious boasting?

It is a comparison few would make. It is not just that *The Making of Americans* is an extremely odd novel for the most part before emptying out the categories of narrative interest. Richard Bridgman writes that "there are three Martha Herslands, three David Herslands, and at least two Julia Dehnings" and that the character of Alfred Hersland changes completely at one point due to Stein's changing conception of the book (*GSIP,* 69). More damning for any standard aesthetic appraisal are the constant authorial asides. The best known is "I am writing for myself and strangers" (*MOA,* 289), which, if one is intent on a kind of damage control, could be at least vaguely assimilated to Joyce's sense of the confident, aloof artist "above his handiwork, indifferent . . . paring his fingernails" (*PA,* 215). But where Joyce thoroughly narrativizes and delicately ironizes Stephen's aesthetic pronouncements in *Portrait* (in *Ulysses* the irony is quite a bit stronger), any sense of irony and artistic mastery that Stein's remark might convey has to be dispelled on looking at the context in which it appears: "I am writing for myself and strangers. This is the only way that I can do it. Everybody is a real one to me, everybody is like some one else too to me. No one of them that I know can want to know it and so I write for myself and strangers" (*MOA,* 289).

"This is the only way that I can do it"—it might seem that nothing could be more destructive to the possibility of aesthetic creation than such a baldly personal admission of lack of means on the part of the writer.[12] Compare the arsenal of styles Joyce displays in *Ulysses.* But in fact Stein often admits not just to stylistic inflexibility but, even worse, to discouragement, apathy, and despair: "I am all unhappy in this writing" (*MOA,* 348); "I am really almost despairing, I really have in me a very very melancholy feeling, a very melancholy being, I am really then despairing" (*MOA,* 459); "You write a book and while you write it you are ashamed . . . you know you will be laughed at or pitied by every one and you have a queer feeling and you are not very certain and you go on writing" (*MOA,* 485).[13] At one point she incorporates an earlier chunk of writing while admitting she doesn't like it: "some then have a little shame in them when they are copying an old piece of writing where they were using words that sometime had real meaning for them and now they have not any real meaning in them" (*MOA*, 441).[14] Such evidence supports Bridgman's claim that *The Making of Americans* is "a disaster" as a novel, and that instead it should be considered as "a psychological and stylistic daybook" (*GSIP*, 61).

Lisa Ruddick has recently explored the dynamics of this daybook in depth, finding a tangle of three voices: that of "the good son, the chronicler of middle-class life," the "psychologist, who uses the characters to illustrate a theory of human nature with serious pretentions of truth," and the voice that eventually takes over, "a hypnotized producer of sentences, someone with moods of her own and bodily rhythms that affect her way of putting words together."[15] Ruddick quite convincingly demonstrates that some of these rhythms are in large part anal, and that in fact *"The Making of Americans* is a spectacularly anal text. . . . Stein experiences her telling as a form of rhythmic accumulation and release."[16] Ruddick's description repeats, though in a positive register, Wyndham Lewis's.

At this point, if not long before, the aesthetic prosecutor could rest his case: how dare Stein place such an obsessive, ill-digested hodgepodge next to the masterpieces of Joyce and Proust? This is not a position I agree with: for one thing, as we have seen with Pound and Joyce and will see with Zukofsky, bodily drives are present to a high degree in other modernist writing—and, anyway, why consider evidence that the writer is conscious of having a body a bad thing? But I am ventriloquizing the prosecutor's case to salvage the grain of truth it contains: that Stein's writing represents an expression of her self and her body that is basic and unaestheticized. This point tends to be overlooked in the principal countermodels that have been developed for reading Stein.

Nevertheless these models are more rewarding than the prosecutorial stance that refuses Stein's rhythms. Her work may be difficult to justify on grounds of conventional literary quality, but read as anti-patriarchal, as mimetic in a Cubist sense, or some other unconventional fashion, or as dialogic, her writing easily regains much of its interest. While none of these approaches will finally provide more than partial justice to Stein, especially when her career as a whole is considered, they are important components in building an informed and sympathetic response.

MODELS FOR READING STEIN

The complete title, *The Making of Americans Being a History of a Family's Progress,* seems to entail a standard family narrative, on the one hand, but, on the other, Stein often claims to be carrying out a supremely grandiose classification scheme—"a history of every kind of them of every kind of men and every kind of women who ever were or are or will be living" (220). While these are two quite different things, both are eminently patriarchal tasks. But the book can be read as the vast effort by which Stein conquered the terror of and desire for such conventional authorial mastery and distance. For Jayne Walker, Stein's agonized abandonment of the Hersland and Dehning family narrative in favor of her own self-creation through writing is the real story of the book; Walker argues that Stein's struggle marks the movement from *plaisir* to *jouissance,* from the readerly to the writerly text.[17]

These Barthesian/Kristevan categories are certainly more generous to Stein and make it possible to read the next twenty years of her work with something other than irritation or scorn. Giving these categories a stronger feminist emphasis, Marianne DeKoven sees Stein's experimental writing as an "anti-logocentric, anti-phallogocentric, presymbolic, pluridimensional . . . antidote to patriarchy," thus valuing just what conventional literary wisdom would condemn.[18] From this point of view, the journalistic insult applied to Stein, "Mother Goose of Montparnasse," would in fact be accurate praise. In abandoning her fantasy of the total schematization of reality in *Americans,* Stein would also be moving away from what Kristeva terms the symbolic toward the semiotic, from post-Oedipal syntax, competence, categorization, separation of subject and object, back to pre-Oedipal bodily process, rhythmic drive, blurred boundaries, disruption.[19] The maternal singsong of Mother Goose, where semantic sense is swaddled and rocked by rhyme and rhythm, would become an oasis of plenitude.

Stein's writing often does sound somewhat like nursery rhymes. To pick three examples from hundreds of possibilities: the refrain "Pigeons on the grass alas" from *Four Saints in Three Acts* (SW, 604); the motto "I am I because my little dog knows me," which becomes an important reference point in Stein's meditations on identity in *The Geographical History of America* (and which in fact *is* a direct quote from Mother Goose); or the following portrait from *Tender Buttons:*

CHICKEN
    Alas a dirty word, alas a dirty third alas a dirty third, alas a dirty
bird.

                                                                    SW, 492

But a reading that is looking exclusively for the semiotic will not be
able to respond to most of what Stein is doing here. The play on the
relation of word and thing, half-hidden in the bird/word rhyme,
mediated deftly by a third rhyming term, which is none other than
the word "third" itself; the sound or number play set up by the
commas, which create a single, a doubled, then a single phrase; the
doubled, mediating phrase ("alas a dirty third alas a dirty third")
functioning like a two-way mirror between the word and the bird;
with the whole refrain governed by a threnody for verbal sin ("Alas
a dirty word"), or is it just grumbling over messy kitchen prep
("Alas a dirty bird")?—all this presupposes a conscious awareness
of linguistic possibilities and philosophical implications that is foreign to the bodily immediacy and pre-articulation of the pure semiotic. Not that the Kristevan textual model DeKoven uses is rigidly
binary; quoting Kristeva, DeKoven sees Stein's work as ultimately
producing an "impossible dialectic," the "constant alternation between time and its 'truth,' identity and its loss, history and the timeless, signless, extra-phenomenal things that produce it."[20] Given
goals this capacious, the model can account for an effect that Stein's
writing often produces: the sudden insinuation of framing and significance amid the rhythmic play of her varying repetitions.
    But there is an important and recalcitrant dimension to her work
not accounted for by the anti-patriarchal semiotic model. Much of
the strangeness of Stein's writing, especially in *Tender Buttons*, is very
difficult to ascribe to some half-hidden semiotic horizon; rather, it
seems to result from the intensity of her commitment to art and to
the specific circumstances of that commitment, principally her association with Picasso and other Cubists. Given her own pronouncements that she was doing in writing what Picasso was doing in
painting, it's hard not to read some of Stein's work as Cubist.[21] Cubist readings and semiotic readings are, however, mutually exclusive.
The semiotic, as the pre-objective expression of the pre-subjective
body, cannot, it seems to me, finally be connected with writing as
art, which implies using language for deliberate subjective purposes

that are also ultimately objective and public. *Tender Buttons* declares itself art from the beginning. Far from blurring the distinction between subject and object, its first section is called "OBJECTS," and the writing, both naming its objects and distancing itself from any conventional closeness to them, creates that sense of distance between writer and reader that is central to the aesthetic. The first object in the book is canonically Cubist, a carafe; and the process of representation—*how* is this a carafe?—arises as a problem in the first few words of the title "A CARAFE, THAT IS A BLIND GLASS."[22]

This brings us to my second category of counterreading, in which the words become a puzzle. The recognition of this aesthetic distance and the desire to overcome it by decoding or otherwise contextualizing what look like Stein's mimetic displacements have motivated some insightful and ambitious critical readings. Marjorie Perloff reads the pieces in *Tender Buttons* as activating many frames of reference at once. Thus, A SUBSTANCE IN A CUSHION, while not "about" buying fabric, sewing, sexual play, and the processes of referentiality, simultaneously activates all these frames in various tangential ways.[23] William Gass attacks the manifest verbal surfaces of the pieces vigorously, often pushing far past them and finding complex systems of "covert" meanings, so that A BOX can be "an ironic argument . . . for lesbianism on the ground that such sexual practices preserve virginity, avoid God's punishment, and do not perpetuate original sin."[24]

By creating narrative or philosophical sense, such readings can domesticate the strangeness of the writing and produce lush supplements, but the strangeness remains. Take the next piece of CHICKEN in *Tender Buttons:*

CHICKEN

    Alas a doubt in case of more go to say what it is cress. What is it. Mean. Potato. Loaves.

SW, 493

These words are deeply resistant to any global reading. I could generalize about domesticity, pointing to the evidence in the last four sentences of a meal surrounding the posited chicken: potatoes, loaves, cress. This would be an easy decoding (although odd decodings are possible). I could read the first sentence as the evidence of a mind in motion: "Alas": taking up the previous piece; "a doubt": abandoning the prior refrain; "in case of more": a sense of the overwhelming specificity of the world; "go to say": go on to say; "cress": cress. But such a narrative of Stein recording small readjustments during an attempt to represent the world covers up the jaggedness of the writing: "Go to say" is not "go on to say"; "Mean" can imply "cruel" or "average" in addition to "signification"; the rhythm of the first sentence is remarkably bumpy, with the first half iambic (singsong) and the second decidedly not ("*go* to say / what it *is* / *cress*"). In addition to creating a tamer simulacrum of the writing, my hypothetical approach would defuse the title's demand or promise; instead of being a portrait of CHICKEN, in the writer's mind if not the reader's, "Alas a doubt in case . . ." would become a record of the writer's struggle with the project of portraiture.

It is precisely this that Wendy Steiner sees as a central focus throughout Stein's career and as an impossible goal, given that Stein rejected conventional descriptive terms and analogies in favor of an absolute equivalence. (In the Peircean terminology Steiner refers to, Stein rejects symbolic [conventional] and iconic [analogic] signs in favor of indexical signs, which are "existentially related to their referent.")[25] If the uniqueness of any object requires a unique language, then the distance between writer and reader will ultimately remain unbridgeable. Steiner sees Stein as uncompromisingly following out these implications to a dead end: "The extension of the artist into the world, dictated definitionally by the portrait, was now impossible . . . virtually all the rest of her writing is caught between audience-directed referentiality and self-reflexive isolation."[26]

In one sense, Stein's account of her practice in writing *Tender Buttons* confirms this conclusion: "This as I say has been the great problem of our generation, so much happens and anybody at any moment knows everything that is happening that things happening although interesting are not really exciting. And an artist an artist inevitably has to do what is really exciting. . . . I became more and more excited about how words which were the words that made whatever I looked at look like itself were not the words that had in them any quality of description" (*LIA*, 190–91). As with many of Stein's public pronouncements, this can be read with varying emphases and ultimately varying meanings. If the emphasis is put on the apparently absolute difference between the words Stein uses to see with and words used for conventional description, then "self-reflexive isolation" will be the result. "The words that made whatever I looked at look like itself" would be indexal words—a unique language for a unique object. If to be an artist means using a separate language, then Stein's position might seem surprisingly close to Pound's. One could take Stein's emphasis on sight as the key process in writing *Tender Buttons* ("I was creating in my writing by simply looking" [*LIA*, 191]), plus her dismissal of conventional description, as analogous to Pound's valorization of the artist's unmediated gaze producing the instant perception that "baffles the man counting on the abacus" (*PD*, 208). But there is a crucial difference. For Pound, genius is a mode of control over the reader, who is not only "baffled" by the writer's insight but obliterated—to Pound's way of thinking, invaginated, becoming the "passive vulva" to the phallic genius (*PD*, 204). Stein on the other hand allows herself to become excited and thus is not the creator of masterful language that simply acts on others, but the one in whom language is acting: "I became more and more excited."

In the above excerpt, then, a second reading would emphasize Stein's submersion in her writing process and would focus not on her superiority or estrangement but on her excitement, which, to some extent at least, she seems to be inviting the audience to share. The fact that she was giving lectures at all does suggest a certain reciprocity. In the next section I will be discussing how complex and qualified this relationship with her audience is. In the overall trajectory of her career, this complexity becomes crucial; the binary dilemma Steiner posits—"caught between audience-directed referentiality and self-reflexive isolation"—does not do justice to the major works of the thirties.

Reciprocity figures in the third countermodel for reading Stein: the dialogic. Before discussing it, I want to point out a progression associated with the three models: a semiotic writing cannot be directly addressed to an audience; a Cubist-mimetic writing, with its emphasis on unconventional analogies, must seek "fit audience . . . though few"; the dialogic would necessarily be audience-centered. The size of the dialogic audience, however, is a question. But whether the public at large is being addressed or just Alice B. Toklas, a great deal of the writing from the period between *Tender Buttons* and the autobiographies is clearly dialogic:

Eat the little girl I say.

Listen to me. Did you expect it to go back. Why do you do
to stop.

What do you do to stop.

What do you do to go on.

I do the same.

Yes wishes. Oh yes wishes.

What do you do to turn a corner.

What do you do to sing.

We don't mention singing. . . .

We were such company.

Did she say jelly.

Jelly my jelly.

Lifting belly is so round.

Big Caesars.

Two Caesars.

Little seize her.

Too.

Did I do my duty.

Did I wet my knife.

No I don't mean whet.

YGS, 22–23

"Lifting Belly," from which this is but a small excerpt, is a remarkable document, incantatory and funny, experimental and sentimental, sexy and analytic. Beyond these binaries, there are qualities
of pleasure, humor, and a deep relaxation in the face of any potential
literary demands along with a pervasive sense that these moments
of living-writing are supremely valuable. In addition to the clearly
legible voices caressing, chatting, writing and rewriting one another,
there are many other sexual and domestic roles, as Stein writes herself in guises that range from the correct husband, or the conquering
husband, to the geologic sex object "Mount Fatty" (*YGS,* 36). Toklas
is variously the delicate wife, the lovely snorer, the Jew lady, the
cow, and even, in two lines of the above, a co-Caesar. It is almost
always difficult to sort out two distinct voices; some lines can be
read as question and answer, but many seem the results of a merged
two-person writing sensibility contemplating a real-life dialogue
that was not written down.

Given the profusion of such pieces in Stein's writing—none quite
as ecstatic as "Lifting Belly," though—Harriet Scott Chessman seems
justified in seeing dialogue as central to Stein: "Stein's model of a
lover-to-lover bond incorporates a profound commitment to lan-

guage as the place in which dialogue becomes audible."²⁷ But to extend this model to all of Stein's work from *Three Lives* (1905) to *The Mother of Us All* (1946), as Chessman does, seems a distortion. It is true that slight signs of this intimate dialogue occur even in *Americans*. As Stein and Alice Toklas became lovers and Toklas began typing the pages Stein had written the night before (a task Toklas hoped "would go on forever"), Toklas, as Chessman points out, appeared in the text as the "some one [who] says yes to it."²⁸

While Toklas is a particularly interactive audience in much of Stein's writing from this point on, the hidden, ecstatic, domestic-sexual-linguistic communion that developed between the two women is hard to equate directly with Stein's relation to the public; at the least there is a great difference in scale, which has greater eventual implications.²⁹ As is indicated by the title of her study, *The Public Is Invited to Dance*, Chessman's sense of dialogue reaches far beyond the lovers' intimacy; dialogue takes place "between characters . . . between the reader and the words . . . between the words themselves . . . between the writer and the words . . . between words and the objects they 'caress' but do not necessarily signify."³⁰ It is only with difficulty that anything can be excluded from such a category. At the same time, it seems inaccurate in another way because Chessman also tries to minimize the importance of the specific Stein-Toklas dialogue; she feels that to interpret "Lifting Belly" as "a conversation between two actual figures" is a mis-emphasis, since Stein "carefully refuses to make her representations of this intimacy stable or certain." This instability is to reach directly out to us as readers: "Stein's dialogue invites our own participation as sharers (fellow 'Caesars') in the act of 'lifting belly,' the composing of the poem so intricately entwined with the conversation of lovers, for we too may become the 'I' or the 'you.' "³¹

This resolution of "I" and "you" into readers masks one of the central difficulties of Stein's writing. Her love for Toklas may well have unlocked her acceptance of her own sexuality and, simultaneously, her courage to venture into new modes of writing. But her relation with the public was far more conflicted. Before turning to this, however, I want to look at the work of one last Stein critic, who avoids Chessman's overestimation of Stein's collaboration with the public but who nevertheless moves toward a similar resolution. Neil Schmitz also sees dialogue as central to Stein's writing, but he emphasizes its covert quality, pointing out that Stein kept "Lifting Belly" and other such works hidden from the public: "So *risque* is the funny feeling in this work, so revealing, Gertrude Stein would suppress the more frolicsome texts in her lifetime. The notable exception is *Tender Buttons* (1914), which gives it away, which doesn't give it away."[32]

The doubleness of these final phrases echoes Schmitz's primary sense of Stein as a humorist, as a writer engaged in double-talk, in a "carefully wrong discourse." Schmitz reads *Tender Buttons* with an accurate responsiveness; where I take issue with him is the social status of Stein's canny "wrongness." On the one hand, in a discussion of "BOOK" (*SW*, 476), he sees the writing as essentially private: "If the reader were informed, he might indeed espy, against a certain landscape, Gertrude Stein, Alice B. Toklas, and their dog, Polybe, and yet the play of this partial disclosure is not primarily with the reader, is not *for* any reader. It is the play of the writer with her intention." However, this private intimacy is, for Schmitz, directly useful for art: "the chatter also expresses at once the intimacy of the sisters and the artistic importance of that intimacy. . . . It is brought, this 'idle' gossip, this jesting sweet-talk, within the scrutiny, the propriety of writing."[33] But "artistic importance" remains an open question and literary "propriety" is exactly what Stein's writing questions so thoroughly. Her notoriety preceded most intelligent appreciation of her work to such an extent that her career dramatizes how disturbingly large the gap between the words "artistic" and "importance" can be.

A recent book club ad in *The New York Review of Books* seems a fitting emblem of how notorious a figure Stein remains, and of how trivial a sense of her writing permeates an improbably wide area of literate culture.[34] In the ad, a small-bodied caricature of Stein sits holding a rose and a teacup beneath the following caption: "A book is a book is a book. Pick any 3 for $3. And you don't have to buy any more. Ever or never." In slightly smaller print below the drawing: "(Translation: 3 books, 3 bucks. No commitment. No kidding.)." Beside the drawing the caption reads, "Gertrude Stein Gertrude Stein." The small print below the picture continues the repetition ("And a great deal is a great deal is a great deal"), but goes on to draw from a wider pool of Steinisms: her association with the young American writers after the First World War ("As a QPB member you'll never be part of the lost generation"); Toklas's exotic cuisine ("every book . . . will earn you Bonus Points [think of them as Alice B. Toklas Brownie Points]"); Toklas's last words to Stein ("What is the answer? To join QPB, of course").

What kind of literary success is this? Stein's biography seems known in some detail, and she herself is still notorious enough to sell books. But of her writing, only the circular "Rose is a rose is a rose is a rose" seems to have survived. The QPB ad offers none of her books, or anything closer to them than Fitzgerald; it features a biography of Stephen King, *20 Years of Rolling Stone, The Microwave Gourmet, The Art of Sensual Massage,* and, most un-Steinian of all, a host of writing manuals: *Get to the Point, The Writer's Handbook, The Elements of Grammar, The Elements of Style.*

An un-Steinian list, and yet Stein's face, biography, and rudimentary but indestructible reminiscences of her writing seem quite at home here. This portion of her fate might seem a pure defeat. After all, she said that it was crucial to keep the difficult originality of art difficult and original: "Every masterpiece came into the world with a measure of ugliness in it. . . . The Sistine Madonna of Raphael is all over the world, on grocer's calendars. . . . It's our business . . . to recover its ugliness" (*FIA,* vii).[35] But the split between Raphael and grocer's calendar is not all that absolute or all that desirable in Stein. She may have been momentarily nonplussed by the burst of fame that followed the publication of *The Autobiography of Alice B. Toklas,* but compared with a writer such as Pound, the fact of being a public figure was, for her, benign. And beyond this, it was a ubiquitous subject of meditation and source of energy in her later work. She addressed a culture that seemingly would have had no way of receiving what she wrote. Yet the ease and the persistence with which she addressed it was remarkable, as was the degree to which she was accepted as a public figure, if not understood as an artist. Whether understanding was finally a very significant issue is the question to which I will now turn.

THE PUBLIC GENIUS

The teens may have been a crucial decade in Stein's development as a writer, but the thirties were the crucial decade in her career. Before that, she had been simultaneously the notorious Mother Goose of

Montparnasse, the proprietor of a chic Paris salon, and the private writer of pieces such as "Lifting Belly." By the forties she wrote as an accepted public figure. This change was effected during the thirties, when she addressed the public as a genius, a more problematic and unstable mode than any of the others, as she had to both assume the status of genius and, contrary to the attributes of that status, demonstrate it. In her major works of this period, *Toklas*, the lectures, *Everybody's Autobiography*, *Four in America*, and *The Geographical History*, she wrote about her writing, herself, society, and history, but these subjects were all variations of the basic theme of genius. In the autobiographies she narrated the outward progress of genius through Paris and America. In her lectures she told the internal story of her struggles and successes with various formal problems visible only to genius. In her less public writing, she combined these two approaches, meditating as a genius on the ontological and social status of genius. In all cases, there is a difficult double insistence: (1) genius is unique, a fact that Stein states emphatically and demonstrates in various ways in the writing itself; and (2) genius is unavoidably perceptible and obviously valuable, a fact that she also states emphatically and that is demonstrated, in however suspect or tautological a sense, by her fame.

Did Stein merely have a genius for publicity, or did her acclaim have to do with her actually being a genius? If this question implies a choice between seeing Stein as a charlatan or an artist it must seem that she would insist on the last option. But her own self-definition is not so uncomplicated. A clear instance of this complexity occurs in her answer to a student's question about "Rose is a rose is a rose is a rose": "Now you all have seen hundreds of poems about roses and you know in your bones that the rose is not there. All those songs that sopranos sing as encores. . . . Now I don't want to put too much emphasis on that line, because it's just one line in a longer poem. But I notice you all know it; you make fun of it, but you know it. Now listen! I'm no fool. I know that in daily life we don't go around saying 'is a . . . is a . . . is a . . .' Yes, I'm no fool; but I think that in that line the rose is red for the first time in English poetry for a hundred years" (CC, 404). These remarks affirm both possible causes of her fame. Stein grants her writing various artistic virtues, standard and advanced: her poems have New Critical integrity (you can't quote just one line); they revivify the great literary tradition, *à la* Eliot and Pound; like the Russian Formalists, she is an exponent of *ostranenie*, defamiliarization.[36] But at the same time, she notices that everybody knows the line. Do they know it because of its literary value, because "the rose is red for the first time in English poetry for a hundred years," or simply because, as the ad quoted above seems to suggest, its repetitiveness sticks in the mind? In Stein's continual meditations upon genius throughout the thirties, her tone, simple and opaque, cannot be confined either to art or to commercialism.

For all of its studied nonchalance, play with narrative sequence, and seeming randomness, *Toklas* holds to the story of the worldly triumph of genius with great tenaciousness. Even in the small opening chapter (*SW,* 3–5), complex distances and connections between genius and the ordinary world are present, mediated by Alice Toklas, a figure who is simultaneously quotidian, like the reader for whom genius is a wild and strange phenomenon; a lover of genius; and, finally, perhaps a genius herself.[37] Extraordinary names and events—Clara Schumann, Napoleon, the Paris Commune—pepper her ordinary ancestral history. One of the first things we see her do is, as a teenager, write to Henry James. Genius may have an affable and approachable side, as is the case when he answers her, but it is still forbiddingly other: his "delightful letter" fills her with shame. Apparently genius cannot be approached from such conventional distances. Outside of this episode, Toklas is the embodiment of complacent gentility: "I . . . have always enjoyed the pleasures of needlework and gardening. . . . [Before meeting Gertrude Stein] I led a pleasant life, I had many friends, much amusement many interests, my life was reasonably full and I enjoyed it but I was not very ardent in it" (3–4).

This complacency assumes gargantuan proportions in Toklas's father, as he shrugs off the San Francisco earthquake with his famous remark, "That will give us a black eye in the East" before going back to sleep, and again when he seems to value decorum over his own son's life, reassuring a mother hysterical at the return of a riderless horse: "Be calm, madam, . . . perhaps it is my son who has been killed." As we will see in a moment, this *sang-froid* and the imaginative power that reduces the fiery ruins of a city to a social black eye have a subterranean resemblance to some of the results of Stein's own genius, but on the surface this remarkable orderliness seems a perfect foil to the entrance of Gertrude Stein, who arrives, indirectly, as the earthquake personified—"The disturbance in the routine of our lives by the fire followed by the coming of Gertrude Stein's older brother and his wife made the difference"—and bells go off in Toklas at the recognition of her genius.

The rest of the book tells the story of that genius, along with fellow genius Picasso, moving through the crowd of lesser and fake geniuses in Paris to worldly triumph, signaled by the publication of *Americans* and the production of *Four Saints in Three Acts*.[38] However, "moving through" is a paradoxical expression because, as we will see, genius never changes or is associated with events or narrative. Nor does genius change the world much. There is no breakthrough: the world of genius is also the ordinary world, and is in fact a little more ordinary than that, more intensely domestic, less patriarchal.

In *Toklas* all signs of struggle are effaced. One of the engaging features of the book is the ease with which it domesticates erstwhile heroic and forbidding modernist figures. Picasso is not exactly made into a teddy bear, but when he asks Toklas if she can see the resemblance his forehead bears to Lincoln's and she comments tactfully but tartly, "I had thought a good many things that evening but I had not thought that" (15), his egotism is rendered charmingly, unthreateningly ludicrous. There are many similar moments. Early in the book, Toklas is confronted by the walls of Stein's atelier, covered "right up to the ceiling" with the terrors of modern art (8–13). The narration does not immediately describe the pictures, however. Instead the strange is made familiar, a gesture the opposite of defamiliarization, as the focus widens to include a plethora of small, reassuring household details—key, lock, stove, inkstand, notebooks—and a phrase or sentence of context is supplied for each. Then there is another abortive attempt at description: "But to return to the pictures. The pictures were so strange that one quite instinctively looked at anything rather than at them just at first" (9). Twice more Toklas says she will describe the pictures, but continues to veer off to chairs, seating habits, lighting fixtures, before finally giving us the impressive roll call: Cézanne, Renoir, Matisse, Picasso, Gauguin, Toulouse-Lautrec, Manet, El Greco.

This domestication of modernist art and writing is carried out even more literally in the following passages: "I always say that you cannot tell what a picture really is or what an object really is until you dust it every day and you cannot tell what a book is until you type it or proof-read it. It then does something to you that only reading never can do," and "Speaking of the device of rose is a rose is a rose is a rose, it was I who found it in one of Gertrude Stein's manuscripts and insisted upon putting it as a device on the letter paper, on the table linen and anywhere that she would permit that I would put it" (106, 130). Apparently one doesn't have to understand difficult modernist art at all; one merely has to live with it: dusting is superior to analysis. As for "Rose is a rose is a rose is a rose," a direct appreciation of it need not involve recognizing how it regalvanizes the tradition of English literature, one can simply stitch it onto napkins and perhaps other personal linen. The shapes the words assume are emblematic of the two approaches: as part of literature they are a (straight) line, in a poem and in a tradition ("in that line the rose is red for the first time in a hundred years"); as an item in the Stein-Toklas household they form a (marriage) ring.

These two shapes may represent mutually exclusive alternatives, but Stein did not choose between them. Genius is both a household word and a literary counter of absolute value. Stein's writing insists on and is based in part on the uniqueness that her relationship with Toklas created and reaffirmed, a difference that was both sexual and creative: Toklas was the first to recognize her genius.[39] But while *Toklas* was one culminating expression of their private union, it was also the vehicle with which she succeeded in reaching and conquering the public, and insisting that they recognize her genius as well: "She realizes that in english literature in her time she is the only one. She has always known it and now she says it" (72).[40] In such a description, as both the message and the pronouns indicate, Stein celebrates, but also objectifies, publicizes, and alienates herself.

A literature composed of "the only one" might easily seem imaginary, a desert island perhaps, especially when the claim is made in a book that in its genre and even more in the way it fulfills its generic obligations has only a tangential claim to be included in mainstream "english literature." But however deserted, the space of literature that Stein maps out is still complex: the book ends with the narrator revealing herself to be Stein writing as Toklas in the same way as Defoe wrote as Crusoe: "About six weeks ago Gertrude Stein said, it does not look to me as if you were ever going to write that autobiography. You know what I am going to do. I am going to write it for you. I am going to write it as simply as Defoe did the autobiography of Robinson Crusoe. And she has and this is it" (237). This says it is simple, and its surface can give that impression, especially at the end: "And she has and this is it." However, the handling of time here creates a mysterious void. There is the past, "about six weeks ago"; there is the future that Stein spoke of then, "I am going to write it"; there is the more immediate past, "and she has"; and finally, at the end, an assertion of the present, "and this is it." But it is a present that vanishes, or clicks neatly shut: the book is over. As a speech act, this paragraph is far from simple. The writer may live in the continuous present but the reader can only stare at the assertion of a present and begin to remember the book in a new way.

While domestic arrangements throughout *Toklas* form a soothing, indirect link between genius and its public reception, Stein and her writing exist there in a Crusoe-like isolation in what could be called the "center" or the "forefront" of English literature—though both metaphors contain a group reference that is not appropriate to Stein's claims. In her lectures, she deals more openly with literature and her place in it, but as a genius she remains just as much of a Crusoe there. Tangentially, one could note the island motif that dominates her explanation of writing in England: "The thing that has made the glory of English literature is description simple concentrated description not of what happened nor what is thought or what is dreamed but what exists and so makes the life the island life the daily island life" (*LIA*, 14–15).

In its dismissal of event in favor of concentration and existence, this description seems to apply more accurately to Stein's own work than to writers like Defoe, Austen, or George Eliot. But the larger similarity to Crusoe occurs in Stein's overall description of her techniques, processes, and goals, which are expressed in ways that cut them off from other literary writing: "sentences are not emotional and . . . paragraphs are" (*LIA*, 93); "Poetry is concerned with using with abusing, with losing with wanting, with denying with avoiding with adoring with replacing the noun. . . . That is what poetry does, that is what poetry has to do no matter what kind of poetry it is" (*LIA*, 231); in *Tender Buttons* "a thing could be named without using its name" (*LIA*, 236). Such claims, while they are quite suggestive about her own work, are absolute and untestable.

At times, she softens this absoluteness, referring, only occasionally, to Whitman, (Henry) James, and Shakespeare as precursors. But her versions of these fellow geniuses deal with predication, comparison, and memory as peremptorily as she does. Stein's James tried to wrest words from all context, so they move without moving against a background; Stein's Whitman replaced all conventional names; Stein's Shakespeare "in the forest of Arden created a forest without mentioning the things that make a forest" (*LIA*, 236).[41] But even such gestures toward a literary tradition, while they may reaffirm her genius by placing her in illustrious company, are problematic in that they involve memory and comparison, functions that Stein repeatedly insists are antithetical to genius. In her lectures she denies any importance to narrative in novels, plot in plays, or pictorial representation: acts of memory, comparison, or identification involve a doubleness that destroys genius. She will nod condescendingly that "a resemblance is always a pleasurable sensation and so a resemblance is almost always there . . . that is just a pleasant human weakness" (*LIA*, 79). But with Cézanne: "The apples looked like apples the chairs looked like chairs and it all had nothing to do with anything because if they did not look like apples or chairs or landscapes or people they were apples and chairs and landscapes and people. They were so entirely these things that they were not an oil painting and yet that is just what the Cezannes were they were an oil painting. They were so entirely an oil painting that it was all there whether they were finished, the paintings, or whether they were not finished" (*LIA*, 76–77). Reading this will not elucidate representation in Cézanne. Attempts to abstract the telling phrase are useless: separately, each phrase borders on (or dwells within) the simpleminded, but together they produce an iridescent sheen as Stein displays an ineffable knowledge that is in her eye at the same time as she dismisses all questions of common recognition. Some readers might feel an intolerable amount of repetition in these words, many of which repeat almost immediately: "The apples looked like apples." Sentence structures repeat without a conjunction to soften the effect: "The apples looked like apples" = "the chairs looked like chairs." There is a similar repetitive play with opposites: "it all had nothing to do with anything"; or, doubly, "if they did not look like apples or chairs or landscapes or people they were apples and chairs and landscapes and people." Not only are "apples" "apples" here despite appearances, but "or" is "and," too. This joining of opposites through repetition also occurs inside the word "they": "because if

they [apples] did not look like apples ... they [apples] were apples. ... They [apples] were so entirely these things that they [ap-
ples] were not an oil painting and yet that is just what the Cezannes
were they [paintings] were an oil painting. They [paintings] were so
entirely an oil painting." This repetition denies the exclusivity of
ordinary oppositions and embodies the prime mystery of genius, its
ability to transubstantiate word and thing. This mystery is reinforced
grammatically by the placement of the name of genius ("the Cezannes") as a fulcrum between the last instance of "they" as apples
and the first instance of "they" as paintings.

Stein's well-known distinction between repetition and insistence—"once started expressing this thing, expressing any thing
there can be no repetition because the essence of that expression is
insistence" (*LIA*, 167)—is not made in the service of a democratic
panacea of increased attention for all. From the story of Stein listening to the chatter of "her very lively little aunts" and realizing that
there could be no repetition, and from her description of the infinite
variety involved when birds sing and frogs hop, it's possible to get
the sense that no two grains of sand are alike.[42] But the genius is the
only one who has the ability to escape the stultifying effects of
repetition.

Stein writes of her genius obliterating her memory and her identity: "I am I, not any longer when I see" (*FIA*, 125). If she is identified,
then she ceases to be a genius: "I am I because my little dog knows
me" is the refrain that runs through *The Geographical History* to dismiss the significance of conventional identity. But she also demands
recognition from the audience: another of her refrains, "When this
you see remember me" evokes the trademarked status of her un-
mistakable style of writing, personality, and appearance.

One could put these refrains together and come to the conclusion
that the audience is Stein's little dog, needing to remember her when
that was precisely what she was too absorbed by the rapture of creation to do. However, recombining Stein's phrases in this way may
seem foreign to the spirit in which they were written. Her approach
to writing was improvisatory, her output was huge, and she was
not a system builder, with the result that individual sentences in her
work are less crucial than the sentences of most other writers. Just
because she wrote "The minute painting gets abstract it gets pornographic" (*EA*, 127) and "I think nothing about men and women

because that has nothing to do with anything" (*GHOA,* 214) does not mean that Stein was a prude or a naturalist, or that she never considered gender important. But this condition of not being easily pinned by her words to a standard social meaning tends to support the more shocking truth that words don't matter in the same way to her as to her readers, thus reinforcing the point that Stein's genius, considered as either a literary or a public-relations phenomenon, does not involve a highly refined degree of communication. She says as much at one point: "It is not clarity that is desirable but force. Clarity is of no importance because nobody listens and nobody knows what you mean no matter what you mean, nor how clearly you mean what you mean. But if you have vitality enough of knowing enough of what you mean, somebody and sometime and sometimes a great many will have to realize that you know what you mean and so they will agree that you mean what you know, what you know you mean, which is as near as anybody can come to understanding any one" (*FIA,* 127–28). The knowledge a genius possesses cannot be translated outside the precincts of genius. Stein begins her lectures in America by saying "One cannot come back too often to the question what is knowledge and to the answer knowledge is what one knows" (*LIA,* 11). In the midst of these rudimentary words, almost commonsense, almost tautological, the ineffability of genius is audible.

"YOU SEE WHAT I MEAN"

Despite her insistence that the meaning of her work was as obvious and immediate as the words of her explanations, her writing was obviously unusual and obscure. In her lecture "Portraits and Repetition" she reads some excerpts from portraits, including the following: "A hurt mended stick, a hurt mended cup, a hurt mended article of exceptional relaxation and annoyance, a hurt mended, hurt and mended is so necessary that no mistake is intended." Then she makes a characteristic comment: "You see what I mean, I did express what something was, a little by talking and listening to that thing, but a great deal by looking at that thing" (*LIA,* 190). Such assertions leave no track for her listeners to follow; they are simply urged to comprehend immediately, somewhat like Gaudier-Brzeska seeing that the Chinese ideogram is a horse. Except that Stein blocks any conventional identification by adding that these "words which were the words that made whatever I looked at look like itself were not the words that had in them any quality of description" (LIA, 191). To recall my earlier discussion, this can imply absolute linguistic otherness or exemplary excitement. But in either case, the public meaning of "you see what I mean" will be problematic.

If one considers the totality of Stein's writing in the thirties, the emphasis falls more easily on "I" than on "mean." That is, it is easier to imagine her audience seeing Stein's "I," and not the writing, as the embodiment of the meaning. If Stein is referring to the meaning of her writing, it is hard to imagine her audience seeing the "thing" that she was looking at and expressing, especially since in the lectures she did not always read the titles of the pieces.[43] The above excerpt is about a twentieth of "BREAKFAST," the portrait from which it is taken. And that portrait, like many in *Tender Buttons,* does not seem to me to portray a single visual object, but rather the relationship between Stein and Toklas, the concomitant change in Stein's writing, and the disappearance of Stein's brother along with his stern disapproval of her literary hopes:[44]

> A change, a final change includes potatoes. This is no authority for the abuse of cheese. What language can instruct any fellow.
> A shining breakfast, a breakfast shining, no dispute, no practice, nothing, nothing at all.
> A sudden slice changes the whole plate, it does so suddenly. . . .
> Anything that is decent, anything that is present, a calm and a cook and more singularly still a shelter. . . .
> What is a loving tongue and pepper and more fish than there is when tears many tears are necessary. . . . A white cup means a wedding. A wet cup means a vacation. A strong cup means an especial regulation. A single cup means a capital arrangement between the drawer and the place that is open.
>
> SW, 483–84

Inside the frame of such a biographical-aesthetic narrative, this seems evocative. "A hurt mended stick, a hurt mended cup" can be read with stick and cup having a sexual dimension, and the whole sentence smoothing out the annoyance of sexual division and soothing it into a necessary and exceptional pleasure. The final quoted paragraph seems almost openly tender and amorous. But this is when the piece is read with the requisite assumptions: that all possible verbal substitutions and connections are to be made to keep the sense moving toward love and literary *jouissance*. Stein in her lectures is not providing such a frame; in the absoluteness of her explanations, she rather is insisting that "language can instruct any fellow" directly, without such critical mediation.

For all of its affability, *Toklas* presented Stein as an inexplicable genius; for of all their insistence on simplicity and clarity, the lectures presented inexplicable bits of difficult writing. Despite this or because of it, Stein's next books, *Everybody's Autobiography*, *The Geographical History*, and *Four in America* were written by a famous person.[45] Stein often seems quite aware of the relation of her impenetrability to her fame. At the beginning of *Everybody's Autobiography*, when she nearly gets her picture taken with Mary Pickford, she writes: "I was very much interested to know just what they know about what is good publicity and what is not. Harcourt was very surprised when I said to him on first meeting him in New York remember this extraordinary welcome that I am having does not come from the books of mine that they do understand like the Autobiography but the books of mine that they did not understand" (*EA*, 8).

Genius can affect history (effect it perhaps) without being understood. Prior to her post-*Toklas* fame, Stein had occasionally considered herself (along with Picasso) as a motor of history in a casual or inexplicable way. In *Toklas*, she and Picasso are walking in Paris during the first winter of the war: "There is nothing in the world colder than the Raspail on a cold winter evening, we used to call it the retreat from Moscow. All of a sudden down the street came some big cannon, the first any of us had seen painted, that is camouflaged. Pablo stopped, he was spell-bound. C'est nous qui avons fait ça, he said, it is we that have created that" (*SW*, 85).

It's not easy to decide here whether the aesthetic or the military is the bigger, more authentic frame. The artists play war, "we used to call it the retreat from Moscow," and the army reproduces Cubism—more or less—on its artillery. In "Composition as Explanation" there is a similarly partial claim, or a spectrum of claims, for the historical efficacy of art. On the one hand "the modern composition," history, is made by society in general: "each generation has something different at which they are all looking" and "nothing changes from generation to generation except the thing seen and that makes a composition" (*WAM*, 26). On the other hand, the artist is ahead of her time and is an outlaw until suddenly becoming a classic. World War One accelerated the perception of society in general so that "we who created the expression of the modern composition were to be recognized before we were dead" (*WAM*, 36). While "the modern composition" and "the expression of the modern composition" are not quite the same thing, artists here seem central in a vague way.⁴⁶

But at times in her earlier work she is provocatively outside history, as "Lifting Belly" demonstrates, mentioning World War One twice in fifty pages, both times glancingly.⁴⁷

> Dare I ask you to be satisfied.
> Dear me.
> Lifting belly is anxious.
> Not about Verdun.
> Oh dear no. . . .
> Lifting belly together.
> Do you like that there.
> There are no mistakes made.
> Not here at any rate.
> *YSG*, 10

The rest of the world may have been caught in the destruction of an enormous tragedy, but Stein-Toklas are unerring. To paraphrase Stephen Dedalus: "Women are geniuses who make no mistakes."

Once Stein is firmly entrenched as a success, however, such cloudy claims disappear and she is a simple fact of history. I don't think the beginning of the *Geographical History*, "In the month of February were born Washington Lincoln and I," is meant as an outrageous joke. But at the same time history itself, everything outside that "I" and its genius, seems to lose all interest: "anybody can know that the earth is covered all over with people and if the air is too what is the difference to any one there are an awful lot of them anyway and in a way I am really only interested in what a genius can say the rest is just there anyway" (*EA*, 118).

Yet her success did not eliminate the need for her to be interested in the rest of the world—the world as audience if not the world as phenomena: in order for that success to exist, other people had to find her genius interesting. The refrain "You see what I mean," repeated throughout the *Geographical History* and *Four in America*, encapsulates the tensions involved. As a speech act, "You see what I mean" feels to me to be a quasi-command, more performative than constative, as if what created the feeling of meaning in the reader's mind was Stein's writing, not any act of the reading mind itself. Often Stein can seem almost bullying in her approach, adding an insistent "yes":

> So you see I am I because my little dog knows me.
> But that has nothing to do with romance but it has to do with government and propaganda.
> Oh yes you do see.
> You do see me.
> And that has to do with government and propaganda but not with money and the human mind.
> Oh yes you do see.
> But do you see me.
>
> GHOA, 168

As often as Stein wrote variants of the phrase "You see" in her work in the thirties, there was a persistent difficulty involved, as she also asserted at least as often that her writing was fundamentally different from all other social uses of language. On one side there was genius, the masterpiece, the present, entity, the human mind, and on the other, society, newspaper writing, memory, identity, human nature. The genius is free from ordinary occupation: "It takes a lot of time to be a genius, you have to sit around so much doing nothing, really doing nothing" (*EA*, 70). The genius is free from ordinary senses of size: "A sentence is an imagined master piece" (*HTW*, 123). The genius is free from ordinary sequence. This means freedom from syntax and from history: "And so I do know what a genius is, a genius is some one who does not have to remember the two hundred years that everybody else has to remember" (*EA*, 121). An ordinary sentence written by a non-genius is transmogrified when a genius reads it word by word: "I found that any kind of a book if you read with glasses and somebody is cutting your hair and so you cannot keep the glasses on and you use your glasses as a magnifying glass and so read word by word reading word by word makes the writing that is not anything be something" (*GHOA*, 151).[48] Stein can turn ordinary words into something fit for the human mind, but human nature, the uninteresting half of the binary, cannot by itself produce genuine writing: "The human mind writes what it is. Human nature cannot write what it is because human nature can not write" (*GHOA*, 105).

Stein often scorns the would-be artistic products of human nature—for example the "encores that sopranos sing" mentioned in her remark about "Rose is a rose." These dismissals are especially prevalent when it comes to literary politics: "Sinclair Lewis is the typical newspaperman and everything he says is newspaper" (*WAM*, 103). Human nature's ontological status is paltry, and, on the other side, the human mind can be an aloof automaton: "The human mind can write what it is because what it is is all that it is and as it is all that it is all it can do is to write" (*GHOA*, 105). Given these conditions, it is surprising that reading is as simple as Stein continually asserts.

At times, she will deny any possibility of a problem with audience reception. The raw fact of her pronouncing her words within an audience's hearing will suffice: "I said to the mother superior when she said that she could not understand what did that matter if the little ones could and she said but little ones always look as if they understand and I said yes but if they look it it is as pleasant as if they do it beside anyway if any one listens to it that is as much understanding as understanding is and she too listened to me so probably she did do as much understanding as any understanding could do" (*EA*, 289–90).

At an extreme, Stein says the human mind is utterly detached from everything: it "has nothing to do with identity or audience or history or events" (*GHOA*, 158). This includes her own history:

> So finally I became so attached to one word at a time even if they were always one after the other.
> Now then let me tell the story of my life.
> The story of my life.
>
> Chapter One
>
> At that time I had no dogs
>
> Chapter II
>
> So I was not I because my little dog did not love me. But I had a family. They can be a nuisance in identity but there is no doubt no shadow of a doubt that that identity the family identity we can do without.

> It has nothing to do with anything if there is no time and iden-
> tity. . . .
> The human mind lives alone.
>
> *GHOA,* 195–96

But there is a substratum of anxiety to all this. While genius, masterpieces, the human mind are detached from the social world, that
world doesn't vanish, even as the writing pronounces its disappearance. In the excerpt above, the nuisance that Stein's family was to
her is detectable. It is much more obvious in *Everybody's Autobiography.* There the story of the birth of Stein's sense of genius at first
seems so unremarkable as to be a non-event: "It is funny this thing
of being a genius, there is no reason for it" (*EA,* 77). But the excessive
unremarkability of this can be seen, in a wider context, as a defense.
The following excerpt, with its repetitions and its rhetorical surface
that is marked as little as possible, can seem to be still warding off
the aggressive critical eye of Stein's brother that it has called up.[49]

> Gradually I was writing.
> About an unhappy childhood well I never had an unhappy any-
> thing. What is the use of having an unhappy anything.
> My brother and I had had everything. Gradually he was remem-
> bering that his childhood had not been a happy one. . . .
> As I say I was writing and well why not I was writing the way I
> was writing and it came to be the writing of The Making of Americans.
> I was writing in the way I was writing. I did not show what I was
> writing to my brother, he looked at it and he did not say anything. . . .
> Then slowly he began explaining not what I was doing but he was
> explaining, and explaining well explaining might have been an expla-
> nation. . . .
> He said it was not it it was I. If I was not there to be there with
> what I did then what I did would not be what it was. In other words
> if no one knew me actually then the things I did would not be what
> they were.
>
> *EA,* 75–77

The accusation that Leo Stein makes here is similar to one that
Robert McAlmon makes in a quite nasty article sent to *The Criterion*
and turned down by Eliot only because "it was too intelligent for
his public." McAlmon's image of Stein's work is clumsily satiric of
her gerund-nouns and repetitions: "The aged elephant mastodoni-
cally heaves to being, breathing in the slow slime, slowly with aged
hope, breathing." He quotes her as damning herself more thoroughly than her brother did: Leo had the meaning of her writing

only extend as far as herself; in the following quite probably spurious remark it doesn't even extend that far: "I sometimes wonder how anybody can read my work when I look over it after a time. It seems quite meaningless to me at times" (*CC*, 289–90).

This slam is uncomfortably close, however, to Stein's luminous sense of the genius continually creating meaning without having that meaning freeze into dead, and hence identifiable, shape. Although it may be an enclave of freedom, genius is narrowly circumscribed. The sentence where genius ignores the preceding two hundred years sounds much less Olympian when it is read in context:

> Every time I go out I meet some one and we talk together of revolutions and the weather. . . .
> Every time we talk about revolutions we know that there is going to be another. After all and that does make me know that when I was frightened when I first knew that civilizations came to an end and cities were buried that it was nothing to frighten because after all the earth is round . . . and so a civilization must end.[50] . . . And two hundred years is as much as anybody can remember.
> And so I do know what a genius is, a genius is some one who does not have to remember the two hundred years that everyone else has to remember.
>
> *EA*, 121

The specific context in which Stein is writing, France in the thirties, is in fact all too historical and full of the uninteresting passions of human nature. The phrase "revolutions and the weather" displays a characteristic maneuver: she admits history into her sentences and instantly neutralizes it. Take the beginning of "The Winner Loses":

> We were spending the afternoon with our friends, Madame Pierlot and the d'Aiguys, in September '39 when France declared war on Germany—England had done it first. They all were upset but hopeful, but I was terribly frightened. . . .
> Well, that was a Sunday.
> And then there was another Sunday . . . and Russia came into the war and Poland was smashed . . . oh dear, that was another Sunday.
> And then we settled down to a really wonderful winter.
>
> *SW*, 615

Here the neutralization, the "really wonderful winter," is a rhetorical shock; more often this escape from history registers as an eccentric perception, tinged with charm perhaps, as when Stein equates war and dancing because both involve going forward and back.[51] This flattening out of all historical consequence, even in the midst of one of the most torturous periods of history, constitutes an extreme denial of Fredric Jameson's credo that "history is what hurts."[52] For Stein, history doesn't even come into contact with the genius.

But for all of this aloofness, the quotidian world is continually the target of Stein's later social and (ahistorical) historical pronouncements, which recreate that world as the world of genius, a world of endless and instantaneous knowledge that is received into the ordinary world and "understood," but understood with a difference, in fact understood *as* difference:

> I cannot tell you how often like and alike are not alike. This I cannot tell you how often.
> What is American religion.
> They all listen to that. . . .
> I cannot help thinking that I can make any of you understand that American religion has spread. Yes it has. In Europe they think nothing is there and that is because the sky is there but in America they know it is there because there is no sky there.
> Now yes you do understand.
> Of course you do understand when I say it like that.
> Any of you of course all of you which is of course any of you, all of you can understand when I say it like that.
>
> *FIA*, 72–73

The knowledge of genius is inseparable from Stein's words. It has to be "said like that," which, to reemphasize an earlier point, is not the same thing as ordinary verbal specification. "That" is not a particular verbal formula but precisely the opposite, an endlessly varied, generalized verbal process that Stein alone can manifest. Nor is it a matter of verbal nuance, of "alike" differing from "like." That would make the knowledge of genius approachable by degree; one could gradually be educated into its subtleties. In the writing of genius, as Stein demonstrates in many places, "like" also differs from "like": each instance of every word is simultaneously exemplary and unique. And in terms of content, there being "no sky there" in America is not an observation for others to corroborate.

The very act of writing always, for Stein, produces knowledge— recall in "Portraits and Repetition" where she speaks of writing "words that *made* [my emphasis] whatever I looked at look like itself." At times Stein admits to not possessing, prior to writing, the knowledge that she then goes on to produce by writing: "What do I know about religion. I know anything about religion. I know everything about religion. I know anything about American religion, but I do not know everything about Hiram Ulysses Grant being a leader in religion. Before I get through I will, I will know anything and everything about Hiram Ulysses Grant being a leader in religion" (*FIA*, 14).

Stein will not gain the knowledge she mentions in the last sentence by going to the library. For "Hiram Ulysses Grant being a leader in religion," one could read "Gertrude Stein (public genius, not biographical person) being a leader in religious (non-temporal, non-spatial, socially untrammeled) writing." But such rewriting, deliverable as it were right to the doorstep of ordinary understanding, is not a work of genius. Ordinary understanding distinguishes between "anything" and "everything," between a particular and the world, between what has happened in history and what could possibly happen in a sentence; genius doesn't.

PASTS AND FUTURES OF GENIUS

Stein may have insisted on her own genius to a greater extent than any other writer, but she was far from the first to avail herself of the category. Though the genius may be free from the baggage of history that everyone else is doomed to carry, the category of genius has a history of course, and it is one that Stein, for all the anomaly of her writing, fits into with surprisingly little difficulty.

The Romantic ideology of the genius may seem today to be unexceptionable if not quaint. The poet resolving the antinomies of subject and object, history and eternity, culture and nature is, while theoretically uplifting, a comfortable enough spectacle and a staple of literary instruction. Issues of gender aside, Wordsworth's widely known image of the poet as "a man speaking to men" and using "the real language of men"[53] casts a veil of self-evident normality over the poet's activities such that it seems eccentric to compare Wordsworth to Stein. Her interest in landscape and "nature" throughout the thirties (especially in *Lucy Church Amiably*, described by Stein as "a return to romantic nature") and the general plainness of her vocabulary would seem to furnish a meager justification for calling her Wordsworthian.[54]

But "Wordsworthian" is an adjective resulting from over a century of school. If we recall the initial and long-lasting outrage that his poetry provoked, Wordsworth becomes more Steinian, especially in his 1802 preface to *Lyrical Ballads* where he discusses the function and reception of the poet and the genius. The poet, he writes, is "under one restriction only, namely, that of the necessity of giving immediate pleasure to a human Being possessed of that information which may be expected from him, not as a lawyer, a physician, a mariner, an astronomer or a natural philosopher, but as a Man."[55]

The poet thus addresses humanity only, not particular people. At the same time, the poet contains the generality of the world: "In spite of difference of soil and climate, of language and manners, of laws and customs, in spite of things silently gone out of mind and things violently destroyed, the Poet binds together by passion and knowledge the vast empire of human society, as it is spread out over the whole earth, and over all time."[56]

This figure of generality, unapproachable by any socially located person, is not that far from Stein's figure of genius, the unconditioned human mind that conditioned, particular human nature cannot read and to which human nature is an open book. More than ten years after the preface, when Wordsworth is writing as an extremely visible literary figure, the parallels with Stein are even clearer. In his essay supplementary to the preface of his 1815 collected poems, the relation of the poet and genius to his audience is nearly as originary, central, and aloof as is the case with Stein:

> every Author, as far as he is great and at the same time *original,* has had the task of *creating* the taste by which he is to be enjoyed. . . . The predecessors of an original Genius of a high order will have smoothed the way for all he has in common with them;—and much he will have in common; but, for what is peculiarly his own, he will be called upon to clear and often to shape his own road:—he will be in the condition of Hannibal among the Alps. . . . Of genius the only proof is, the act of doing well what is worthy to be done, and what was never done before.[57]

All of Stein's literary activities from *Toklas* on could very accurately be described as creating the taste by which they are to be enjoyed.

In "Composition as Explanation" Stein speaks of the genuine artist as "an outlaw until he is a classic. . . . There is almost not an interval" (*WAM*, 27–28).

"There is almost not an interval" can be taken simply as a quite accurate prediction of the rapid storm of acclaim that *Toklas* occasioned. But in a more pervasive sense it can stand for the difference in kind between the unapproachable genius and all others. There is no set of graduated steps from outlaw to classic. This is where Stein does part company with Wordsworth: in the above excerpt "an original genius" will, despite his originality, have predecessors and will have much in common with them, and Wordsworth also writes of the poet as "differing nothing in kind from other men, but only in degree."[58] Stein, on the other hand, posits a difference that is absolute. In this she is closer to an even more surprising precursor, Kant.

One of the seemingly slighter and giddier moments in *Toklas* occurs after Stein, in Oxford, has given her second public lecture. She writes, "It was very exciting," which, if we accept the rest of her description, must be an understatement, as she apparently had the deans and dons literally jumping:[59]

> Then up jumped one man, it turned out afterwards that he was a dean, and he said that in the Saints in Seven he had been very interested in the sentence about the ring around the moon. . . . Another man, a don, next to him jumped up and asked something else. They did this several times, the two of them, jumping up one after the other. Then the first man jumped up and said, you say that everything being the same everything is always different, how can that be so. Consider, she replied, the two of you, you jump up one after the other, that is the same thing and surely you admit that the two of you are always different. Touché, he said and the meeting was over. One of the men was so moved that he confided to me as we went out that the lecture had been his greatest experience since he had read Kant's Critique of Pure Reason.
>
> *SW*, 221–22

"Everything being the same everything is always different" is another of the gnomons or sphinxes of genius. The froglike academics who are unable to grasp it nevertheless furnish, by their hopping, an illustration of the ability of genius to create variety out of what the ordinary eye sees as the automata of nature. Given the exaggerated, anxious comedy of this passage, it's easy to assimilate the reference to Kant to the same satiric moment. But Kant is quite relevant to Stein. Using the genius terminology she explored in the "Henry James" section of *Four in America*, one could say that such relevance is not an "accident" but a "coincidence." ("An accident is when a thing happens. A coincidence is when a thing is going to happen and does" [*FIA*, 119].) The coincidence of Stein and Kant didn't just happen, it was going to happen and did. A university, it turns out, was the perfect place for them to meet.

In the *Critique of Judgment* Kant, like Wordsworth, aligns genius with nature and with originality. "Nature," Kant writes, "gives the rule to art. . . . beautiful art is only possible as a product of genius." No definite rule can be given beforehand for the products of genius: "*originality* must be its first property." Genius cannot be taught or imitated; while Newton differs only in degree from a student, who can retrace Newton's steps and learn what Newton discovered, in aesthetic matters there is an absolute difference between the genius and any other. No one can follow in the steps of a Homer, not even another genius: "the product of a genius (as regards what is to be ascribed to genius and not to possible learning or schooling) is an example, not to be imitated (for then that which in it is genius and constitutes the spirit of the work would be lost), but to be followed by another genius, whom it awakens to a feeling of his own originality and whom it stirs so to exercise his art in freedom from the constraint of rules, that thereby a new rule is gained for art."[60] The genius embodies a paradoxical exemplariness: while he is not bound by prior, learned rules, he generates new rules that are useful for society to imitate but useless to a further genius. David Lloyd points out that a similar paradox is constitutive of the pedagogical situation, where the inimitable products of genius furnish the materials for the formation of taste. "The opposition of genius to learning is absolute," yet "genius remains exemplary . . . produc[ing] for humanity at large exemplary products for the judgment of *taste* . . . the progressive formation of taste is inseparable from an exemplary pedagogy. The problem that arises here is that although the concept of genius indicates an example of human freedom independent of imitation, it provides no solution to producing that freedom in the sphere of pedagogy."[61] Stein and Kant are, of course, an even more unlikely pair than Stein and Wordsworth, who at least began as an aesthetic revolutionary. Kant, on the other hand, preferred to find exemplary passages "in the old dead languages, now preserved only as 'the learned languages,' " and he warned that originality doesn't necessarily guarantee genius: it "also can produce original nonsense," which is surely the category to which he would have assigned Stein's writing, seeing her only as an outlaw, not a classic.[62]

But consider the following sentences:

> A sentence never needs to be like what there is where there is some of it that is the same.
> She stays longer to look than he does and he walks away and she stays longer to look than he does.
> This is a sentence which may mean that it is thought to be alike. If they feel that it sounds as it does it will be very well to have it helped and held when they do. . . . There is a difference between what I like and what they like. And they do it. They do like what I like.
> Now this whole thing is a very good example of just what he means by very nearly to and please. That is a sentence that has not been needed. A sentence that is needed is one that initiates their sealing. She is very fond of sealing.
> What is a sentence. They will not need to know where she has been.
>
> *HTW*, 209

These sentences seem to accord with Kant's demand that "beautiful art" not "be derived from any rule which has a *concept* as its determining ground."[63] These sentences are examples only of themselves, and thus they illustrate the impossible exemplariness demanded of the genius. If school were taught by a genius instead of a teacher, the lesson might look like *How To Write*.

But Stein's "scholarly" output was relatively small: *How To Write* (1931) and *Stanzas in Meditation* (1932) are the principal books. In them "I" or "she" stands for the genius and "they" are the students or outsiders to whom she proffers her endless examples, which are created out of no other subject matter than the difference between her position in language and theirs:

> I think I could say what nobody thought
> Nobody thought I went there
> This is however that they add sufficiently
> Because it is not better allowed
> All will come too.
> Just joined how to houses
> But they will like an only name
> They could be thought why they had a weakness
> To be sure.
> Now this is only how they thought.

Let no one leave leaves here.
Leaves are useful to be sure
Who can or could be can be sure
I could think add one add one advantage
That is how they like it.

YGS, 367

But this grammatical, ontological separation is not maintained in her post-*Toklas* work. Not that genius becomes any the less impossible in worldly terms when she writes as a celebrity. But the later Stein can be made into a textbook illustration of the Romantic ideology of the aesthetic genius only if the temporal dimension of her relation to her readers is ignored.

In both Wordsworth's practice and Kant's theory, the consonance embodied by genius exists as both origin and goal for society at large. Wordsworth's sense of childhood fullness and his model of poetry as, in the words of *The Prelude,* a record of "the growth of the Poet's mind," imply a narrative of progression that is matched in Kant's thinking by the placement of the exemplary periods of human culture both at the dawn of history (Greece) and at the end, when genius will have fully formed the universal taste. Getting from origin to conclusion may involve an impossible narrative. That, in the aesthetic sphere, is what school is for and also is the problem with school—the "perpetual deferral" and "the inexpungible melancholy of the pedagogical scene," as Lloyd puts it.[64]

Hegel tries to short-circuit this narrative contradiction; by claiming to embody the synthesis of objective and subjective knowledge, the Hegelian system also claims that the story of the aesthetic has been told. This is what is implied, according to Paul de Man, in Hegel's statement that "art is for us a thing of the past." Not surprisingly, de Man will find the aporia in Hegel's claim. The thinking subject, who plays a role analogous to the genius, will turn out to be impossible, to exist as a contradiction. De Man quotes the following "quite astonishing sentence" of Hegel's: "When I say 'I,' I *mean* myself as *this* I at the exclusion of all others; but what I say, I, is precisely anyone; any I, as that which excludes all others from itself." The implied narrative here in the passage from the particular to the general "I" is, as de Man writes, "the plot and the suspense of Hegel's history of the mind. . . . [The mind] has to recognize itself as itself, that is to say, as I. But how are we to recognize what will necessarily be erased and forgotten, since 'I' is, per definition, what *I* can never say?"[65]

Hegel's "astonishing sentence" seems quite aptly exemplified in Stein's title *Everybody's Autobiography,* which embodies this impossible "I." But while this makes her at least obliquely Hegelian as well as Kantian and Wordsworthian, her fate as a genius was distinct. The transformations asserted or embodied in Wordsworth's poetry are, as I said, a staple for poetic criticism and pedagogy; to what extent the Kantian genius or the Hegelian thinker resolves the antinomies of nature and history is certainly now matter for further study. But the trajectory of Stein's genius is not so easily directed toward deferral, study, refinement, entanglement—toward school, at least as it has existed over the last two centuries.

She states her own opposition to school quite emphatically: "Identity is recognition, you know who you are because you and others remember anything about yourself but essentially you are not that when you are doing anything. I am I because my little dog knows me but, creatively speaking the little dog knowing that you are you and your recognizing that he knows, that is what destroys creation. That is what makes school" (*WAM,* 84–85).

This can seem too absolute: after all, she did tour America giving lectures and occasionally teaching classes. But her account of first being invited to teach is revealing. The invitation was the result of an angry blowup upon meeting Robert Hutchins and Mortimer Adler of the University of Chicago. This is the only place I can recall in her work where she represents herself as losing control. Adler's list of "all the ideas that had been important in the world's history" causes Stein first to get "excited" and then "violent" (*EA,* 205–7). She is invited to teach Adler's class the next week, where, predictably, she triumphs. Afterward she explains to Hutchins: "You see why they talk to me is that I am like them I do not know the answer, you you say you do not know but you do know if you did not know the answer you could not spend your life in teaching but I I really do not know . . . that is the trouble with governments and Utopia and teaching, the things not that can be learnt but that can be taught are not interesting" (*EA,* 213). What Stein recoils from so violently is the pedagogical narrative of spending one's life as a teacher trapped inside the forever-receding perspective of the great ideas and representing that impossible distance to students who are thus doubly trapped. Stein's relation to her listeners and readers is not narrative or temporal but immediate.

This is not to deny what I have been saying about Stein. As a genius, she is utterly distinct from all others. But she does not represent a lesson they will one utopian day be able to master; she is present to them: they "see [present tense] what she means [present tense]" even if they are unable to articulate, reproduce, or understand that meaning by studying it and making it theirs.

If Stein's genius will not fit in the Romantic mold, there are more immediate contexts. One possibility grows out of a concern she mentions frequently in her post-*Toklas* writing: money. Suddenly she gets paid for what she does, and this finite recognition from the public provokes tremendous anxiety. Her concern over money is clear throughout *Everybody's Autobiography*. She writes of buying an expensive car, coat, and two studded collars for Basket (40), of money as it relates to Jews and Communists (41), of the equivalence of the genius and the miser (154). She supplies a narrative for the origin of her rhetorical trope of counting by ones: it was the way her Aunt Fanny counted money (153–54).[66] Most tellingly, she even suffers writer's block, an extraordinary condition for such a prolific writer: "Before one is successful that is before any one is ready to pay money for anything you do then you are certain that every word you have written is an important word. . . . And then it happens sometimes sooner and sometimes later that it has a money value I had mine very much later and it is upsetting" (*EA*, 39).[67] The eponymous heroine of *Ida* (1940) can easily be considered a self-portrait of Stein as a literary celebrity. Ida travels and marries constantly, but is never fully possessed by husband or location.[68] Her typical action is "to go away." But Stein's celebrity status was also a pleasure. In the following excerpt, that pleasure is quite visible:

> Every class has its charm and that can do no harm as long as every class has its charm, and anybody is occupied with their own being. Of course the French do believe in metier that is in knowing your occupation and so do I.
>
> And so we were on the Champlain [an ocean liner]. Being a celebrity we paid less than the full price of a small room and we had a very luxurious one. That was a very pleasant thing. . . . I used to say that I would not go to America until I was a real lion a real celebrity at that time of course I did not really think I was going to be one. But now we were coming and I was going to be one.
>
> In America everybody is but some are more than others.
>
> *EA*, 167–68

It is certainly possible to dismiss what Stein is saying here about métier, class, and celebrity as patrician narcissism. (One could also place in evidence statements such as her claim that it is difficult to get people to work when there is a great deal of unemployment [*EA*, 54]). But in a way the above picture of Stein gives an accurate account of why her assertions of genius met with such a positive response.

In this passage, Stein is a celebrated genius with special privileges, while at the same time she is a member of the universal class of celebrities: "Everybody." Throughout *Everybody's Autobiography* she lives in the immediacy of the entertainment and media world, hobnobbing with Chaplin and Dashiell Hammett, having tea at the White House with Mrs. Roosevelt, and almost having her picture taken with Mary Pickford. One of the first things she sees on arriving in America is her name in electric lights in Times Square, and later she sees herself in a newsreel. She is initially troubled by these sights of herself as simulacrum, but overall the book is anything but a critique of the shallowness of a publicized existence.

In this state there is nothing standing between Stein and the rest of the world, which is presented as hardly to be distinguished from her own art. She flies in an airplane, looks down and sees Cubism (191–92); she sees Burma Shave signs in Minnesota and is delighted (225–26); she reads a billboard in Georgia and speculates:

> Let's make our flour meal and meat in Georgia.
> Is that prose or poetry and why.
> Let's make our flour meal and meat in Georgia.
> This is a sign I read as we rode on a train from Atlanta to Birmingham and I wondered then and am still wondering is it poetry or is it prose.[69]

These reactions might be taken as signs of a totally aestheticized life, but they can also, without erasing that aestheticization, be taken as signs of a life given over to consumerism. Stein, as genius, who never touches or is touched by history, who "sit[s] around so much doing nothing really doing nothing," and for whom the world is a perpetually exciting, novel, countable, and abstract spectacle, is an ideal consumer as well as an ideal commodity, never sullied by anything resembling use value.

I do not mean to dismiss Stein's writing as shallow. But Stein as writer needs to be differentiated from Stein as genius. The writer, to put it in Steinian terms, wrote the writing, every word of it. The genius was present intermittently, as subject matter, goal, or authorizing source of the writing. Genius was Stein's trademark: what she wrote had to be "Gertrude Stein," unfathomable and glamorous as art but as immediately available as the shine of goods in a store window, where memory and comparison are not wanted:

> We did have trouble with Chicago.
> Muriel Draper has just been here she has been in Spain and we talked about all that and we said she said that and I said that and that was that and then we said yes it is good to look at and New York and Chicago are good to look at and Oklahoma and we said that.
>
> *EA,* 188

Here, Steinian repetition and lack of punctuation mask a pretentious exchange. But Stein's writing is rarely so banal. Genius, while always a social role, did not merely function as a kind of reversed protective coloring, enabling her to stand out and so survive. Throughout her career genius was also an emblem of the pleasure she felt as she wrote, whether that resulted from the control of writing word by word in the linguistically reduced universe of *The Making of Americans,* or from the freedom of writing the erotic and social conversation portraits, or from the deep humor of instantaneously remodeling history and society in the sentences of her later work. Every assertion of her genius and every stylistic display of it can also be seen as the desire for this pleasure to be socially validated.

Her fame was an indication that, in some sense, it was validated. However, she was celebrated not for her writing but for her identity as a genius, an eccentric—for being "Gertrude Stein." Her freedom from the trammels of society also meant her exclusion from society. This is poignantly demonstrated by her last major piece of writing, *The Mother of Us All.* It is somber, and, most uncharacteristic, historical. The writing is motivated not so much by its own processes as by the external question of whether Susan B. Anthony will succeed in getting the vote for women, and more importantly, in changing the world. There are also a cluster of related subplots dealing with potential marriages and questions of changing last names. Outwardly, Anthony succeeds; women get the vote, but "it will do them no good because having the vote they will become just like men" (*LOP,* 81).

This ineffectual success is mirrored in the diction of the writing throughout the play, where the plot doesn't really fit into the words that are supposedly its vehicle. In the following excerpt, lilting rhyme, a Stein trademark connoting genius and play, makes the social applicability tenuous; her attempt to make a difference in the world loses traction by the fact of its difference as writing: "Will they remember that it is true that neither they that neither you, will they marry will they carry, aloud, the right to know that even if they love them so, they are alone to live and die, they are alone to sink and swim they are alone to have what they own, to have no idea but that they are here, to struggle and thirst to do everything first, because until it is done there is no other one" (*LOP*, 72). Not that this could have been "improved" by reducing the rhyme and increasing its functionality. The fears of men (and eventually women) that Stein castigates in the play are bound up with just such assumptions of instrumentality and domination. The rhyme of "they are alone to have what they own" catches the isolation of the property owner at a deep level. But a noninstrumental writing will not, to echo the final dialogue between Stein and Toklas, be "the answer"; it will not challenge such dominion, and will only exist as difference.

Stein's writing was committed to motion without repetition, remembrance, or identity; her faith in her impulse to write is exemplary and the body of writing that impulse produced is vivid throughout most of its wide range. As she wrote in "Portraits and Repetition," "if the movement, that is any movement, is lively enough, perhaps it is possible to know that it is moving even if it is not moving against anything" (*LIA*, 165). But in a life devoted to writing, such movement not only begins again and again, in each work and each sentence, it also repeatedly comes to an end. At these points questions of its social trajectory remain. Because any of us reads it, Stein's writing does not move in a vacuum.

5

The Allegory of Louis Zukofsky

If poetic reputation arose simply from the words on paper and their richness of verbal possibility, then Louis Zukofsky would be a major American poet and "A," the long poem in twenty-four movements he wrote from 1928 to 1974, a major poem of the century. His collected shorter poems would be widely studied, as would *Prepositions*, his collection of criticism. The two large and complex productions of his later years, his translations of Catullus (in collaboration with his wife, Celia), and *Bottom: On Shakespeare*, his encyclopedic, collaged ruminations on Shakespeare, Spinoza, Wittgenstein, and much else, would be accorded great respect.

I think these evaluations are right, and in this I join a small but growing number of poets and, more recently, of critics. But Zukofsky's separation from his own contemporaries was almost total and was a primary fact conditioning his writing. He garnered some slight notice for his early efforts to promote the "Objectivists" in the early thirties, but his own work was barely published and hardly read at all until it began to be issued by major presses in the last years of his life.[1] He has been lauded by members of the Black Mountain school, especially Robert Duncan and Robert Creeley, and for many involved with language writing he is an exemplary poet, but for most readers he has remained a difficult figure to assimilate.[2] Some critics have celebrated the remarkable intricacies of his poetry, treating him as something of a *miglior fabbro* to Pound; others have paid attention to the left-wing politics expressed in his work up to World War Two, especially in the first half of "A," but the two sides have hardly been brought together.[3] Until recently, his work has been generally ignored.

His early gestures toward communism (with a small c) coupled with his ambitious verbal engineering can be seen as contributing to this outcome, though difficult writing and uncircumspect politics do not necessarily keep a poet from being read, as the case of Pound demonstrates. But Pound is a compelling figure, with his claims for the heroic role of the poet, his obsessive literary and cultural interventions, his hatreds, his monumental failure—even his final silences had public impact; this, coupled with his attempts to make *The Cantos* an instrument of social change, renders the poem visible from afar as a site of conflict and social significance. Zukofsky is often a more accomplished craftsman than Pound: he completed complex writing structures, where Pound increasingly gestured and improvised. Zukofsky, beneath his later rhetoric of densely philosophical accommodation, is as contradictory a figure: the politics and aesthetics of *The Cantos* may make an unsavory combination, but the break in *"A,"* where the first ten movements (Zukofsky's term for sections) are deeply political while the final fourteen are not, also expresses an intense conflict between being a poet and existing in history. Unlike Pound, however, Zukofsky ultimately found the role of the poet as a figure in society to be untenable; he compensated by trying to maximize the possibilities for meaning in the writing itself. Without the frame of the exemplary writer to organize their responses, the majority of contemporary readers have not found the resulting linguistic complexity worth the labor. In recognition of this, Zukofsky has sometimes been granted the gilded booby prize of being a poet's poet—in fact, Guy Davenport has called him a "poet's poet's poet."[4]

Zukofsky's work offers few places where a persona-centered poetics can latch on with any certainty; his reticence and his focus on language make him seem a candidate for structuralist and poststructuralist readings. Hugh Kenner and Ron Silliman, who hold quite different critical viewpoints, agree that for Zukofsky language as a system is more important than any singular track left by the poet. Kenner remarks that "anything you can write is already somehow immanent in the language, a baffling fact. . . . Zukofsky . . . caught on to it early . . . it forestalled his becoming anything of a rhetorician" (*PR*, vii). Silliman sees Zukofsky as central among those poets who "have increasingly emphasized that meaning in poetry falls on the side of the signifier—and that it is not deferred to any hierarchic abstraction such as character, plot or argument." One should not, Silliman argues, turn one's "attention away from . . . the page, toward some (always deferred) moment of total 'unification.' "[5] These statements contain the basic perspective necessary for baffled readers vainly looking to find narratives in much of Zukofsky's work and to empathize with him. The following exchange with Davenport gives a good sense of the wide play Zukofsky found within the narrowest compass of letters: "I once asked Zukofsky what the 'mg. dancer' is who dances in *"A"*-21, a milligram sprite, a magnesium elf, a margin dancer, or Aurora, as the dictionary allows for all of these meanings. 'All,' he replied."[6] Zukofsky's answer affirms more than his allegiance to the polysemy of language; it also points back to his own career. It is typical of his explosive conciseness that in the space of three letters he indicates the generalized space of potential meaning in the dictionary while simultaneously naming his own collection of short poems.[7]

Zukofsky's career should not be ignored. While it is possible to read the narrative of his life's work as a dissolution of the genius paradigm into the free play of textuality, this less conflicted reading depends on ignoring the obsessiveness of his identifications with a variety of masters. To focus on language *per se* will not answer the further question that can so easily arise in reading any of Zukofsky's lines: why *that* language? I will be arguing that Zukofsky, very much in spite of himself, *is* a rhetorician—that is, he is not a disinterested experimenter combining words but is writing to an audience out of a specific set of social needs—and that meaning in his work cannot be grasped by concentrating solely on the words. Though often jarringly displaced, the words are *his* words, and they are built on his life in remarkably strained ways, while always laboring toward total unification with that life.

Consider one of the final twenty-six lines of *"A"*-23: "*Kalenderes enlumined 21-2-3, nigher* . . fire—(A 23, 563). The passage as a whole marks the conclusion of the actual writing of *"A"* (the final movement, 24, is a collage of his writing made by his wife) and Zukofsky has packed it with tokens of literary and ontological completeness:

> A living calendar, names inwreath'd
> Bach's innocence longing Handel's untouched.
> Cue in new-old quantities—'Don't
> bother me'—Bach quieted bothered;
> since Eden gardens labor, For
> series distributes harmonies, attraction Governs
> destinies.
>
> *A 23, 562–63*

While the capitals rehearse the letters of the alphabet, the lines also merge music, gardens, and mathematics in a utopic fullness. The *"Kalenderes"* line quotes Chaucer's similar alphabetic device, "An A.B.C." But in addition to reembodying Chaucer, the line also commemorates—quite obliquely, to be sure—the birthdays of Zukofsky, Celia, and their son, Paul.[8] The continual reappearance of minute personal details amid capacious generalities makes *"A,"*— unlike *The Cantos*—narrative, assuming one's microscope is in focus.

Why *that* language? seems to have been a question that haunted Zukofsky himself, judging by his incessant rewriting and the increasingly labored structures he produced. Word choice becomes more pronounced while sentence boundaries blur; this makes the writing meaningful to a very high degree—a close reading of almost any passage will involve a great deal of explication—but the social significance of the whole, the possibility of an intervention in the present, tends to decrease as the complexity increases. Zukofsky's writing is not separable from Zukofsky writing, laboring over words in isolation, producing meaning but not quite embodying it. The resulting words tend to resist falling into conventional social categories of meaning and to provoke a reader into manufacturing multiple possibilities of meaning.

To include Zukofsky's unresolved labor in the meaning of the writing will involve going beyond his repeated claims that *"A"* is ultimately music or that it is the result of "nature as creator." Although Zukofsky always protested against being labeled difficult and insisted that his words were not diffuse or mediated but were present as an indissoluable unity, these claims need critique more than affirmation. All his elaborate structures, when finally decoded, claim elemental simplicity. It is just for this reason that his writing will need to be read allegorically in the sense that this term has been used by Paul de Man and Joel Fineman.[9] Their sense of allegory as enacting an inevitably displaced significance, both temporal and linguistic, will furnish a useful critique of Zukofsky's claims for a writing that is musical, natural, and fully present.

In a number of places Zukofsky's writing is specifically allegorical, as some movements of *"A"* are violent point-by-point reworkings of other texts. Zukofsky's relation to certain artists—Pound, Cavalcanti, Catullus, Bach—is allegorical in the sense that he identifies with their achievements and tries to reconstitute them in his own work by means of various displacements rather than by simple imitation. In an overall sense *"A"* with its plethora of procedures and structures in the service of a most uncontextualized goal of "song" becomes an allegory of what it means to be a poet. The implications of this could be used to situate the poem athwart the imaginary boundary between modernism and postmodernism, though in what follows I will be more concerned with the specific words Zukofsky wrote—their extreme particularity makes them nearly inassimilable—than with global theoretic implications. This specificity, combined with his insistence that his writing has an ontological status equal to that of the world, is what makes the problematics of genius as relevant to Zukofsky as to the more obvious cases of Pound, Stein, and Joyce. Zukofsky was, both bitterly and resolutely, not a public figure, but a similar refusal to accept any mediation is as much the ground of his writing as is the case with the other three.

"THE WORDS ARE MY LIFE"
(THE WORDS OR MY LIFE):
CHRONOLOGY VERSUS TELEOLOGY

It will be useful, especially for those readers not familiar with Zukofsky, to begin with two partial and opposing approaches, which in places will produce conflicting readings. Zukofsky's work can be read either as a narrative or, as he himself preferred, as a teleological filling out of an organic structure. The narrative will tell of conflict, focused on a break at the midpoint of his career. The teleological reading, naturally, will be harmonious.

Zukofsky began his literary career as an outsider. His parents were Yiddish-speaking immigrants; he attended Columbia and was interested in literature and Marxism.[10] This is hardly a unique story, but the swiftness with which Zukofsky stepped into the modernist arena was remarkable. Although it was written soon after he left Columbia, his "Poem beginning 'The' " effects a total break with his juvenilia; it takes *The Waste Land* as both norm and rival.[11] Like Eliot, Zukofsky builds out of direct or modified quotation; where Eliot numbers every tenth line as if the poem were already a classic, Zukofsky numbers every line, and his notes, which preface the poem, give evidence of a rapid and comprehensive response to modernism, referring to a wide range of literary figures, including Eliot, Pound,

Joyce, cummings, Moore, Woolf, and Lawrence.[12] The epigraph from Chaucer, "And out of olde bokes, in good feith," has an ironic ring, since some of the citations and comments are so contemporaneous that in places the poem resembles a newsletter. For example, lines 11, 12, and 13, "Residue of self-exiled men / By the Tyrrhenian / Paris." seem to refer to Pound's move from Paris to Rapallo in 1924 and the appearance of *The Exile* in 1927.[13] But beyond the irony, Zukofsky's extensive appropriation of his immediate predecessors seems an aggressive gesture aiming to place himself in the "olde boy" network. Eliot's onomatopoeic warning, "Immature poets imitate; mature poets steal," must have marked an ominous divide for an unknown, ambitious writer in his early twenties.[14]

Some of the same allegorical clouds hang over Zukofsky as over Eliot. Both are non-originary, since the use of quotation, no matter how recent and how cleanly stolen, inevitably involves a secondariness. In Zukofsky's case the secondariness was compounded by the cultural deficit he felt in being Jewish. Nevertheless, given the attraction the modernist arena held for him, he found the voices he had to deal with a source of optimism and energy, and he treated his own cultural specificity with a mordant wit that displays no nostalgia for a golden age of cultural authority. In places he almost can seem to anticipate current debates over multiculturalism. Here at the beginning of his career Zukofsky's Marxism allows him to perceive history as progress (though, as we will see, he disavowed all linearity later), thus providing for a major contrast to *The Waste Land*: a rhetorically happy ending.

> 321 We shall open our arms wide,
> 322 Call out of pure might—
> 323 Sun, you great Sun, our Comrade,

But the core of the poem is not so much political as cultural. While the gestures toward an Eliotic poetics of quotation depend at least in part on the university, Zukofsky finds his identity in opposition to his education. As an outsider, the elitism of its universalist assumptions was quite obvious: for him, cultural appropriation would not automatically resolve into unity.[15] Nevertheless, while his own progress in this arena is far from an inevitable outcome, he is as charming in this opposition as he will ever be:

166   It's the times don'chewknow,
167   And if you're a Jewish boy, then be your
              Plato's Philo.

168   Engprof, thy lectures were to me
169   Like those roast flitches of red boar
              . . . .
175   Thy heavy jowl would make me fit
176   For the Pater that was Greece.
177   The siesta that was Rome.
              . . . .
251   Assimilation is not hard,
252   And once the Faith's askew
253   I might as well look Shagetz just as much
              as Jew.
254   I'll read their Donne as mine,
255   And leopard in their spots
256   I'll do what says their Coleridge,
257   Twist red hot pokers into knots.

The satire directed against Paterian aesthetics in line 176 is sharp;
Zukofsky's later work would, however, aspire fanatically to the condition of music.

Zukofsky's early confidence in his power to wield cultural markers is such that he can cast himself not only as an atheist Shylock but
as a pretentious aestheticizing Marxist, criticized by a figure further
outside the cultural pale than himself (note the opposed moral and
cultural codings present in the letters "aw" in the following two
voices):

245   Dawn't you think Trawtsky rawthaw a
              darrling,
246   I ask our immigrant cousin querulously.
247   Naw! I think hay is awlmawst a Tchekoff.

The narrative of Zukofsky's career cannot escape Ezra Pound,
who plays the role of originary genius-poet to Zukofsky's displaced
and allegorical follower. Whether this pattern, which Zukofsky repeated with other masters, would deny the problematic title of genius to Zukofsky himself would be a continual issue. In itself, "Poem
beginning 'The' " displayed Zukofsky's precocious mastery of modernist techniques and affirmed his independence by the suppleness
of the cultural identifications, but as a poem put into circulation

under Pound's auspices in *The Exile* it marked Zukofsky as something of a footnote to Pound, a status that would trammel him from then on. Pound positioned Zukofsky to edit the "Objectivists" issue of *Poetry* in 1931, and Zukofsky followed Pound's advice/instructions closely (*PZ*, 45–75). As far as visibility goes, this was to be Zukofsky's high-water mark until near the end of his life. But to most readers the "Objectivists," carefully encased in quotation marks by Zukofsky, could look simply like imitators, more scientistic and left-wing, of Pound's *Imagistes*. *"A"* and *The Cantos* continued this resemblance. Although Zukofsky vigorously denied that his poem was influenced by Pound's, nevertheless, there are major similarities, both specific and general, especially in the early sections of *"A"* (*PZ*, 77–83). As I noted in Chapter One, Pound begins with Homer in an attempt to reembody a lost presence and then comments somewhat ironically at the end of the first canto on his separation from that presence; Zukofsky begins *"A"*-1 with the aesthetic and social completeness of Bach's *St. Matthew Passion* and finds his own status as an outsider quite problematic. In subsequent movements, especially 6 and 8, history is articulated through collaged voices just as in *The Cantos*. In Canto 36, Pound translated "Donna Mi Prega"; four years later Zukofsky translated it and reproduced its syllabic scheme exactly in *"A"*-9. And Zukofsky's *A Test of Poetry*, a would-be textbook written in 1938 but not published for ten years, resembles the *ABC of Reading* closely.[16]

Even though, as we will see in a moment, Zukofsky's writing after World War Two broke free from the Poundian model, nevertheless significant parts of Zukofsky's later work can be seen as echoing Pound. *Catullus* is a translation that utterly transforms the original Latin in an attempt to revivify it, thus recalling "Homage to Sextus Propertius." Zukofsky's surprising choice to devote *"A"*-21 to a translation-transformation of Plautus's *Rudens* can be explained, as Barry Ahearn does, by noting echoes of *The Tempest* and of *Pericles* (which Zukofsky's wife set to music), but the closer formal parallel is with Pound's *Women of Trachis*, which was published ten years before Zukofsky wrote *"A"*-21.[17] Pound's translation is deliberately anachronistic in tone, and while Zukofsky far surpasses Pound in straying from the conventional semantic meaning, his license is Poundian in its complex gestures toward contemporary speech.[18] The final congruity between Zukofsky and Pound is the largest and most significant: each spent the majority of his writing life on a single poem that, while it may have started as an articulation of history, ended as a specimen of autobiography or at least as needing to be read through the lens of the poet's life.

Zukofsky's relationship with Pound was not smooth. While at times they saw each other as allies in the literary wars, the positions they occupied on the battlefield were quite different, with Pound by the thirties looking rather desperately for recruits from anywhere and Zukofsky looking for an imprimatur primarily from Pound. Zukofsky was also looking for literary guidance. In his initial letter accepting "Poem beginning 'The'," Pound suggested editorial improvements. Zukofsky followed most of Pound's suggestions and was quick to pick up on the possibility for more poetic advice in his answering letter: "actually 5 volumes by L.Z. exist, none typed. When they are, will you at that dim time indicate what should not see the light of day?" (*PZ*, 6). In one turn of phrase that is hard not to load with pedagogical and psychic significance, Zukofsky asks for Pound's reactions as follows (note the Poundian diction): "Here y'are—give Boy a mark" (*PZ*, 39).[19]

Initially in their correspondence they would share a bantering anti-Semitism, but it clearly was a matter of great conflict for Zukofsky, as the following reference to Pound's favorite economist, C. H. Douglas, indicates: "C.H.D.'s leaning to the Nazi side of anti-Semitism in *Soc. Credit* not very reassuring—in spite of the fact that I'd betray & immolate most of my people for 1 [Tibor] Serly etc etc" (*PZ*, 156). Zukofsky did eventually ascend from this level; a few years later he condemned the dangerous simplemindedness of Pound's anti-Semitism quite forcefully, though insisting that his rapport with Pound concerning poetic matters was unaffected.[20]

But on matters of literary business—advice, contacts, publication—Pound was a most volatile mentor, first praising then increasingly threatening to excommunicate: "The next anthology will be econ/ conscious and L/Z won't be in it. . . . I can't even advise N/E/W [*New English Weekly*] to print you. . . . Be careful or you'll fall back into racial characteristics, and cease to be L/Z at all. . . . J/HEEZUSS, you aint even caught up with Jules Romains//" (*PZ*, 162–63). Zukofsky dedicated *An "Objectivists" Anthology* to Pound, but Pound's contribution to it was the anti-Semitic, anti-Black, misogynist doggerel of "der YIDDISHER Charleston BAND"—which Zukofsky saw fit to print.[21]

It is easy to imagine that Pound's indifference would have been even more troubling than his aggression. *"A"*-9 marks a crucial moment in Zukofsky's career: as it turned out, it marked the end of his active political hopes. At the height of their increasingly bitter exchanges on Marxism and anti-Semitism, Zukofsky sent the first two stanzas of his translation of Cavalcanti's canzone to Pound in a moving attempt to maintain a purely poetic connection free of the various chasms of politics:

> I enclose the first two stanzas of a canzone—knowing what you know about poetry is more than most of us know I'm not ashamed to send you uncompleted work, if you care to be bothered. The local small fry would no doubt accuse me of being a fascist for having lived with the Guido as basis day in & day out for the last two years. You will probably see how far gone I am on the Marx side of it, & attribute all my faults to the influence of his unenlightened use of language. But no matter if there's any poetry in ⟨it⟩, you'll still see it, I believe. Some insight a man never loses.—But let's not correspond about politics, etc.
>
> *PZ,* 199

Zukofsky is here poised impossibly between local Communists he considered insufficiently literary ("local small fry") and the (Fascist) reader whose opinion he most valued; the astounding amount of labor that went into *"A"*-9 is at least in part the result of this social vacuum. Pound's laconic reply encapsulated Zukofsky's pedagogic afflictions; he "gave Boy a Mark" (a *B*-, say) in the dourest way: "The canzone seems to me harmless undergrad/ exercise" (*PZ,* 200).

The advent of World War Two and Pound's broadcasts for Mussolini made Zukofsky's relationship with Pound impossible. Zukofsky made little attempt to enter the literary arena during the forties, and his writing moved sharply away from overtly Poundian concerns. *"A"*-10, written in 1940, marks the point at which *"A"* ceases to be a politically motivated poem.[22] The piece is an agonized and strident condemnation of French collaboration; events are too destructive to be articulated by his poetics, and the lines "Let a better time say / The poet stopped singing to talk" (120) signal a temporary surrender of poetic privileges.[23] *"A"*-11, written ten years later, marks the beginning of the familial and lyric half of Zukofsky's work, and the end of all concern to unite poetry and politics.[24] It is an impacted lyric, densely rhymed, celebrating the musicianship of

Celia and their son, Paul, a child prodigy and eventual concert violinist. *"A"*-12, also started in 1950, is longer than the first eleven movements combined; in its familial and Spinozan concerns, it outlines the thematic territory for the rest of the poem, though there is tremendous formal variety throughout subsequent movements.

Grossly obvious events must have helped push Zukofsky's writing away from politics. The war forced serious reappraisal on most American leftists, and postwar anti-communism must have been traumatic for Zukofsky, especially since he had been a friend of Whittaker Chambers.[25] But in addition to these external pressures, Zukofsky himself, in a 1939 letter to Pound, gives evidence that the oncoming break in his writing would stem from his break with Pound: "there is no use, the way I'm made up, reasoning with your convictions as they are now. If I'm good enough, I'll reach more fruitful ground. In your case, the best I can do is shut up. That does not mean I don't respect yr. integrity. I've gone on respecting it ever since you got yourself drowned in the batter of credit economics— at a loss (to myself) of every practical & helpful contact in U.S. & Europe. I don't regret it" (*PZ*, 198). In a literary sense, Zukofsky did more or less "shut up"; the bulk of his writing was written after the war, but it was done with little attempt at outreach. Even after the war, however, Zukofsky remained quietly loyal to Pound: a note written during the Bollingen Prize controversy praised *The Cantos* and absolved Pound of all personal anti-Semitism.[26] In his first letter to Pound at St. Elizabeths, Zukofsky still centers his literary horizons around Pound: "Contacts? Practically none—except occasional correspondence with about three people we once knew (of) in common" (*PZ*, 206). (Note how the "(of)" makes Zukofsky secondary: Pound knew them; Zukofsky knew of them.) In this same letter Zukofsky diffidently urges Pound to read the now-completed *"A"*-9. The temporal gap between the first and second halves of the poem is ten years; with respect to Pound there seems to have been no gap for Zukofsky at all: he picks up where he left off in 1940.

A final letter (1963) to the older poet attempts to lighten Pound's precipitous despair over his work—"the *song* . . . yours, **always right**"—and, characteristically, asks what Pound thinks of Zukofsky's latest writing: "I understand Mary de R[achewiltz] has been receiving my Catullus translations in *Origin*—sometimes wonder what **you*** might think of 'em if you ⟨can⟩ read 'em. *Don't matter what anyone else thinks—even the praise. Still obstinate you see" (*PZ*, 218).

There is more to the narrative of Zukofsky's career than Ezra Pound—marriage, years of teaching at Brooklyn Polytech, the quick breakup and long silence of the "Objectivists," friendship with Williams, Zukofsky's rediscovery by Duncan, Corman, Creeley, and others. But the pattern in which Zukofsky posits his own existence as an extension of the work of a single master continues to be crucial, beyond the psychology of his relation to Pound. In a late talk on Stevens, Zukofsky grants Stevens some of the same centrality. Zukofsky denies the importance of his own autobiography and simultaneously gives quite a bit of autobiographical detail based on tenuous parallels with Stevens. For example, "I appeared in print more frequently, again of no consequence except I sometimes wonder whether Stevens read me" (*PR*, 32). In a gesture that recalls Pound's inflation of his single meeting with Mussolini, Zukofsky reads a genuine confirmation of his own work into the perfunctory note that Stevens sent him in answer to *A Test of Poetry*—the only communication he ever received from Stevens—"The contents pick up a particular interest." Zukofsky comments, "I was especially comforted by the word *particular* because it could have been general" (*PR*, 32).

Zukofsky disavowed biographical approaches to his work. The teleological reading is the one consistently supported by the poet, who claimed that his words and his life formed an organic whole, and who insisted that any biographical attention was misplaced. Zukofsky grew to be a reclusive poet, but for one so reticent he made quite a few statements about the relation of his words to his life, which suggests that it was a problem he kept solving and reencountering. The following is a description of *"A"* Zukofsky wrote when the poem was half-finished: "In a sense the poem is an autobiography: the words are my life. The form of the poem is organic—that is, involved in history and a life that has found by contrast to history something like perfection in the music of J. S. Bach (a theme threaded through the entire poem). . . . [The] poet's form is never an imposition of history but the desirability of projecting some order out of history."[27] Words and life are equated, but not just any words, or life in all senses. "The form of the poem is organic" is balanced by "the poet's form": both poem and poet must achieve form in order to avoid the chaos of history. "The words are my life" takes that life out of time, makes it organic and musical. *"A"* is a formal project, not a diary: from *"A"*-9 on, the movements were not written in strict sequence.[28] One does not have to look at many pages of *"A"* to see that Zukofsky was not interested in autobiography in any usual sense. His *Autobiography*, a small book published in 1970, seems to have been composed to make precisely that point. The book consists of eighteen mostly short and impersonal lyrics set to music by his wife. Six laconic paragraphs are interspersed (one reads, "As for subsistence I can only quote with affection e.e. cummings: 'no thanks.'"); one prefatory sentence warns the reader away from the person of the poet: "As a poet I have always felt that the work says all there needs to be said of one's life."

But while the social self of the poet seems to disappear in such a model, the life remains central. In a different context from the quotation cited above, Zukofsky calls *"A"* "a poem of a life," which to my ear seems to emphasize the autobiographical over·the formal and to reverse the accent of "the words are my life."[29] A large area of *"A"*-12 is built around the claim that "each writer writes one long work whose beat he cannot be entirely aware of" (*A 12*, 214), which suggests that the unifying capacity of his life goes beyond *"A"* to include all his writing.[30] Zukofsky not only suggests this, but acts it out: the above sentence comes from a letter to "L.N." [Lorine Nie-decker]; some pages after this he devotes hundreds of lines to presenting discarded notes and early poems, scraps of dialogue for plays, ideas for movies, westerns, etcetera. This is far from being egocentric in any usual sense: Zukofsky does not disguise the odd results of his early efforts. But the following lines, which evoke the poet contemplating the fading substantiality and comprehensibility of the words he once wrote and then speaking of them to his wife, seem to grant a meaningfulness to his life and writing as a whole that any particular moment or scrawl might lack.

> A theatre that for atmosphere
> Smells like water at the bottom of
> A swimming pool
> (Too expensive to produce?)
> Lines for a play?
> How tell her
> On a night after such lightness
> He held her reflection without

> An envelop. (That is all I make of it,
> Celia.)
> *A* 12, 253–54

This process of auto-production culminates in *"A"*-24, which ends the poem by using nothing but recycled passages from earlier in *"A"* and from Zukofsky's other writings.

The last statement Zukofsky made affirming the unity of his life writing was in the apparatus for the publication of *"A"* by the University of California Press, which occurred in the last year of his life. The edition begins with a table of contents giving the dates the twenty-four movements were written, stretching from 1928 to 1974, and it ends with an index focusing on such items as "a," "an," "ear," "eye," "the," "thing," "world," and "word," leavened by scattered particulars such as "Tick-Tack Uhr," "Toonerville Trolley," "holluschikies," and "Ezra Pound" (as a crossword puzzle entry). The references are more gnomic than informative: for instance, it seems impossible to determine why the first of the nearly one hundred references under "the" begins with page 175. But the apparatus makes a schematic statement by its framing. *"A"* can be said to move from the contingent chronology of its author to the spatialized existence of eternal matters: the writer in time is to be lifted beyond time. Throughout, Zukofsky works with the tension between particulars and totality, between the process of writing and the structures that result.

This tension can be read even in the title, which is deeply bifurcated: *"A"* can be read as both the first letter of the alphabet, the Aleph, icon of cosmic beginnings and inclusiveness, and as the indefinite article, sign of contingency. Zukofsky suggests both meanings in the following: "a case can be made out for the poet giving some of his life to the use of the words *a* and *the:* both of which are weighted with as much epos and historical destiny as one man can perhaps resolve. Those who do not believe this are too sure that the little words mean nothing among so many other words" (*PR,* 10).

"A" is both letter and word, a graphic analytic element and a synthetic constituent of language. It also stands for a musical note—the one orchestras use for tuning up. The quotation marks around this letter/word create their own split: they can denote speech, and thus, while not quite implicating "historical destiny," they do at least suggest a writer speaking, acting in history. But at the same time,

they mark "A" as a quoted word, an example of itself, with no defense against being taken ironically. Perhaps the quotes in the title mean that "*A*" is to be read as a "poem." The quotation marks in *An "Objectivists" Anthology* are similar, signaling Zukofsky's resistance to being labeled—objectified—by society. Along the same lines, there is a tinge of comedy in the way "*A*" points obliquely back to the author: it seems odd and then deliberate that someone with a name as alphabetically postponed as Zukofsky would call his life's work "*A*." And perhaps "*A*" is the grade Zukofsky would like to get for his writing—"give Boy a mark."[31]

Similar plays of meaning can be read into the words throughout. And yet for all the intellectual and technical achievement, the beauty, or even, to use a key Zukofskian term, the "perfection" of "*A*," the poem reflects its origins and is modified by them in ways that severely limit and ultimately disrupt its verbal autonomy. Syntactic possibility, semantic suggestiveness, and realized form are so prominent that it is easy to focus on the richness of meaning that the writing provides—as if ambiguities and multiple possibilities automatically accrued in some ideal readerly account—and to forget the other side: the lack of actual readers, the absence of social impact, the obscurity of the language. "*A*" was written in an intense literary vacuum, one that is only partially filling in today. If the notoriety that eventually enabled Pound to merit space in a *Times* crossword has to be considered a key goal of his poetics, then the lack of response Zukofsky received also needs to be seen as an important cause of the ambitious meanings he balanced upon his words. And if Zukofsky's summary of the relations between a wise and faultless generality ("eye," "love," "word," "world") and quirky particularity ("holluschikies," "Tick-Tack Uhr," "Toonerville Trolley") might seem whimsical in his index, in the writing of the poem the struggle was not genial.

"*A*" exhibits abundant signs of both structural and thematic completion: the poem as a whole is finished and, especially after the first six movements, each movement exhibits full formal elaboration and deliberate choice. But the extravagance of its means sends out an opposing message of randomness and unsatiated desire for social significance. The clearest instance of this might be the final movement, "*A*"-24, also called the *L. Z. Masque*, a collage of Zukofsky's words set by his wife to Handel's music (although the voices are spoken, not sung). The four voices of the *Masque* (Thought, Drama, Story, and Poem) are taken from the poet's single collection of criticism, single novel, single drama, and the rest of *"A,"* thus treating all modes of his work as complete, coherent, and mutually reinforcing. That the final movement is his wife's arrangement of Zukofsky's words affirms the utopian domesticity celebrated throughout the second half of the poem. And most importantly, the musical treatment seemingly literalizes Zukofsky's aspirations for his poetry to be sounded as music. As he wrote in *"A"*-12:

> I'll tell you.
> About my *poetics*—
>
> $$\int_{\text{speech}}^{\text{music}}$$
>
> An integral
> Lower limit speech
> Upper limit music
> *A* 12, 138

But *"A"*-24 is precisely where Zukofsky's claim on music is most clearly revealed to be allegorical. To hear the piece performed is to be struck by the fact that words, no matter how "musical" their sound or their syntax, are *not* music.[32] Where European music (the kind Zukofsky was concerned with) uses a scale of twelve notes, English uses a "scale" of a few hundred phonemes, and more significantly, hundreds of thousands of words. The simultaneity of sound and significance that constitutes music and allows for single lines to build up into immediately perceptible chords does not occur with words.

To take a simple case, *"A"*-24 ends with two voices speaking over a cadence in C minor. The Drama voice says, "Darling, meet my mother. New gloves, mother?" as the Poem voice, concluding an apostrophe to ivy, says, "I wonder what makes thee so loved," with the typography showing that "gloves" and "loved" are to be spoken together. A misleading analogy could be made to two contrapuntal instrumental voices meeting on a C. But the verbal lines do not meet. "Gloves" and "loved" form a near rhyme, but that only involves part of their sound. Where C, E ♭, G, and C sound a single C-minor

chord, "gloves" and "loved" interfere with one another when pronounced simultaneously. (What happens in hearing and more
clearly in reading *"A"*-24 is that *isolated* words and phrases are viv-
idly foregrounded.) Rhyme is not a transparent, absolute property
that is sensed immediately. Rather it involves—to evoke Freud un-
analytically—an "uncanny" suppression of time. The last two words
of "New gloves, mother?" give pleasure in sounding more or less
the same precisely because they are not the same: "mother" calls
back a simulacrum of "gloves" after it is irrevocably gone.[33]

The identity of his writing and music was crucial for Zukofsky,
especially after he abandoned his political aspirations. He filled *"A"*
with thematic references to and structural analogs of music. A few
examples: *"A"*-11 is a song meant to be set to music by Celia and
played by Paul. The five sections of 13 are meant to mime the dance
forms of a Bach partita. The "narrative" core of 19 (though exegesis
is needed to comprehend it) involves Paul winning a prize in the
Paganini competition in Rome, and the words of the piece have been
felt to imitate the down strokes, trills, and tremolos of Paul's bowing.[34] *"A"*-20 presents Paul (on his twentieth birthday) with a verbal
tone row of the titles of his compositions. And of course, throughout
"A" Zukofsky venerates the music of Johann Sebastian Bach. But by
literalizing the organic unity of the meaning of the poetry and its
music, and of *"A"* and Zukofsky's life, *"A"*-24 reveals music as Zukofsky used it to have been an extended metaphor, that is, an
allegory.[35]

"MY ONE VOICE. MY OTHER":
THE OBJECTIFIED SUBJECT

In his introduction to the "Objectivists" issue of *Poetry*, Zukofsky
maintains a similar essentializing premise concerning sight, which
has led to attempts to assimilate the work of the "Objectivists" to
photography.[36] In the essay, Zukofsky makes sight immediate and
unquestionable, proclaiming his *"Desire for what is objectively perfect,
inextricably the direction of historic and contemporary particulars,"* and
calling for writing "which is the detail, not mirage, of seeing, of
thinking with the things as they exist, and of directing them along
a line of melody. . . . This rested totality may be called objectification" (*PR*, 12–13). Even though sight is meant as an immediate con-

nection to the solidity and totality of "things" and a barrier to false and easy metaphors, the metaphorical quality of his claims for sight can be deduced from the fact that the discussion switches metaphors from sight to music.

But whether it is music or clearsightedness that guarantees the quality of genuine poetry, the point is that the poet becomes unquestioned and impervious. Zukofsky dismisses subjectivity as a deformation: "Strabismus may be a topic of interest between two strabismics; those who see straight look away." And because of this looking away, strabismics—unseeing poetasters—do not exist as far as literary history is concerned. He quotes with approval a "Chinese sage" (though in actuality he got the quote from Pound) who wrote, "Then for nine reigns there was no literary production."[37] Zukofsky amplifies: "None at all; because there was neither consciousness of the 'objectively perfect' nor an interest in clear and vital 'particulars' " (*P*, 12). However, the definition of objectification is taken from "*A*"-6, where in context it is far from being either "rested" or a "totality" and courts the risk of remaining thoroughly subjective writing, thus of not counting as "literary production" at all:

> Thus one modernizes
> His lute,
> Not in one variation after another;
> Words form a new city,
> Ours is no Mozart's
> Magic Flute—
> Tho his melody made up for a century
> And, we know, from him, a melody resolves
>   to no dullness—
> But when we push up the daisies,
> The melody! the rest is accessory:
>
> My one voice. My other: is
> An objective—rays of the object brought to a focus,
> An objective—nature as creator—desire
>   for what is objectively perfect
> Inextricably the direction of historic and
>   contemporary particulars.
>
> J.S.B.: a particular,
>
>   *A 6, 24*

At first, melody, perfection, and untrammeled sight seem to be bound up with the elimination of subjectivity. But even here, in the poem's most programmatic statement of its poetics, though "objective," "focus," "perfect," and "inextricably" suggest absolute definition, the meaning floats more loosely than first appears. "The melody!" seems to be the essence of art set against all else, both history ("his melody made up for a century") and the poet's own mortality ("But when we push up the daisies, / The melody!"). However, in the next phrase, "accessory" has opposed connotations—support or secondariness. "Rest" also can be read two ways: either as opposed to "melody" ("The melody! The rest" = melody and not-melody) or as its necessary background (= the pattern of the sounds and the silence). "My one voice" and "My other" seem opposed, but the spacing and the colon after "other" tend to unite rather than separate them. If subjectivity is being eliminated, nevertheless the objective is still personal: "*My* other." In the next lines, "An objective" is used cannily, under the guise of being repeated: the first time it is a noun signifying a lens and connoting impersonal science; the second time it is—or can be read as—an adjective modifying "desire," thus forming a phrase that is finally an oxymoron, since desire has to be felt by a subject. This tension is hard to notice because in both lines the word is interrupted by a dash. In the second line, however, the dash is not a sign of a copula but signals the interruption of the phrase "nature as creator."

These are narrow subtleties. Is art to be separated from life or not? More pointedly: is perfect art to be separated from Louis Zukofsky's life or not? "An objective desire for what is objectively perfect" is a verbal Moebius strip affirming and delaying achievement of perfection. Perhaps one could reacquire certainty here by saying that in any event the definition of desire is framed by references to the perfect music of Mozart and Bach. But if we look beyond the quoted excerpt, the distinction between contemporary particulars (inevitable materials for art) and what a strabismic might see (private distortions of no interest) becomes more blurry:

> The song—omits?
> No, includes Kay, Anybody.
> Ricky's romance
> Of twenty-three years, in
> Detail, continues

> He—a—pyjamas off—
> Invites ants upon his ankle
>   Up-up, ta-ta,
>   minus, but quite there:
>
>   "I beg your pardon
>   I've a—"h" begins the rhyme here,
>   Shall we now?"
> . . . .
> "A — sole, a — sole
> A soldier boy was he
>
> Two—pis   two—pis
> Two pistols on his knee"
>   *A* 6, 23, 34

There is a surprising amount of such material in *"A"*-6: scurrilous, childish, private. That Zukofsky does not mean to break his musical model is indicated by his applying the praise word "Detail" (echoing "particular") to "Ricky's romance"; but clearly he is aggressively testing the absorptive capacities of his composition.[38] He does this also by featuring the sententiousness of Henry Ford: "Many people are too busy to be unemployed" (the initial version of *"A"*-6 was published in 1931); "I read poetry, and I enjoy it / If it says anything" (*A* 6, 26). The present is not described with total irony: Lenin and the Russian Revolution occur as progressive clarities. But Lenin does not lend his blessing to the poet's vocation:

> "It is more pleasant and more useful,"
> Said Vladimir Ilytch,
> "To live thru the experience
> Of a revolution
> Than to write about it."
>   *A* 6, 30

In fact the relation of "particulars" to "history" is at its most blurry precisely at the point of Zukofsky's own attempt to be a poet. In his introduction to *An "Objectivists" Anthology* he may grant poems a secure ontological status and call them jobs as well ("The good poems of today are—as jobs—not far from the good poems of yesterday"), but in the writing of *"A"*-6, the poet's vocation is anomalous if not nonexistent:[39]

History: the records of taste and economy of a
                                        civilization.
Particular: Every fall season, every spring, he needs
                                        a new coat
            He loses his job—
Poetry? it has something to do with his writing of
                                        poetry.
                                        A 6, 26

Compare Lenin's imperious proclamation of self-employment:

Be prepared, well and completely prepared
To make use, with all our forces,
Of the next revolutionary wave.
That is our job.
                                        A 8, 91

For a contemporary poet to appear to lead a fully poetic life is indicted as a fraud. As part of a sketchy synopsis of a trip across country, Zukofsky lampoons Robinson Jeffers living in Tor House in Carmel:

Parched earth and fog here:
Type of mind faking a thirst for itself—
Land's jest—
Concoctors of 'hard' poetry—
Dramatic stony lips, centaurs, theatrical rock—
Living in a tower beyond rock,
In the best imitation of Sophocles.
                                        A 6, 35

(Zukofsky's sarcasm here could be seen as a displaced criticism of Pound, a fanatic proponent of "hard" poetry and an enthusiastic promoter of the Greeks.)

The attempt to bridge the gap between poetry and music ends tentatively in *"A"*-6. Zukofsky asks near the end:

Can
The design
Of the fugue
Be transferred
To poetry?
                                        A 6, 38

The answer is not an unqualified yes. The movement ends unquietly: "With all this material / To what distinction—"

This uneasiness is much amplified in the earlier version of "A"-6 published in *An "Objectivists" Anthology*. There, Zukofsky's fugal designs are more clearly affirmed at one point, but with violent irony, and with the recalcitrant, nonmusical nature of the "themes" more highly foregrounded than in the final version:

> Zoo-kaw-kaw-someone opens his mouth and you copy,
> When you're phosphates, they'll look you up and discover
> For six years you was out of a job—
> But J.S.B.—Polyphony—'e was a Latin instructor—
> *Ye daughters!*—tiaras, tantrum, tiaras—or taught 'em something of that
>   sort or other—
> Six jobs, six themes at once and fughatta, and all music—
> The sea, yeh, yeh, the sea.
> But who are we—[40]

This was edited down to:

> "When you're phosphates
> They'll look you up and discover—
> J.S.B. was a Latin instructor—
> Some individual you were!",
> Croaked Mr. Anybody.
>   *A 6, 27*

The beginning of "A"-2 was also edited most significantly. The final version:

> —Clear music—
> Not calling you names, says Kay,
> Poetry is not made of such things,
>   *A 2, 6*

The initial version:

> The clear music—
> Zoo-zoo-kaw-kaw-of-the-sky,
> Not mentioning names, says Kay,
> Poetry is not made of such things,[41]

It could be said that in both cases Zukofsky simply eliminated some out-of-control lines. But what is embodied so glaringly by the juxtaposition of the first two lines above is a problem that never goes away in Zukofsky's writing. "The clear music" is meant to signify perfection, but the actual line is bland—not to say trivial. "Zoo-zoo-kaw-kaw-of-the-sky" is something else again. It is not just a "barbaric yawp" uttered by a picturesque Whitmanian eagle standing in for Nature; Zukofsky's phrase is the energetic but horrible noise of his name, ethnicity, and class, self-deformed: his subjectivity objectified in the bad sense—a stuttering crow. But "Zoo-zoo-kaw-kaw-of-the-sky" is also a formalization, reading all sorts of semantic echoes into the oddness of the poet's name—zoos, zoology, crows, caca, and whatever meteorological or heavenly associations the sky might conjure. This particular objectification would be edited out of the final version of the poem, but the pattern of transmuting contingent, trivial, and nonpoetic bits of everyday life into quite formalized writing continued, becoming more pronounced after the political hopes of the first half evaporated. It is reminiscent of Rumpelstiltskin: Zukofsky spins straw into gold (his life into song) but must keep his name a secret. But Zukofsky's writing does not resemble elfin magic; rather, the transmutation involved endless translation and reworking of verbal material, rewriting and editing instead of writing. In "*A*"-2, Zukofsky writes sardonically of culture: "Music, itch according to its wonts, / Snapped old catguts of Johann Sebastian, / Society, traduction twice over" (*A*, 6). His later career demonstrates the tangle of cultural production with traduction, although his commitment to marriage, music, and originary presence attempted to mask all feelings of betrayal.[42]

BACH: *IUS PRIMIS NOCTIS*

The use of Bach throughout "*A*" makes an instructive contrast to the status of Zukofsky writing within his own poem. Bach's music represents "something like perfection," and a number of lyric evocations of it occur, both in the politically committed first half:

> Leaf around leaf ranged around the center;
> Profuse but clear outer leaf breaking on space,
> There is space to step to the central heart:
> The music is in the flower,
>
> *A* 2, 7

and after the politics have vanished:

> The order that rules music, the same
>   controls the placing of the stars and the feathers
>   in a bird's wing.
>
>   *A 12*, 128

But beyond this pure organicism, Zukofsky also presents Bach's music as immediately available to the community for which it was written. *"A"* begins with the poet attending a performance of the *St. Matthew Passion*. In contrast to the patrician philistines at Carnegie Hall in 1928, Zukofsky imagines, two hundred years earlier, the "motley / Country people in Leipzig—"

> "Going to Church? Where's the baby?"
> "Ah, there's the Kapellmeister
>   in a terrible hurry—
> Johann Sebastian, twenty-two
>   children!"
>
>   *A 1*, 1

Given the status Bach would attain as patron of Zukofsky's marriage as well as his art, it seems significant that *"A"* opens with Bach in the dual role of artist and father extraordinaire. Bach wrote for the people ("Choruses comparatively simple, / Within the competence of singers / Not called on to sing figural music . . . Two orchestras composed of the town's musicians" [*A 8*, 43]), and the people made his music part of their everyday lives ("Singing Bach as they dug" [*A 8*, 103]).[43] Bach's music united nature with a homogeneous society, therefore his labor was unalienated.[44] He was a hard worker but the results were Einsteinian in scope:

> Asked Albert who introduced relativity—
> "And what is the formula for success?"
> X = work, Y = play, Z = keep your mouth shut."
> "What about Johann Sebastian? The same formula."
>
>   *A 6*, 23

Bach's music was also a wholesome and unproblematic inheritance from his fathers:

> Tree of the Bach family
> Compiled by Sebastian himself.
> '   Veit Bach, a miller in Wechmar,
> Delighted most in his lute
> Which he brought to the mill

> And played while it was grinding.
> A pretty noise the pair must have made,
> Teaching him to keep time.
> But, apparently, that is how
> Music first came into our family!'

> A carousel—Flour runs.
> Song drifts from the noises.
>
> *A 4*, 15

Such natural social harmony is not available to Zukofsky. Initially, this makes for irony. As a Jew and a leftist, Zukofsky is unable to bear the performance of the *St. Matthew Passion* at the beginning of the poem; he highlights the contradictions, beginning a stanza, "It was also Passover," bitterly quoting the chitchat of the diamond-encrusted audience ("Such lyric weather"), and giving prominence to the Wobblies in the street. The result is that he is alienated from the music ("The next day the reverses / As if the music were only a taunt") and that he can hardly write ("Not boiling to put pen to paper" [*A 1, 3, 4*]).

"*A*"-4, the movement that contains Bach's genial account of his ancestors, is in contrast mostly given over to the voices of Zukofsky's fathers, who severely reprove his fall from orthodoxy: "We had a Speech, our children have evolved a jargon"; "Our own children have passed over to the ostracized." One couplet alludes to the opening lines of *The Cantos*, associating Pound with the condemning (and unapproachable) fathers: "My father's precursors / Set masts in dinghies, chanted the Speech" (*A 4, 12, 13*).

Bach's name acquires, in Zukofsky's eyes, a natural meaning. Bach wrote fugues on the theme *B-A-C-H* (in German the letters signify the notes B♭, A, C, B) and Zukofsky tries to do the same, giving over a key moment of "*A*" to a reworking of Bach's letters. "*A*"-12, the midpoint of the poem, is a 130-page elegy for Zukofsky's father and celebration of the poet's marriage and fatherhood; its 20-page finale is built around the letters of Bach's name printed in caps, and the movement ends by merging Zukofsky's marriage and "BACH":

> Blest
> Ardent
> Celia
>   unhurt and
> Happy.
>   *A 12*, 261

But in writing the natural meaning that is embodied in Bach's music and name, Zukofsky, while overcoming the ironic distance between himself and Bach in *"A"*-1, perpetuates a pattern of quotation, separation, and allegory. The conclusion of his epithalamium for his own marriage names an alien bridegroom.

THE LIFE OF THE POET: "THERE SHALL BE A COMPLETE FRAGMENT"

The following lines from the fourth poem of the early *55 Poems* demonstrate what happens when Zukofsky confronts experience unfocused by a larger framework, such as Bach, or the epos of "a" and "the."

> Buoy—no, how,
> It is not a question: what
> Is this freighter carrying?—
> Did smoke blow?—That whistle?—
> Of course, commerce will not complete
> Anything, yet the harbor traffic is busy,
>   there shall be a complete fragment
>
> Of—
>
> Nothing, look! that gull . . .
>
>   *CSP,* 23–24

This poem has been read as a "devastating indictment of capitalism's destruction," but the principal dissonance to be counted does not seem so much to be the result of capitalism and commerce as to arise out of the gap between Zukofsky's non-writing experience and the words he uses to represent it.[45] The poem makes a good reminder of the fact that the "Objectivists," disparate as their poems were, were interested in poems as objects, not in objects themselves. Most of the sensory particulars are mentioned in ways that question if not dismiss them ("Did smoke blow?—That whistle?"); the sound and words of the poem are full of the "nothing" of Zukofsky's own speech gestures: broken phrases, questions, sarcastic rhetorical dramas (the spatial suspense surrounding "Of"), and exclamations. The social self here is recognizable as the same private Zukofsky who dourly inhabits some of the less memorable lines of the early parts of "*A*." That self is not audible in lines such as "The music is in the flower / Leaf around leaf," but rather in the preceding line: "Listen, Kay . . ." (*A* 2, 7).[46]

When Zukofsky wrote "J.S.B.: a particular" in "*A*"-6, he was, in his understated way, writing a line of the highest praise, invoking the valid functioning of history and nature. But in his own case, being a private individual made him, at the beginning of "*A*," not a "particular" but a "fragment." This deficit was to be made up by the labor of writing. As Barrett Watten puts it, "The act of writing . . . replaced the empty space reserved for the 'poem of the life.' "[47]

But this "empty space" is not so easily filled in. Nevertheless, early in his career Zukofsky has great hopes for the act of writing. "*A*"-7 is a good example of what he expected a high degree of formality to accomplish. It is a sequence of seven sonnets and seems to have been intended to function as a sublation of the ironic thrashing-about of the first six movements: it concluded the published installments of the poem in Zukofsky's three major early appearances in print: *Poetry, An "Objectivists" Anthology,* and Pound's *Active Anthology.* As a "narrative" it starts from the same condition as the short poem quoted above, with the poet looking out on a foreclosed social scene, but the conclusion is quite different: Zukofsky overcomes his alienated social position through the act of writing:

> Horses: who will do it? out of manes? Words
> Will do it, out of manes, out of airs, but
> They have no manes, so there are no airs, birds
> Of words, from me to them no singing gut.
> For they have no eyes, for their legs are wood,
> For their stomachs are logs with print on them;
> Blood red, red lamps hang from necks or where could
> Be necks, two legs stand A, four together M.
> "Street Closed" is what print says on their stomachs;
> That cuts out everybody but the diggers;
> You're cut out, and she's cut out, and the jiggers
> Are cut out. No! we can't have such nor bucks
> As won't, tho they're not here, pass thru a hoop
> Strayed on a manhole—me? Am on a stoop.
>
> *A* 7, 39

The formality is strict, though given a manic quality by the diction, which Zukofsky allows to lapse into sing-song. This condition increases until it is unequivocally reached by the fifth sonnet:

> See! for me these jiggers, these dancing bucks:
> Bum pump a-dumb, the pump is neither bum
> Nor dumb, dumb pump uh! hum, bum pump o! shucks!
> (Whose clavicembalo? bum? bum? te-hum. . .)
> Not in the say but in the sound's—hey-hey—
> The way to-day, Die, die, die, die, tap, slow,
> Die, wake up, up! up! *O Saviour*, to-day!
> Choose Jews' shoes or whose: anyway Choose! Go!
>
> *A 7*, 41

It would be easy to see Zukofsky as acting out his aggressions toward a formal model that he considers alien.[48] There is worry behind the humor of "from me to them no singing gut," with the referent of "gut" oscillating between a Bach violin string and his own intestines. Violent oscillations are taking place in a number of other words as well. "Horses" refers to sawhorses—props fit for many thirties poems about labor—and to the Zukofskian horse, a lifelong obsession, combining elements of Pegasus and a Houyhnhnm-like, Chagall-like image of the perfection and opulence of living organisms.[49] Similarly, "manes" moves between the divine and the physical, referring both to horses and to the Roman *manes,* ancestral spirits.[50]

By his gross emphasis on the functionality of each word, he is continually announcing "This is form; this is writing"; if one is willing to read a lot into the words—as Zukofsky reads "A" and "M," his own existence, into the sawhorses he stares at—the sequence makes the very largest claims of poetic creativity, implying the transformation both of Zukofsky and "*A*" and of society as a whole.[51]

> Sea of horses that once were wood,
> Green and, and leaf on leaf, and dancing bucks,
> Who take liveforever! Taken a pump
> And shaped a flower. "Street Closed" on their stomachs.
> But the street has moved; at each block a stump
> That blossoms red . . .
> . . . the sun's, bro', no months' rent in arrear—
>   Bum pump a-dum, no one's cut out,
>
> *A 7*, 41–42

Zukofsky presses toward the claim that he can transmute the materials of everyday life into poetry and thus into a just world: "Taken a pump / And shaped a flower." This is even more emphatic at the end of the movement, where in the last line the (saw)horses come alive and the distinctions between thing and word, subject and object, are dissolved: "Spoke: words, words, we are words, horses, manes, words."

But this merging is evanescent, and Zukofsky embeds his transcendent affirmations in local ironies of the immediate scene.[52] In the few lines just before the end, a threesome seems to ask the poet for money, and seven workers come and take the sawhorses away—which is when the transformed sawhorses speak:

> three said: Bother,
>
> Brother, we want a meal, different techniques."
> Two ways, my two voices. . . Offal and what
> The imagination. . . And the seven came
> To horses seven (of wood—who will?—kissed their stomachs)
> Bent knees as these rose around them—trot—trot—
> Spoke: words, words, we are words, horses, manes, words.
>
> *A* 7, 42

Zukofsky's excited arrival into the status of poet (and demiurge) coincides with the fact of the formal completion of "*A*"-7, but the concomitant renewal of society is much less evident. It is only gestured at by the vaguely Communist "sun" and "red," and communal action remains at the level of an analogy with aesthetics: "fellow me, airs! we'll make / Wood horse, and recognize it with our words." In the following lines, the extreme jaggedness makes Zukofsky much more the sonneteer trying to include the hard to hide word "revolution" than the revolutionary writing sonnets (even though the sonnets might be aesthetically "revolutionary"):

> Two legs stand "A"—
> Pace them! in revolution are the same!
> Switch! See! we can have such and bucks tho they
> Are not here, nor were there, pass thru a hoop
> (Tho their legs are wood and their necks've no name)
> Strayed on a manhole—See! Am on a stoop!
>
> *A* 7, 40–41

The effacement of all problems of the self seems complete in "*A*"-9, where Zukofsky's commitment to technique reaches an extreme—not only for him, but for any poet who has written in English. This commitment is only hazily visible on initial readings: the opening five stanzas form a canzone with a highly intricate rhyme scheme that is then almost exactly duplicated by the final five stanzas, written ten years later, although the ostensible subject matter changes from "labor" in the first half to "love" in the second. But the density of the syntax limits casual perception. For instance, the fifth stanza begins:

> Light acts beyond the phase day wills us into
> Call a maturer day, the poor are torn—a
> Pawl to adorn a ratchet—hope dim—eying
> Move cangues, conjoined the coils of things they thin to,
> With allayed furor the obscurer bourne, a
> Stopped hope unworn, a voiced look, mask espying
> That, as things, men want in us yet behoove us,
> Disprove us least as things of light appearing
> To the will gearing to light's infinite locus:
> Not today but tomorrow is their focus.
>
> *A* 9, 107

Clearly the simultaneous display of technique and occasionally obtrusive self that marks "*A*"-7 ("Am on a stoop!" . . . "o! shucks") is not present here. But turning to the original publication of the first half of the poem will be instructive. Zukofsky self-published *The First Half of "A"-9* in a mimeographed edition of fifty-five copies in 1940.[53] In addition to the opening five stanzas of the final version, the pamphlet contained the rationale for the work, its sources, and some conflicted explication. Taking this material as a whole we can see some of the same tensions that animated "*A*"-7, though here they are wound to a tighter pitch.

"*A*"-9 is the apotheosis of writing as labor, where Zukofsky sets himself simultaneous tasks on the levels of word, sound, and letter. The words are selected from the Everyman edition of Marx's *Capital* and from a textbook on the physics of light; the rhyme scheme exactly duplicates Cavalcanti's "Donna Mi Prega," with each strophe requiring fourteen terminal and twelve inner rhymes; and the letters of each strophe "are the poetic analog of a conic section," which means that the frequencies of r and n stand in for the x and y coordinates of a circle.[54] This last requirement seems more deeply fanatic than the other extravagances: readers wanting to fashion a more human Zukofsky would probably be relieved to know that, as Michael Davidson acknowledges, the distribution of the letters "is irregularly performed and gradually breaks down by the poem's end." Davidson sees this as deliberate: "Zukofsky is interested less in the perfection of formal method than in the way that it defamiliarizes and rematerializes," but his justification, to my mind, makes Zukofsky more pliable and relative than *"A"*-9 as a whole and the rest of his work demonstrates him to have been.[55] As I think the exchange with Pound over the poem shows, Zukofsky was trying for an impossible political synthesis through the formal achievement of the poem. When Zukofsky identifies himself as "having lived with the Guido as basis day in & day out for the last two years" (*PZ*, 199), it indicates that the act of translation seems not to have been an instrument of defamiliarization for the reader in general, but to have functioned for Zukofsky as the one familiar thing in the world.

There is a most ambitious meaning intended for the resulting poem—Marx's theory of surplus value is reproduced, along with hints that the physics of light will be congruent with Marx's explication of the laws of history—and Zukofsky hopes that his poem will contribute toward the largest of social consequences, writing that "a Briton pronounces *capitalism* with the accent on the second syllable: ca-pit´-al-ism. *"A"*-9 may mean more if it be taken also as a sign that ca*pit*alism will capitulate" (1).[56] Along with this ambition, Zukofsky also displays a strong desire to keep the reader's attention strictly within the boundaries of the poem: "These aids ["Donna Mi Prega," excerpts from *Capital,* concepts in physics, conic sections, other Cavalcanti translations] have been presented in the following order, the poem last, so that if the intention to have it fluoresce as it were in the light of seven centuries of interrelated thought has at all been realized the poem will explain itself. In any case, the aids may forestall exegesis" (1).

Despite the coldness of Zukofsky's prose, there is an immense literary ambition visible in the procedures of *"A"*-9. That any writer would complete such a series of tasks has been a more striking fact to most readers than any "fluorescence" provided by the text itself.[57] What *"A"*-9 actually means is intensely problematic: the words of the poem are so overdetermined and the models of meaning that Zukofsky proposes in the pamphlet as a whole are conflicted. His intention, however, is for meaning to be immediate—or at least not mediated via exegesis. The inclusion of two odd slang translations of the Cavalcanti is said to "prove that a living poem can retain its essential emotion in whatever language" (1). But the status of *"A"*-9 is most ambiguous and multiple. If "Donna Mi Prega" is a living poem because it is independent of its words, then *"A"*-9, which is utterly dependent on heterogeneous words and structures, may qualify only as a simulacrum of a poem. While Zukofsky hopes "the poem will explain itself," he doesn't put the poem last: he adds a prose pony that he tries to de-emphasize by claiming, "The *Restatement* at the end of the volume is intended merely as restatement." However, the pony is necessary if we are to decipher the rhetorical frame of the poem, which, following the trope in *Capital*, has commodities speaking of their condition. The lines from "*A*"-9 quoted earlier translate to:

> As duration, things would cite their physical existence in light, an energy the action of which ultimately explains them. For now appearing in the working day, they are together with the poor nothing but mysterious, worn springs, appendages to the extant material conditions of production. They would call out against the exploitation of the poor, who have had and still have fastened (as in China) large circular pieces of wood round their necks, as human cattle. And they would sense the poor's hope that the unpaid labor in things will voice its right desire to be completely paid to the poor in things.
>
> 41

The difficulty any reader would have in coming close to producing this meaning from the words of the poem indicates how far Zukofsky was from realizing his intentions for the poem to embody an essential meaning while having, at the same time, a social existence through labor.

The second half of "*A*"-9 is a further complication. Written ten years later, its surface mimicry of the first half masks a great transformation in Zukofsky's poetics and the evaporation of his hopes for social impact. The lines parallel to those quoted before read:

> Love acts beyond the phase day wills it into—
> Hate is obscure, errs, is pain, furor, torn—a
> Lust to adorn aversion, hope—love eying
> Its object joined to its cause, sees path into
> Things the future or now, that poorer bourne, a
> Past, a step, a worn, a voiced look, gone—eying
> These, each in itself is saying, "behoove us,
> Disprove us least as things of love appearing
> In a wish gearing to light's infinite locus,
> Balm or jewelweed is according to focus.
>
> *A* 9, 110

By repeating his procedure but substituting Spinoza's "love" for Marx's "labor," Zukofsky may be proposing to complete labor with love, dialectically. But the duplication has the effect of making the first, absolute claims relative. That is, rather than having literature, science, and Marxism add up into a perfect whole of unalienated labor, the canzone becomes, in retrospect, more of a game.

This is in fact the status that Zukofsky's techniques move toward in the second half of the poem. It is consonant with his abandonment of history that, unlike the canzoni, sonnets, and sestinas of the early work, the latter patterns that Zukofsky uses are of his own invention. In the second half of *"A"* Zukofsky has no more hopes for any correlation between society and his writing. Bits of daily life appear, but always in an aesthetic frame that is eternal and asocial. When the father is putting his child-prodigy son to bed at the beginning of Zukofsky's novel, *Little*, the following conversation takes place:

> Little Baron looked serious and tearful. "I don't want to die and I most certainly don't want to sleep. Is Mozart dead?"
> "Not really, if you play his music he's alive."
> "Then composers don't die?"
> "And—poets don't either." . . .
> "You know, Dala, we picked a good profession."[58]

"Profession," however, would have to be a loaded word for a poet who, in the contemporaneously written *Autobiography*, described his career as follows: "It was thru Pound's efforts that Harriet Monroe invited me to edit the February 1931 issue of *Poetry* (Chicago). But it was not until 1965 that an easily accessible volume of my poetry appeared on the American scene. . . . My wife Celia and son Paul have been the only reason for the poet's persistence."[59]

Without public recognition, Zukofsky's profession perforce became that of immortal poet. But there the obvious problem remained: if immortality was a function of being read, what if no one read him? From *"A"*-12 on, there are a number of extremely bitter passages about his neglect as a writer.[60] These tend to call into question the numerous gestures that assert that all personal questions are gone, irrelevant, alchemized into song:

> the blood's motion—arteries to
> veins and back to the
> heart: come at last into
> ample fields sip every cup

>a great book great mischief
>perched dwarf on a giant
>may see horse race or
>hidebound calves out to pasture:
>poet living tomb of his
>games—a quiet life for
>an ocean:
>
>   *A* 22, 530–31

As this late passage from *"A"*-22 suggests, such writing gainsays its existence as something produced by a person in time. Emblems of vivid totality such as body, fields, horse, and ocean don't completely hide elements that name the particular act of writing something produced by a hidebound dwarf. The allusion to the ancient Greek proverb "A large book is a large evil," appearing after five hundred pages and a lifetime of writing, is symptomatic of the contradiction. Zukofsky's description of himself as a "living tomb" indicates that such a natural life is hardly to be distinguished from death, a condition contemplated repeatedly throughout the poem, which begins to resemble a speaking cenotaph. In *"A"*-11 this makes for a rapt lyricism with no irruption of any untoward content: "River that must turn full after I stop dying / Song, my song, raise grief to music . . . this much for honor" (*A 11*, 124). But the outcome of this self-sublation is not always smooth. *"A"*-18 is also a proleptic meditation on his own death—"I know always / it is I who have died"—but it goes on to include a most heterogeneous content:

>Rather noted a statesman hump TV-
>free face between a pumpkin and a shark.
>For a roman à clef all resemblance to living or
>dead obviously intended if these find their identities
>in them. For the young starting out: better
>ordure than order's arrogance of 'ideas' and 'ideals.'
>We warm us may ah Lesbia what cue
>may maim us the theatre marquees too big
>to read, a friend writes 'the song preserves
>recurring saves us' the song preserves a store's
>*preserves* packed rancid: death wars' commonplace no hurt
>wars not Old Glory's archaic even for MacArthur
>'How many killings per Diem Phu on Nhu'
>housewife alarmed veteran unpacking from the supermarket 'I
>told him not to put the encyclopedia with
>the vegetables, PENTHOUSE FLOOR send the elevator down.'

> When I am dead in the empty ear
> you might ask what was he like away
> from home: on his job more patient with
> others than himself more patient with strangers that's
> always so: what if the song preserves us?
>
> .　.　.　.　.　.　.　.　.　.　.　.
>
> No not an efficient man only an observant
> sits down with an aspirin without a prayer
> eight words a line for love
>
> *A 18, 389, 392–93*

Although both the sense of personal obtrusiveness that earlier spurred the writing of "Zoo-zoo-kaw-kaw-of-the-sky" and Zukofsky's initial sense of fragmentation and insignificance are in theory neutralized by the formal distance of "eight words a line for love," they are nevertheless still quite present, putting love, honor, and the immortality traditionally promised to the poet under pressure. The song may be eternal, but its preservative power may not necessarily be great enough to transubstantiate its contents, which may in fact be "packed rancid." The love that Zukofsky speaks of and whose sign he often writes under, labeling short poems and various movements of "A," including this one, "valentines," makes a closed and successful circuit as far as writing is concerned, since Celia is also his reader, typist, and, in the case of "A"-24, writer-composer. (In "A"-12 he calls her "My one reader / Who types me" [246].) However, art as a social activity (as opposed to his own writing, his wife's composing, and his son's performing) receives sour treatment here and throughout the last half of the poem: Zukofsky seems to disapprove of new developments such as using "elbow and arm boards to / cover the whole keyboard" or "Op-and-Pop art" (*A 18*, 391; *A 21*, 456). While ashtrays, apartment-window vistas, his wife's conversation, or his son's earliest drawings are granted full meaning, the bits of everyday life outside the personal, familial sphere are mere content, and the wit that plays over them can sometimes verge on the bathetic, especially when public matters such as Humphrey ("hump TV- / free") and Vietnam ("How many killings per Diem Phu on Nhu") come up. Zukofsky is still interested in politics here; but where "A"-9 was written as a contribution to the overthrow of capitalism, the political contents in "A"-18 are cited from TV and the press. Similarly, "A"-15, in part an elegy for John Kennedy, takes that material from TV. Politics has become a distanced enterprise, secondary to the formality of the writing.

"*A*"-18 contains over seven hundred lines, which, contrary to the scrambled appearance of the surface, develop a number of densely interwoven themes. Of all the lines, the one quoted near the end of the last paragraph might easily be the least satisfactory, politically and poetically: "*A*"-18 as a whole can be read as voicing a sincere though distant opposition to the Vietnam War.[61] But the line is still worth examining. Extravagant puns such as the one equating "phooey on you" with "Phu on Nhu" and *apo koinu* constructions that merge "killings per diem" and "Diem Bien Phu" are ubiquitous in the second half of the poem and are symptoms of Zukofsky's attempted dismissal of time.[62] The early, overt politics tend to mask this, as the presence of a topical meaning is almost always more prominent than the synchronic semantic alternatives. But in the second half of the poem, Zukofsky, who originally aspired to make organically complete social statements, has developed into a writer who continually uses allegory on the phonetic and syntactic level. The layering of meanings overshadows the action of statement: topicality fades into polysemy. The forward motion of the words no longer matters.

To revert to "*A*"-9 for a moment, compare the final lines of each canzone. The second "repeats" the first, but the question remains as to whether difference or identity, "approximation" or "equation," predominates.

> We are things, say, like a quantum of action
> Defined product of energy and time, now
> In these words which rhyme now how song's exaction
> Forces abstraction to turn from equated
> Values to labor we have approximated.
>
> . . . .
>
> Love speaks: "in wracked cities there is less action,
> Sweet alyssum sometimes is not of time; now
> Weep, love's heir, rhyme now how song's exaction
> Is your distraction—related is equated,
> How else is love's distance approximated."
>
> *A* 9, 108, 110–11

In the first case, despite the immense totalizing ambition, the element of history remains: things are produced by time; there is still work to be done before labor is redeemed. Zukofsky's hopes—"capitalism will capitulate" and that the poem will "fluoresce . . . in the light of seven centuries of interrelated thought"—involve designs upon history; his "fluorescence" is distinct from Pound's transhistorical, originary light. In the second canzone, however, history can vanish—"sweet alyssum sometimes is not of time"—and identity no longer involves struggle: "related is equated." Zukofsky, by miming Cavalcanti and Spinoza so well, is related-equated to the masters, is a true son of an ahistorical lineage.

THE SOUND OF ALLEGORY

Though there is a crucial allegorical dimension to Zukofsky's writing, his poetic goals seemingly precluded any use of allegory in the received sense. He consistently defined the poet's expertise in terms of measurement and scorned any "poetic" prerogatives such as allegory. In his introduction to the "Objectivists" issue of *Poetry* he had dismissed "strained metaphor," which "carries the mind to a diffuse everywhere and leaves it nowhere," preferring instead "the economy of presentation in writing," which he found to be "a reassertion of faith that the combined letters—the words—are absolute symbols for objects, states, acts, interrelations, thoughts about them" (*PR*, 14). In his essay "Poetry," written at the midpoint—or nadir—of his career (1946), he compared poetry and science in a way that registered his distaste for the kind of secondariness that allegory entails: "When poetry is defined as indirect or 'desirably' incapable of definition, symbols standing for sound, and words which are the semblances of the things, events or susceptibilities of science are conceived as echoes occurring out of nowhere. The choice for science and poetry when symbols or words stop measuring is to stop speaking" (*PR*, 7).

But in both cases precision leads to what could certainly be seen as a "diffuse everywhere." The assertion that "words are the absolute symbols for objects"—a sentiment nearly worthy of Bishop Sprat's desire for "so many *things* in so many *words*"—opens out to the endlessness of "objects, states, acts, interrelations, thoughts about them," and in "Poetry," while the correct choice for a poet when confronted with a lack of measurement should be silence, Zukofsky also writes of "words, whose effect as an offshoot of nature may (or should) be that their strength of suggestion can never be accounted for completely" (*PR*, 7), thus implying that any measured word in a poem never stops speaking.

Zukofsky displayed little overt interest in the Romantics, but in writing of "absolute symbols" and invoking nature as the root of words he is quite close to them. From this perspective, Paul de Man's account of the entanglement of symbolic and allegorical structures in Romantic writing is surprisingly relevant to Zukofsky's writing, though the intensity of Zukofsky's writing practice goes far beyond the nicety of de Man's discriminations.

The symbolic reading of Romanticism is a critical commonplace de Man wants to complicate; for him, the symbolic world is eternal, free of conflict, and shallow. Part and whole, poem and world, are organically continuous; "the symbol is always a part of the totality that it represents." Coleridge, one of the tutelary spirits of such organic thinking, is quoted by de Man: "such as the life is, such is the form."[63] In contrast, Romantic allegory is (re)born after this cocoon of coincidence has been shattered by doubt. De Man sees this as a much more valuable state; allegory appears at "the most original and profound moments . . . when an authentic voice becomes audible" (205). Symbolic aspirations move toward a naive simultaneity of language, self, and world; in the case of allegory "time is the originary constitutive category" (207) and the author's recognition of his or her own belated separateness, "the unveiling of an authentically temporal destiny" (206), is a painful and valuable advance. As we will see, this critical judgment (which contains its own absolutist perspective in its discrimination of what is "authentic") will not be all that applicable to Zukofsky, but the temporal structure that de Man sees in allegory will be central: "allegory designates primarily a distance in relation to its own origin, and, renouncing the nostalgia and the desire to coincide, it establishes its language in the void of this temporal difference. In so doing, it prevents the self from an illusory identification with the non-self, which is now fully, though painfully, recognized as a non-self" (207).

The tensions de Man sees in Romantic poetry are present to a high degree in Zukofsky's work, but they do not resolve into a dramatic (and critically convenient) "unveiling"; there is no way that "*A*" can be read as a progression from symbolic innocence to allegorical insight. The later parts of "*A*" contain repeated assertions of simple symbolic consonance even while the writing is allegorical in highly complex ways.

Recognition of the difference between self and non-self was, so to speak, mother's milk to Zukofsky, who realized from the first that the role of writer was not his natural inheritance: "254 I'll read their Donne as mine, / 255 And leopard in their spots / 256 I'll do what says their Coleridge" (*CSP*, 18). Or take a passage like the following from "*A*"-5, where the friction between self and non-self is registered in the most bodily terms:[64]

> New are, the trees,
> Purple in the violets' swath,
> Birds—birds—birds,
> Against bark a child's forehead
> tormented red,
> (No glasses between eyes and bark)
> Face to bark.
>
> *A* 5, 19

The estranged quality of the non-self shows up not only in the final image but in the rhetoric of the first three lines, which, if looked at closely, are wryed in three different directions: the first line a deliberately awkward inversion, the second an upside-down Impressionist blur with the violets coloring the trees; the third nearly as mindless as a bird call. Despite such local jaggedness, however, symbolic aspirations clearly govern "*A*" in its overall ambition of being "a poem of a life." To create consonance between self and world was a prospect that to Zukofsky as an unknown poet must have appeared, no matter how carefully hedged, heroic.

The poem contains a number of passages that look like textbook illustrations of Coleridgean organicism:

> I walked on Easter Sunday,
> This is my face
> This is my form.
> Faces and forms, I would write
> you down
> In a style of leaves growing.
>
> A train crossed the country: (cantata).
> A sign behind trees read (blood red as intertwined
> Rose of the Passion)
> Wrigleys.
>
> *A* 2, 8

The second half of this, however, as well as the first line, should remind us that Coleridge's universalist assumption blandly embodied in "such as *the* life is, such is the form" is exactly what Zukofsky challenged by his self-identification as *a* life. And by defiantly appropriating the central mystery of the dominant (foreign) culture—Christ's eternally performative "This is my body"—Zukofsky is scrambling the elements de Man sees as constituting the sad drama of allegorical lucidity. Rather than realizing his own belatedness *vis-à-vis* Christ, Zukofsky is asserting that the organic process of his writing ("In a style of leaves growing") is predicated upon the alienating artificialities of the present.

Zukofsky's use of language here involves both temporal and social displacement. Temporally the mention of Easter alludes to that eighteenth-century communal performance of the *St. Matthew Passion* he will never get back to; socially, the mystery of Christ's incarnation standing behind natural forms is replaced here by a literal sign standing behind trees: "Wrigleys."[65] But these distances do not constitute a void, as they would in de Man's scenario; here they are the social space in which Zukofsky tries to maintain his symbolic (not allegorical) claims to creativity. "Wrigleys," to my mind, wavers between an ironic literariness and a nonironic Marxist teleological acceptance of the here and now.

De Man cites, disapprovingly, Gadamer's remark that a symbolic aesthetics "refuses to distinguish between experience and the representation of this experience. The poetic language of genius is capable of transcending this distinction" (188). However, while Zukofsky retains this goal of symbolic consonance, his practice is not naive. In the first sections of *"A"* there are passages that can be read as autobiographical reportage, but there are also passages that anticipate the aesthetics of the latter half of *"A,"* where instead of representations of the poet's experience there is simply writing, a practice that ignores any chasm between experience and its representations.

If "Wrigleys" is emblematic of the initial state of *"A,"* where experience and representation are at odds, the word that exemplifies the condition that the latter half of the poem aims at is "this." While "This is my face / This is my form" can refer to the poet's body, "this" can also be read as performative in an extremely local sense. The word would then refer, incontrovertibly, to itself and to the lines it occurs in: "This is my form" = "This writing creates my valid existence." A similar self-referential turn enlivens the following colloquy between Zukofsky and Kay:

> Our voices:
>   "How? without roots?"
>   "I have said *The courses we tide from.*"
>   "They are then a light matter?"
>   "Let it go at that, they are a light matter."
>   "Isn't it more?" "As you say."
>   "Your people?" "All people."
>   "You write a strange speech." "This."
>
> > *A 5, 18*

The physics pun on "light" and "matter" aside, Zukofsky's registration of social tones seems pedantic (or one could say that his experience is not supplying the necessary materials for interesting writing) until the last line when, to my ear, the fiction of a conversation between supercilious, insecure poet and earnest literature student drops away. As if Zukofsky had become a Derridean *avant la lettre,* "You write a strange speech" seems, in spite of its quotation marks, more written than spoken; and in answering the implied challenge, "This" defines itself as an example of writing where there is no distance between sign and meaning, between experience and the achieved objectification of art. Unlike the naive, symbolic "desire to coincide," where the coincidence would be between world and the poet's language, here Zukofsky's art and his life would coincide only in writing, conceived of as both act and resulting structure.[66] The "empty space" of his life would seem to be filled.

If Joel Fineman's remarks on allegory are valid, Zukofsky's goal is still chimerical. A key concept in Fineman's discussion is the distinction between the terms heterologic and autologic. Autologic words are self-descriptive: "short" is a short word, "English" an English word; "monosyllabic" and "French" would be heterologic. For Fineman, autology represents the dream of philosophy to speak the truth, whereas heterology, which both etymologically and in practice resolves into allegory, is "the paradigm of literary language." Fully dressed out, the paradox runs, "literary language . . . can never mean what it says because it never means anything except the fact that it is saying something that it does not mean."[67]

Fineman's conclusion—a nicely epigrammatic version of what much poststructuralist theory has implied over the last few decades—puts literature firmly in its place. It is a place that might either be high or low, but whether it is thought of as utopia or as a funhouse mirror, literature here is denied the social meaning that other language has. As we have seen, this is a conclusion that Zukofsky worked all his life to avoid, yet it is one toward which his writing inevitably drifts. The claims for absolute, immediate meaning that are built into *"A"*-9 and *"A"*-24 produce some of the most elaborately displaced literary structures of the century. One of the central contradictions in *"A"* is that "music" is heterologic: it is a word, not music.

Such tensions reach an easily perceivable extreme in *Catullus*, where the English aspires to fit exactly into the sound scheme of the Latin. Thus, in the classroom standard, number 85, "Odi et amo" [I hate and I love], the opening phrase is translated "O th'hate I move love," while the final phrase, "sed fieri sentio et excrucior" [but I feel it happen and am crucified] becomes "say th' fiery scent I owe whets crookeder" (*CSP*, 310). Zukofsky's claims are far-reaching: "This translation of Catullus follows the sound, rhythm, and syntax of his Latin—tries, as is said, to breathe the 'literal' meaning with him" (*CSP*, 243). Here the Zukofskian notions of poetic measurement and music are at their most intense and are most clearly fictive. The "sound, rhythm, and syntax" of "Odi et amo" are the music aimed at, but the finer Zukofsky whets his stylus the crookeder the resulting letters. The first three Latin words present a blunt antithesis in balanced sounds, beginning and ending on long *o*'s. In the English, on the other hand, both "hate" and "love" are sonically encumbered or overshadowed: "th'hate" and "move love." This is not to be judgmental; the translations contain a wealth of glosses and turns of phrase and can certainly be defended.[68] But the results point to a pattern that is central to the strain in Zukofsky's work: the stronger the claims of symbolic consonance, the more glaring the displaced allegorical quality of the writing; the faithfulness is a pious aggression.[69]

To "breath the 'literal' meaning" as Zukofsky says he is doing is to treat the Latin letters and sound as a living body. At one point in *"A"*-14, Zukofsky describes his "Cats" (that is, the translations) and his method of producing them as

> chaste—eyeing passionate
> Italian lips two
> thousand years near
>
> to sharp them
> and flat them
> not in prurience—

> of their voice—
> eyes of Egyptian
> deity that follow
>
> each half step
>
> *A 14, 356*

Catullus's lips and voice are present in his text and, as the vocabulary suggests ("sharp," "flat," "half step"), they form a divine music. Zukofsky's religious veneration here is similar to his attitude toward Bach, Pound, Cavalcanti: making their works and bodies absolute confirms his distance from them.

Bottom: On Shakespeare, written during the same period as *Catullus* and the section of *"A"* quoted above, extends this pattern to Shakespeare. David Melnick has demonstrated how Zukofsky here attempted to obliterate all motion and context in order to posit the changelessness of Shakespeare's work.[70] The four-hundred-plus pages of *Bottom* can be reduced to two basic postulates: (1) that Shakespeare's plays and poems comprise a single work, "always regardless of time in which it was composed, and so, despite defects of quality, durable as one thing from "itself never turning" (*B*, 13); (2) and that the theme of this work is the excellence of sight over reason: "*love: reason : : eyes: mind* . . . Love needs no tongue of reason if love and the eyes are *1*—an identity" (*B*, 39) or "that it is best to actually look with the eyes—otherwise reason is not happy love; that thoughts without the eyes' judgment are strays. . . . It is not merely history Shakespeare figured at the beginning, but the *seeing love* of all the Plays and Poems that followed" (*B*, 267).[71] Melnick shows how Zukofsky went directly against the dramatic sense of some lines in order to extract from them a praise of dispassionate sight (63). For Melnick, this dismissal of context and action means that Zukofsky "deals with Time by not dealing with it, by denying its reality, by making it into an unfortunate and self-deceptive quirk of the mind" (58). In denying time, Zukofsky also dismisses social conflict; Melnick concludes that "Zukofsky's world has no room for people in it: he will not deal with more than one pair of eyes at a time" (64).[72]

Such a conclusion is too stark: three—the number of the family—is always the minimum number in the later Zukofsky. A fourth member could be added if we include the continuous interplay between the biographical writer and his various projections of incorruptible wholeness. Given the simplicity and power he attributes to these originals, and his own extravagantly displaced imitations, he can be seen as fulfilling one of his early ironic prophecies: he does become something of a "Plato's Philo." Though where Philo "formulates the theological necessity for philosophical, allegorical exegesis in the face of divine ineffability," Zukofsky works from the absolute sound of his predecessors and his attempts to conserve it create a distance almost as absolute as that Philo posits.[73]

What of Zukofsky's own voice and immediacy? A short interlude, one of a number of such that punctuate the *Rudens* of "*A*"-21, gives an answer:

> *(Voice off)*
> > nine
> > men's
> > morris
> >
> > this
> > is
> > my
> > form
> >
> > a
> > voice
> > blown
>
> > > *A* 21, 445

All the elements of this are overdetermined. The first three lines are of course from Shakespeare, but they also pun, elegaically, on the name of Zukofsky's recently dead brother, to whom the movement is dedicated.[74] "A voice blown" is from "*A*"-8, where "Voice a voice blown, returning as May" was a vaguely Marxist refrain uniting the May Days of Puck and Lenin.[75] The semantic oppositions built into "a voice blown" are extreme: in Elizabethan usage "blown" would designate a voice that has flowered to perfection; as contemporary slang it implies fatigue or failure. "This is my form" is written a word to a line for maximum emphasis, but at the same time it is impossible to pin down. Referents for "this" include Shakespeare's writing and the organic folk dance presumably behind it, the ambiguously blown voice, and the whole project of translating Plautus, identifying with Plautus, and producing writing that is in social terms utterly distant from Plautus—which, after all, is closer in tone to *I Love Lucy* than to Homer. (If the plot of *Rudens*—child found, family reunited—is to rhyme with the condition of Zukofsky's own family, it does so only by ignoring the context of prostitution and slavery so integral to *Rudens,* where satisfying the economic claims of the "evil pimp" forms a major part of the action. In fact, it is the lack of any consideration of economic and power relations within the family that makes Zukofsky's use of it often sentimental.)

As an emblem of the relation of poet to poem, the would-be symbolic and in fact highly allegorical lines "this / is / my / form" seem properly conflicted. Within the boundaries of their own sound, they are unarguably performative and control their own meaning, but in the context of "A" and in the larger context of literature that necessarily surrounds "A" such claims are irrevocably subject to interpretation.

In an interview, Zukofsky and L. S. Dembo act out the consequences of this pattern. Dembo is more or less sympathetic but does not seem to understand the poet's work or his remarks. Dembo wants not so much to read Zukofsky's work as to place it in a social context and map it onto a literary continuum. Zukofsky, on the other hand, keeps fending off the questions and coming back to the words he has written. In answer to one question he quotes from "The Old Poet Moves to a New Apartment 14 Times," ending with the line, "All the questions are answered with their own words."[76]

The tendency revealed by such a line, and such a social response as quoting that line in answer to a question about the "Objectivists," would be identified by de Man as symbolic, by Fineman as autologic, and perhaps by Zukofsky as genuinely musical and poetic. The power that he saw in Pound's work, "the *song . . .* yours, **always right**," cannot be questioned and finally is not in social circulation. Zukofsky aspired to that same modernist unity, for his life-poem and for his fragmented life. As a final example of this, I will quote the following lines, the beginning of "A"-22:

> AN   ERA
> ANY TIME
> OF   YEAR
>
>
> Others letters a sum owed
> ages account years each year
> out of old fields, permute
> blow blue up against yellow
> —scapes welcome young birds—initial

transmutes itself, swim near and
read a weed's reward—grain
an omen a good omen
the chill mists greet woods
ice, flowers—their soul's return

let me live here ever,
sweet now, silence foison to
on top of the weather
it has said it before
why that was you that

is how you weather division

A 22, 508

The title proclaims the poem's imperviousness to time, and a symbolic consonance of self and world is suggested by the generalized
natural lyricism. It is also affirmed in the specific moments where
landscape and page blend: "read a weed's reward" can be para-
phrased as "look at seaweed" or as "read an outsider's poem"; similarly, the "here" of "let me live here ever" can be both "in this
natural setting" and "in this poem."[77] But any clear synecdochal and
synchronous union of part and whole is complicated by a number
of allegorical gestures, the first of which appears in the opening line.
The syntax is effaced, but the general tenor of "Others letters a sum
owed" implies that writing is a foreign medium—the letters are "[of]
others" or are "others" themselves—and that the writer, far from
being autonomous, is in debt.

"Out of old fields, permute" refers to the Chaucerian epigraph to
"Poem beginning 'The' ": "*out of olde bokes, in good feith.*" By treating
his initial literary gesture as contemporaneous, Zukofsky affirms the
unity of "a poem of a life"; the change from "bokes" to "fields"
makes the symbolic consonance all the stronger. But affirming that
books have been transmuted to fields also highlights the separation
of the elements involved, a pattern that becomes more obvious when
"let me live here ever" is recognized as lifted from *The Tempest*.[78]
"Here" then acquires other referents: Prospero's isle, Shakespeare's
text. The distance activated by Shakespeare's language seems to provoke the next lines: "*it* has said *it* before / why *that* was you *that*,"
which emphasize in their repetitions both identity and difference.
"That / is how you weather division" appeals to natural, cyclical
time rather than history to resolve the dilemma, but elsewhere in

Zukofsky's work the divisions resulting from alien sources and temporal distances are so prominent that such appeals cannot paper them over. The lyric weather of *"A"*-22 could be taken as an organic apotheosis of the line "Such lyric weather" in *"A"*-1; but the irony of the earlier line, which was the result of the specific, painful, historical position of the younger poet, is subsumed and overcome by the later lyricism only at the cost of the complete effacement of any social position for the older poet. The free play of the later language has been paid for by Zukofsky's social marginalization.

In a late talk on Wallace Stevens Zukofsky both affirms poetry's victory over time and reveals his own isolation, exhibiting a touching need for connection with the older poet. They never met and corresponded only in the most minimal sense, but Zukofsky is at great pains to find parallels in their poems and lives. He goes beyond this to claim that the act of one poet reading another creates an identity, no matter how many centuries may have elapsed between their lives: "sometimes a word impels . . . a feeling a duration, best defined I think as Spinoza defined it, an indefinite continuance of existence. It is not a temporal thing, may be felt only an instant, but that instant call it love, eternity, infinity. . . . [What endures] is a reading removed from yet out of time, without actual mutual influence or conscious awareness of tradition, literary handbooks or chronometers" (*PR*, 24–25). Zukofsky may have hoped to eliminate the literary handbooks that, at the time, had eliminated him, but at one point he focuses on the physical conduit of this transcendent communion, the page. Looking up two especially Stevensian words, "gubbinal" and "joost," in his *Century Dictionary*, he wonders if Stevens had the same dictionary and also looked up the words: another possible moment of union between the two poets. He describes the physical pages lovingly: "The volumes of *The Century* are heavy; their white refractive leaves were meant to last. Not much darkened, still unfoxed, page 3243, volume IV. . . . It seemed then as to influence that the very paper of *The Century* had brought us together" (*PR*, 36).

That paper can be "read" as an attempt to imagine a unity between Zukofsky's labors as a writer and his early Marxist concerns with materiality that later became so etherealized. I see in that excellent paper Zukofsky's image of a just, well-functioning society, where communication between people would be, if not immediate, at least more direct than it is now, and where a poet's labor would be adequately valued and would be permanent. But it's hard to imagine that *"A"* would have been written in such a world.

Afterword:
Afterward

I have been reading modernist genius as a career construct, though I do not mean that it is merely a superficial pose. Rather than wearing a cape and eating roses at dinner parties, the part requires a lifetime of attention to and ambition for words on the page. But the pages produced are not enclaves free from such social conflicts as seating arrangements, publishing practices, or wars. The effort called for is continual: since language is the social medium *par excellence,* the social authority of genius cannot simply manifest itself as discrete points of inexplicable distance.[1] Genius has to be continually displayed in writing, but both the passage of time outside the writing and the very temporality of the medium conspire to recontextualize genius, to reduce its sheen to words that eventually will be stylistically and socially decodable.

Genius and narrative thus coexist in conflict. While the writing is underway—while the generic title is still *Work in Progress*—to be fully legible dooms genius to ordinariness. Once completed, a work of genius should, in theory, be recognizable as sublimely new and astounding; after the fact, the narratives of literary history take over and place *The Cantos,* however uneasily, in the heterogeneous category of the modernist long poem, alongside *The Waste Land; A Cloud in Trousers; Paterson; Helen in Egypt; The Bridge; "A"; Harlem Gallery; Testimony: The United States; The Maximus Poems,* etcetera. This three-step process is nondialectical: would-be cutting edges fall back into the matrix without necessarily producing syntheses. From the vantage of the nonspecialist, this pattern might look suspiciously like the primal problem facing any producer in the marketplace where the imperative to "Make It New" applies at least as urgently to cars as to poems.

However, while works of genius have such problems with history, the lives of geniuses can make effective narratives, which can

become commodities in their own right: Pound's life is more interesting to a wider range of people than is *The Cantos*.[2] But the writing
that remains is neither fully expressive of nor aloof from these lives.
The contested space in between writing as display of genius and
writing as formal entity continually calls the writer's agency into
question, undercutting its reach while sharpening the personal necessity for it.

The reading I've been proposing follows out the dynamics by
which totalized claims rested on contingent acts of writing. These
claims have ranged from the explicit pronouncements of Pound and
Stein to the implicit demonstrations of a completed world in *Ulysses*
or a completed life in *"A."* Genius has served as something of an
indecipherable shorthand for the accomplishments and contradictions involved. Poundians especially must have noticed that I have
not used the word as a transcendental compliment; the notion of the
immediately authoritative genius consistently mars Pound's cos-
mopolitan panache, proposing a fundamentalist lexicon and syntax
that must embarrass attempts at a humanist reading. But genius is
not simply a critical demerit to be applied whenever a writer over-
steps generic and aesthetic boundaries. In writing about Pound,
Joyce, Stein, and Zukofsky, I have also been investigating the writing
that I have found most challenging and still generative for contemporary writing.

ENDS OF GENIUS

In spite of Pound's railing against it in *The Cantos*—"Time is not,
Time is the evil, beloved" (*C 84*, 458)—and in spite of the autonomous articulations and circular structurings of Joyce and Zukofsky;
in spite of Stein's dismissals, the worst thing that could happen to a
work displaying modernist genius did happen: time passed.

Zukofsky's career bridges the period of modernist heroism and
what came next. Moments from both ends of his career mark the
boundaries of modernist genius. Late in his life he characterized his
writing as no more intentionally shaped than *"found objects* in late
exhibits—which arrange themselves as it were, one object near another—roots that have become sculpture, wood that appears talisman" (*PR*, 168). This echoes and to some extent undoes the imagery
in Kant's discussion of genius. There, Kant had said that no one

coming upon "a bit of shaped wood" in a bog would think that it
was a product of nature rather than of art.[3] But the provinces of art
and nature, as easily distinguished as a board from a tree, are to be
reunited by genius, "the innate mental disposition through which
Nature gives the rule to Art." In claiming that the naturalness of his
work has subsumed its artistry, Zukofsky turned down any public
role. He was apparently resigned to having his work appear, like
the found objects, in the museum of literary history.

By the time these remarks were written, however, Zukofsky finally had at least a small, specialized audience. As emblem of his
earlier hopes for a much more widely efficacious writing, I'll cite
what I assume is an accidental pun in his least public pages: the self-
published *First Half of "A"-9*. The table of contents lists a "Foreward," while the page in question is labeled "Foreword." Isolated
as he was, and hermetic as the piece was, Zukofsky intended *The
First Half of "A"-9* to move history forward by dint of the exquisite
engineering of its words. The gap where genius writes can be read
in the discrepancy between "foreward" and "foreword." Read typologically, a foreword tends toward the divine, echoing the original
Word that will direct the world or that has already effected the
world. *The First Half of "A"-9* is Marxist in its verbal matter and its
political goals, but Zukofsky intended more than a material act; he
made claims on both the past and the future in his intention for the
poem to "fluoresce . . . in the light of seven centuries of interrelated
thought." (See the discussion in Chapter Five.) Yet events did not
move forward in the light of the words of the poem.

Zukofsky had already sent the world's rejection letter in *"A"-8*:

> China, the one place it could happen:
> "Most honorable Sir,
>   We perused your MS.
> with boundless delight. And
> we hurry to swear by our ancestors
> we have never read any other
> that equals its mastery.
> Were we to publish your work,
> we could never presume again on
> our public and name
> to print books of a standard
> not up to yours.
> For we cannot imagine
> that the next ten thousand years

> will offer its ectype.
> We must therefore refuse
> your work that shines as it were in the sky
> > *A 8,* 94–95

This was written in the thirties when Pound's China, the site of the direct seeing described in *ABC of Reading* and projected in Canto 49, was a place that Zukofsky had some faith in. This faith would have made the contemplation of such a rejection a pleasant joke, a minor moment in one voice of the eight-part fugue of *"A"*-8. But for the next twenty-five years the world did reject *"A,"* not even "perusing it with boundless delight" first. The poem ended in great privacy, and if it was going to "shine as it were in the sky" it would have to invoke that condition for itself. Zukofsky's late work does attempt to create a purely autonomous world harmony. The final lines written by Zukofsky—the end of *"A"*-23—affirm an eternity without significant dissonance at the same time that they site themselves in a very local point that could have little claim on society:

> > sawhorses silver
> *all these fruit-tree tops:* consonances
> and dissonances only of degree, never-
> Unfinished hairlike water of notes
> vital free as Itself—impossible's
> sort-of think-cramp work x: moonwort:
> music, thought, drama, story, poem
> parks' sunburst—animals, grace notes—
> z-sited path are but us.
> > *A 23,* 563

The sawhorses, which in the sonnets of *"A"*-7 were figures of labor transformed by poetry to poetry, are purely natural here. The words of the passage name their own perfection; they are, they say, always complete, musical and fluid, and microscopically filiated to one another: "never- / Unfinished hairlike water of notes / vital free as Itself." In their freedom they also fend off the kind of critical repackaging I'm engaging in here, naming it "impossible's / sort-of think-cramp work x." But if, to paraphrase *"A"*-9, their "locus is infinite" (110), their social location is private: the last line can be unfolded to say that there is no one but Zukofsky's family at the end of his path; anecdotally we know that the last three words pun on the name of the street where the poet's son lived: Arbutus.[4]

This conclusion typifies, on a quirkier and more private scale, the strains over narrative and social placement that occur at conclusions in the other three cases. While Molly's Yes pronounces the marriage of art and the world, her soliloquy also solidifies the conflict between authority and transgression. Pound's failure to complete *The Cantos* demonstrates non-conclusiveness in another way: it is significant that the last three editions have different endings: such editorial uncertainty accurately reflects Pound's quandaries. The end that is currently in place is tellingly provisional. Labeled "FRAGMENT (1966)," and thus naming Pound's fundamental structural anxiety, it begins as a brief paean to Pound's companion: "Her name was Courage / & is written Olga." In this dimension it could be seen as a tenuous recurrence of the pattern embodied by Celia Zukofsky and Molly, where woman is placed at the conclusion as the emblem of totality. But what is interesting about the final lines of "FRAGMENT" is the way they try to posit an ending even as they struggle beyond it to acknowledge that they are simply a dated moment in a potentially never-ending stream of words:

> These lines are for the
> ultimate CANTO
>
> whatever I may write
> in the interim.
>
> [*24 August 1966*]
>   C, 818

There's a ghostly, wry humor here. Though he was quite painfully aware of how hard it had become for him to produce any words, spoken or written, Pound is saying—in formal terms at least—"Stop me before I write again."

I have discussed the problematic contextualization of Stein's last major self-presentation in *The Mother of Us All*, where the very fact of social victory implies ontological defeat. In the first half of her career, however, Stein's final sentences were not usually momentous: they were not conclusive and did not involve any change in content or rhetoric from what came before. This is no surprise, given her commitment to a continuous present.[5] The ending of *Toklas* is atypically emphatic: "I am going to write it as simply as Defoe did the autobiography of Robinson Crusoe. And she has and this is it"

(*SW*, 237). Here the end snaps a new frame around the whole book: Stein turns out to have been the writer of the pages we have read; she has put herself in the company of Defoe and named herself a classic.

She has also placed herself in society, which becomes a fact that her subsequent endings need to encompass. With the approach of the Second World War this became a difficult task. *Picasso* ends with Stein flying above American farmland and seeing the fields manifest designs that Cubist painters had already painted: "yes I saw and once more I knew that a creator is contemporary, he understands what is contemporary when the contemporaries do not yet know it . . . and as everything destroys itself in the twentieth century and nothing continues, so then the twentieth century has a splendor which is its own and Picasso is of this century, he has that strange quality of an earth that one has never seen and of things destroyed as they have never been destroyed. So then Picasso has his splendor. Yes. Thank you."[6] The largeness of Molly's Yes and its parallel, the "splendour" that ends Canto 116, are here; but there is a choice too. The ending can be read as apocalyptic, with Stein pointing to the imminent outbreak of war and affirming that art will transcend it. But there is a second conclusion: "Thank you," one of the calling cards of genius for Stein. It is the most ordinary social speech, but for Stein to write it does not imply sociability: a rough translation is "Thank you for my being a genius."

The end of *Paris France* is similar:

> The century is now forty years old, too old to do what it is told.
> It is old enough to like to live quietly and well, to go to heaven or to hell as they like, to know that to live as they please is pleasanter than to be told.
> So this is what England and France are going to do and this book is dedicated to them because I want them to do what they are going to do. Thank you.[7]

Typically, this is contradictory. The sentence that informs us it is pleasant not to be told what do is followed by a sentence telling England and France what they are going to do. Perhaps this is just humor, but I read it as a more absolute assertion, one that is in line with Zukofsky's foreword dictating the forward path of history: genius tells the world what to do in ways the world can't quite hear.

Is the lesson that genius must learn simply that there is a world outside, independent of the most perfect words? (Even *Ulysses* tends more to the assertion that the world is within it, not outside it.) Do the following lines of Wallace Stevens sum up the problem?

> Mesdames, one might believe that Shelley lies
> Less in the stars than in their earthy wake,
> Since the radiant disclosures that you make
> Are of an eternal vista, manqué and gold
> And brown, an Italy of the mind, a place
> Of fear before the disorder of the strange,
> A time in which the poet's politics
> Will rule in a poet's world. Yet that will be
> A world impossible for poets, who
> Complain and prophesy, in their complaints,
> And are never of the world in which they live.[8]

This is a clear, delicately elegiac presentation of the problem, but the very clarity of these lines compromises the power of their answer. Steven's lament for the social reality of poetry fits easily within a socially well-defined sense of poetry. The lines mention "an Italy of the mind," but are not actually written in such a mental Italy (or mental China) as is displayed so often on Pound's pages. The charm and ironized beauty of Stevens's lines make him very much a poet of the world in which he lives.

I have quoted Stevens for more than his lucidity, and that is simply to affirm that there is something outside the writing of Pound, Joyce, Stein, and Zukofsky. There is an outside, and, of course, an afterward.

THE PRESENT OF MODERNIST GENIUS

These writers and their works have met with sundry complex and contradictory fates. Joyce can claim more widespread pockets of triumph than the other three. His work is analyzed or mentioned with reverence by a broad range of literary critics and philosophers, and it has been an emblem of daunting intellectuality in popular culture for decades: *Ulysses* is shown on the floor of Frank Sinatra's apartment in *The Manchurian Candidate*, and when Captain Picard in *Star Trek* says he is going to read it on vacation, the first mate's jaw drops. The components of this success may be the book's serious brush with melodrama combined with the narrative and stylistic transgression, plus the ambitious inventiveness of the patterning, which gives the work a scientific aura. Somewhat similar elements can be found in *"A"*: dense patterning, a "plot" that revolves around marriage and self-realization, as much syntactic and referential difficulty as you like. But aside from the context of language writing, Zukofsky has had very little impact. This can be set down to fiction's wider appeal, to the unconventionality of his language, and perhaps to the lack of the tender, parodic distances to be found in *Ulysses:* the valentines to Zukofsky's wife that dot the latter half of *"A"* and *All* are not ironic. Pound is still attended to by some critics and remains notorious in wider cultural circles. The influence of his writing, especially his aggressive prose, among poets has been great: for a number of New American writers such as Creeley, Dorn, Duncan, and Olson, he has been the model of the activist poet, and for many, especially Olson, the model of the masculine poet as well. Stein is mildly notorious, though in the contemporary cultural landscape her eccentricities would be modest. Her influence in language writing circles and among feminist and lesbian poets (none of them mutually exclusive categories) has been considerable.

Compared to the totalizing effect that was posited by these writing projects, this range of impact is mixed and minor. In 1949, Basil Bunting wrote of *The Cantos,* "There are the Alps, / fools! Sit down and wait for them to crumble!"[9] The monuments of modernism may not have exactly crumbled, but they certainly have been outflanked as cultural shrines. The three groups who still read this writing make very different uses of it: the specialists read it carefully, accept its value, and naturalize the problems of its social rhetoric. Poststructuralism and critical theory allude to it glancingly and at times claim its effect. Contemporary poets, in some cases, read it for instigation.

Before noting a few representative moments, however, I need to mention a fourth area in this mapping: the culture at large. Here genius has become a washed-out, ubiquitous compliment, and, in regard to literature, an outmoded, faintly ridiculous term (it still seems to have non-ironic value when applied to scientists). A Bugs Bunny/Wile E. Coyote cartoon furnishes an apt cultural X ray of its current status. It is not surprising that it would be a cartoon: it is a medium where the information is primarily visual, where causality is dreamlike without the sententiousness of surrealist dreaming, and where the goal of narrative desire involves the elementary satisfaction of eating rather than the social gymnastics of sex and status. And in this case the Bronx sarcasm of Bugs's voice—"Ehnn, what's up, Doc?" accompanied by carrot crunchings—stands nicely for a popular critique of overcomplexity.

The plot revolves around the title of genius. Coyote keeps naming himself one, pronouncing the title with obsequious self-congratulation, "Wile E. Coyote, *Genius*," and informing Bugs that it's no use running because he is doomed to be eaten by his superior. Of course, the prophecy is false: each of Coyote's overbrained Rube Goldberg schemes inevitably blows up in his face. Charred one last time by his own intellectual dynamite, the shattered coyote relinquishes the title of genius and confesses that his name is Mud as he topples eponymously into it. From this cartoon perspective—a perspective that intellectuals who aspire to live in the present are in no position to look down on—the devaluation of genius is striking. The lightning Goethe saw flashing from Beethoven's soul has become the lightbulb turning on above Coyote's head in token of his incipient ridiculousness.

The discourse of the exceptional individual has been delegitimated from another quarter as well: poststructuralist theory. Although its relations to modernism are not easily summarizable, theorists frequently allude to modernist experiment and frequently make claims for the efficacy of writing almost as large as those Pound and Stein made. And at times they deny modernism any contemporary importance: "It is not surprising that the medium of a *post*modern literature should be the critical text wrought into a paraliterary form. . . . Barthes and Derrida are the *writers,* not the critics, that students now read."[10] Gregory Ulmer cites Elizabeth Bruss as affirming that "theory is not only the most interesting of contemporary literary forms, it is the mode best suited for moving out of the impasse reached by the modernist movements in the arts."[11] In contrast to such dismissals of modernism, the comments of Anthony Easthope and John O. Thompson provide a useful reminder that theory and modernist writing are more permanently intertwined: "A conservative response to the great theory wars which have devastated conventional author-based literary criticism . . . has been to claim that such theory has little or no relation to the practice of creative writing in the twentieth century. We would disagree entirely. For it is arguable that these powerful theoretical movements were themselves . . . reorientations made necessary by a previous artistic movement."[12]

But whether theory has superseded modernism or is just starting to catch up with it (positions that need not be mutually exclusive), Foucault's well-known citation of Beckett is still representative of the second-hand existence modernist writing currently undergoes in the world of theory. In his essay "What Is An Author?" Foucault urges us not to concern ourselves with the author's subjectivity but to ask about the "modes of existence of [the] discourse," the patterns of circulation and control, the possibilities of subjective placement, and the functions of subjectivity that the work reveals. He ends by citing Beckett: "Behind all these questions we would hear little more than the murmur of indifference: 'What matter who's speaking?' "[13] The important words here are not those from *Texts for Nothing* but rather Foucault's characterization of them as "the murmur of indif- ference." This makes Beckett underwrite a fungibility of subject that is quite false to the comedy, farce, and tragedy of his own writing. As is the case with all of Beckett's work, *Texts for Nothing* is far from an indifferent murmur: it is a funny, bathetic, and painful paring down of an eccentric subjective voice. The keepers who surround the speaker are possibly torturers. The range of effect flickers rapidly between tragic and comic, but the focus on the speaker's bodily and mental displacements is obsessive. The tone of the following passage is typical: "This evening the session is calm, there are long silences when all fix their eyes on me, that's to make me fly off my hinges, I feel on the brink of shrieks, it's noted."[14] The abyss between a shriek and the passive "it's noted" of recording grammar is the site from which the self-absorbed and self-defying rhythm of Beckett's writing is endlessly proclaimed. Indifference is only one half of the story. The hero, though squashed, is still heroic: "the sky and the earth, I've heard great accounts of them, now that's pure word for word. . . . Between them where the hero stands a great gulf is fixed, while all about they flow together more and more, till they meet, so that he finds himself as it were under glass, and yet with no limit to his movements in all directions, let him understand who can."[15]

In touching on Beckett here, I am also gesturing toward the im- pact of these modernists on subsequent writers. The gesture will remain minimal; the subject is book-length to say the least and the paths of influence have not been simple. But it's safe to say that the social location of genius is no longer even a remotely likely goal for a writer. Shadows of the former mode remain on the landscape, where a partial history of recent poetry could trace the subsequent modification of genius into insistence on singularity, starting with the confessional poets and devolving, in some poetry circles, into an allegiance to "voice." But this mode has become unambitious: it precludes effort toward political solidarity and mystifies investigation into language. While some contemporary poets have had an impact comparable to what the modernists strove for, unlike the modernist genius they have written to make contact with their constituencies. Certainly such politically involved writers as Adrienne Rich, Amiri Baraka, and Allen Ginsberg are writing for social impact; they are not writing as geniuses.[16]

But I don't want to conclude by simply urging that genius be critiqued and put in the museum. The work I have read also embodies immense social and aesthetic ambitions, although—to say it a final time—the split between social and aesthetic was at the heart of what was being contested. The aestheticization of society can be censured as symptomatic of a variety of outcomes ranging from Fascism to Disneyland. But to keep the aesthetic in a purely decorative or neutral place does not feel like much of an answer. Not that there aren't reasons for wanting to do so. It has been tempting to ignore the social problematics of modernist writing and to concentrate on the potential verbal richness of technique.[17] But it we try to boil down, say, Pound's writing to the safe area of technique, the following lines should give us pause:

> not a lot of signs, but the one sign
> etcetera
> plus always Τέχνη
> and from Τέχνη back to σεαυτόν
> Neither by chinks, nor by sophists,
> nor by hindoo immaturities;
> C 85, 560

This embodies Pound's technique more than do the sensible strictures of "A Few Don'ts." The fact that *"Tekne"* is written in Greek script is emblematic of the idiosyncracy of his technique. Consider how compactly incoherent the first two lines are: there is "the one sign" and there is "etcetera": the host of nonsigns, presumably. An insistence on "the one sign" is recognizable as the modernist striving for totalization; but the poem contains as much "etcetera" as anything else. As happens so often, he insists on race; we can focus on his condescension—which is so near to phobic hate—and declare the passage simply bad. But even here the range of reference should remind us that the variety of cultures, content, and languages in *The Cantos* makes Pound one of the most multicultural poets. If this seems too counter-intuitive a statement, considering his deeply entrenched racism, at least we could say that his work, in spite of Pound himself, opened up possibilities for a thoroughly multicultural poetry. The double-edged quality of Pound's work holds true, less dramatically, for Joyce, Stein, and Zukofsky as well. Technique and career are not casually separable.

Bruss wrote of a modernist "impasse"; Easthope and Thompson mentioned problems with "conventional author-based literary criticism" as an accepted fact. But writing, poetry especially, will remain extremely "author-based" until it is more integrated into society, and the impasses poets face are not automatically translatable into opportunities for theoretical survey.

There are great gulfs in the contemporary intellectual landscape with the contesting viewpoints of critics, theorists, and poets constituting a kind of paper/rock/scissors game: poet = rock (autonomy or solipsism); critic = scissors (discrimination); theorist = paper (blanket discourse). Victory is claimable from each angle: rock breaks scissors (poet beats critic—explication never does justice to the original); scissors cuts paper (critic finds flaws in theoretical writing); paper covers rock (theory subsumes any specific writing).

These professional triumphs of framing are also symptoms of a larger social defeat, as each sphere remains separate and not all that relevant to those outside it. While none of the particulars of the work fit the present, the writing of Pound, Joyce, Stein, and Zukofsky still provides provocative models of a more totalized yet highly individual writing. They will remain most useful if considered with an attitude that is neither dismissive nor monumentalizing. What is at stake is a condition in which reading and writing, now so professionally separated, can be brought closer together.

Notes

CHAPTER ONE

1. It is easy to overdramatize words like "illegibility" and "unreadability." Here, I am simply referring to the fact that it is not easy for many readers to make a lot of sense out of a page of, for instance, the *Pisan Cantos.* In *Paperspace: Style as Ideology in Joyce's "Ulysses"* (Lincoln: University of Nebraska Press, 1988) Patrick McGee makes a telling case against more absolute uses of the concept: "Calling a book unreadable, after all, is a reading of it; and I would go a step further to argue that it is the most hegemonic reading practicable on a text. The reading that excludes all readings withdraws from the political and social space in which textuality is realized in practice. It retreats into the idealism or fetishism of the text" (6).

2. Quoted in J. W. N. Sullivan, *Beethoven: His Spiritual Development* (New York: Knopf, 1958), 8.

3. Charles Altieri, *Painterly Abstraction in Modernist American Poetry* (Cambridge: Cambridge University Press, 1989), 104.

4. Michel Foucault, "What Is An Author?" in *Language, Counter-Memory, Practice: Selected Essays and Interviews,* trans. Donald F. Bouchard and Sherry Simon (Ithaca: Cornell University Press, 1977).

5. See Leo Bersani, *The Culture of Redemption* (Cambridge, Mass.: Harvard University Press, 1990), 171–78, for amplification of this point.

6. See Dominic Manganiello, *Joyce's Politics* (London: Routledge & Kegan Paul, 1980), 175–89, for numerous examples.

7. See *JM,* where the September preface is almost breathless is its adulation of Roosevelt: "As I write this 18th September, anno XI, there is NO American daily paper contemporary with the F. D. Roosevelt administration" (8). In the foreword, written two years later, Pound recants.

8. Leo Braudy, in *The Frenzy of Renown: Fame and Its History* (New York: Oxford University Press, 1986), demonstrates that beginning with the Romantic poets, distinctions such as Wordsworth's between the negative "PUBLIC" and the positive "PEOPLE" were common. In Whitman's case the positive term was "democracy" and the negative "the people." See 428, 467.

9. Fredric Jameson, *The Political Unconscious: Narrative as a Socially Symbolic Act* (Ithaca: Cornell University Press, 1981), 106.

10. Theodor Adorno, *Aesthetic Theory,* trans. C. Lenhardt, ed. Gretel Adorno and Rolf Tiedemann (London: Routledge & Kegan Paul, 1984), 7.

11. Theodor Adorno, *Prisms,* trans. Samuel and Sherry Weber (Cambridge, Mass.: MIT Press, 1981), 23.

12. See especially Hugh Kenner, *The Pound Era* (Berkeley: University of California Press, 1971).

13. Certainly, Joyce's mind is venerated by many critics as well. Criticizing this pattern, Leo Bersani writes that "Where *Ulysses* really leads us is to Joyce's mind; it illuminates his cultural consciousness. At the end of the reader's exegetical travails lies the promise of an Assumption, of being raised up and identified with the idea of culture made man." *Culture of Redemption,* 176.

14. For readings of Joyce stressing the linguistic displacement of the subject, see, among many others, Mcgee, *Paperspace,* and Jean-Michel Rabaté, *James Joyce, Authorized Reader* (Baltimore: Johns Hopkins University Press, 1991); for readings stressing the Symbolic and the Imaginary, see Alan Durant, *Ezra Pound: Identity in Crisis* (Totowa, N.J.: Barnes & Noble, 1981), and Jean-Michel Rabaté, *Language, Sexuality, and Ideology in Ezra Pound's "Cantos"* (Albany: State University of New York Press, 1986); for readings of antipatriarchalism in Stein, see Marianne DeKoven, *A Different Language: Gertrude Stein's Experimental Writing* (Madison: University of Wisconsin Press, 1983), and Lisa Ruddick, *Reading Gertrude Stein: Body, Text, Gnosis* (Ithaca, N.Y.: Cornell University Press, 1990).

15. "Poetry is the image of man and nature. . . . The Poet writes under one restriction only, namely, that of the necessity of giving immediate pleasure to a human Being possessed of that information which may be expected from him, not as a lawyer, a physician, a mariner, an astronomer, or a natural philosopher, but as a Man." William Wordsworth, preface to *Lyrical Ballads,* in *William Wordsworth,* ed. Stephen Gill, The Oxford Authors (London: Oxford University Press), 605.

16. Peter Bürger, *Theory of the Avant-Garde,* trans. Michael Shaw (Minneapolis: University of Minnesota Press, 1984).

17. Walter Benjamin, "Theses on the Philosophy of History," in *Illuminations,* ed. Hannah Arendt, trans. Harry Zohn (New York: Schocken, 1969), 256.

18. Zukofsky makes the claim of a final organic frame around all his writing. In Chapter 5 I will discuss the strains involved. Here, I am simply pointing to the obvious superficial difference between the overdetermined rationales behind Joyce's styles and the fact of Zukofsky counting eight words per line in *"A"*-18 or writing *"A"*-20 as a "tone row" using the titles of his son Paul's musical compositions.

19. "Gertrude Stein concluded that negroes were not suffering from persecution, they were suffering from nothingness. She always contends that the african is not primitive, he has a very ancient but a very narrow culture and there it remains. Consequently nothing does or can happen" (*SW,* 224).

20. Perry Anderson, "Modernity and Revolution," in *Marxism and the Interpretation of Culture,* ed. Cary Nelson and Lawrence Grossberg (Urbana: University of Illinois Press, 1988), 332.

21. See Samuel Taylor Coleridge, *On the Constitution of Church and State,* ed. John Barrell (London: J. M. Dent & Sons, 1972).

22. Charles Olson, *The Maximus Poems,* ed. George Butterick (Berkeley: University of California Press, 1983), 75.

23. See James R. Mellow, *Charmed Circle* (New York: Praeger, 1974), 291.

24. See Frank Budgen, *James Joyce and the Making of "Ulysses"* (Bloomington: Indiana University Press, 1960), 67–68.

25. Eliot, in "Ulysses, Order and Myth," *The Dial,* November 1923, spoke of Joyce as a scientist manipulating mythic parallels. Pound, in his first review, "Ulysses," pegged Joyce as a satirist in the tradition of Rabelais and Flaubert. Later, in *Guide to Kulchur,* this perception had intensified and simplified: "The sticky, molasses-covered filth of current print, all the fuggs, all the foetors, the whole boil of the European mind, had been lanced" (96). The fact about *Ulysses* that seems most salient today, its technique, is only mentioned by Pound in his earlier review as secondary: "And on the home stretch, when our present author is feeling more or less relieved that the weight of the book is off his shoulders, we find if not gracile accomplishments, at any rate such acrobatics, such sheer whoops and hoop-las and trapeze turns of technique that it would seem rash to dogmatize concerning his limitations" (*LE*, 405).

26. Franco Moretti, "The Spell of Indecision," in Nelson and Grossberg, eds., *Marxism,* 344.

27. "History . . . is a nightmare from which I am trying to awake" (2:377); "Count me out, he managed to remark, meaning work" (16:1148); "Ireland must be important because it belongs to me" (16:1164–65).

28. The question primarily seems directed toward Joyce ("How could Joyce write again . . ."), but the wording accommodates a generalized reference ("How could anyone write again . . ."). Such competitiveness was not foreign to these modernists. See Pound's congratulations to Eliot on *The Waste Land:* "Complimenti, you bitch" (*L,* 169).

29. In *Time and Western Man* (London: Chatto and Windus, 1927), Wyndham Lewis accuses Stein of "counterfeit," childishness, and "deadness" (69–81). Her "prose-song," he writes, is "a cold, black suet-pudding . . . of fabulously reptilian length" (77). Also see *The Childermass* (London: John Calder, 1965) for a particularly phobic reaction to what Lewis perceives as her infantile prose:

> Satters day-dreams and stares and steins while he clings to his new-found instrument [his companion, Pullman] for all he's worth.
> Pulley has been most terribly helpful and kind there's no excusing himself Pulley has been most terribly helpful and kind—most terribly helpful and he's been kind. He's been most terribly kind and helpful, there are two things, he's been most kind he's been terribly helpful, he's kind he can't help being—he's terribly.

(44)

The subsequent infantilization of Satters is described with remarkably vivid hatred. For a kinder imitation of Stein (and a kind one of Pound), see Joyce's letter to Harriet Weaver, 13 June 1925, in *LJ,* 228.

30. See Peter Quartermain, " 'Not at All Surprised by Science': Louis Zukofsky's *First Half of "A"-9,"* in *Louis Zukofsky: Man and Poet,* ed. Carroll F. Terrell (Orono, Me.: National Poetry Foundation, 1979), 203–26.

31. Louis Zukofsky, ed., *An "Objectivists" Anthology* (New York: To Publishers, 1931), 22.

32. Zukofsky had, in a vague way, planned the twenty-four movements of the poem from the beginning. See Barry Ahearn, *Zukofsky's "A"* (Berkeley: University of California Press, 1983), 38–39. And *The First Half of "A"-9* makes clear by its title that a second half was going to be written. Nevertheless, Zukofsky could not have anticipicated the fissure the Second World War would make in his writing.

33. Georg Lukács, *History and Class Consciousness,* trans. Rodney Livingstone (Cambridge, Mass.: MIT Press, 1971), 120.

CHAPTER TWO

1. Donald Hall, *Remembering Poets: Reminiscences and Opinions* (New York: Harper & Row, 1978), 121.

2. A similar passage occurs in *GK,* 128–29.

3. Adolf Hitler, *Mein Kampf,* trans. Ralph Manheim (New York: Houghton Mifflin, 1943), 57.

4. Robert Casillo has shown how thoroughly congruent Fascist thought was to Pound's language: "Far from being adventitious or extraneous to Pound's texts, anti-Semitism is a characteristic manifestation of Pound's thought and language, a virtually inescapable response to the most pressing intellectual and poetic difficulties." Robert Casillo, *The Genealogy of Demons: Anti-Semitism, Fascism, and the Myths of Ezra Pound* (Evanston, Ill.: Northwestern University Press, 1988), 16. Casillo's sentence is quoted in Leon Surette's review in *Paideuma* 19 (1990): 233–39.

5. See Leon Surette, *A Light from Eleusis: A Study of Ezra Pound's "Cantos"* (Oxford: Clarendon, 1979), for thorough discussion of Pound's devotion to the Eleusian mysteries.

6. Pound is approvingly jocular in referring to a charge of rape against Malatesta, evoking it and brushing it off in a single line: "And there was the row about that German-Burgundian female" (*C* 9, 36). In the lines that end Canto 10 on a rhetorical high point, Malatesta's military success is premised on his antihomosexual prowess:

> All I want you to do is to follow the orders,
> They've got a bigger army,
>   but there are more men in this camp.
> *C 10, 47*

7. Such reminiscing does not occur only after Pisa. In *Guide to Kulchur* Pound tells some small anecdotes from his past and then adds, italicizing for emphasis: "*I am not in these slight memories, merely "pickin' daisies". A man does not know his own ADDRESS (in time) until he knows where his time and milieu stand in relation to other times and conditions*" (*GK,* 83).

8. Randall Jarrell, excerpt from "Five Poets," quoted in *Ezra Pound: The Critical Heritage,* ed. Eric Homberger (London: Routledge & Kegan Paul, 1972), 440–41.

9. My attention was called to this passage by Peter Nicholls's discussion in *Ezra Pound: Politics, Economics and Writing: A Study of the "Cantos"* (Atlantic Highlands, N.J.: Humanties Press, 1984), 161–201.

10. Carroll F. Terrell affirms this: "To me, *The Cantos* is a great religious poem." *A Companion to the Cantos of Ezra Pound* (Berkeley: University of California Press, 1980), viii.

11. See Tim Redman, *Ezra Pound and Italian Fascism* (Cambridge: Cambridge University Press, 1991), 233–74, for a detailed account of Pound's involvements with the Salò Republic.

12. Guy Davenport, *The Geography of the Imagination* (San Francisco: North Point Press, 1981), 173.

13. Ibid., 174, 172. In his recent memoir, James Laughlin is similar in his cut-and-dried dismissal of the problem: "Ezra was paranoid and . . . anti-Semitism is a recognized element in paranoia. Pound could not control himself." *Pound as Wuz: Essays and Lectures on Ezra Pound* (Saint Paul: Greywolf Press, 1987), 15. On the other hand, Wendy Stallard Flory, *The American Ezra Pound* (New Haven: Yale University Press, 1989), devotes a book to the problem. She situates Pound's passions in the tradition of the American jeremiad (see 5–12), but for the most part the frame of her reading is ultimately Pound's psyche: "His conscious intentions [in making the radio speeches] were frequently overridden by his unconscious motives, which were of such a nature as to guarantee that the speeches would have no destructive effect on others" (140).

14. My perception of Pound's politics is indebted to the work of a number of critics in addition to the work of Casillo, Flory, Nicholls, and Redman, already cited: Massimo Bacigalupo, *The Forméd Trace: The Later Poetry of Ezra Pound* (New York: Columbia University Press, 1980); Michael André Bernstein, *The Tale of the Tribe: Ezra Pound and the Modern Verse Epic* (Princeton: Princeton University Press, 1980); William Chace, *The Political Identities of Ezra Pound and T. S. Eliot* (Stanford: Stanford University Press, 1973); Cairns Craig, *Yeats, Eliot, Pound, and the Politics of Poetry* (Pittsburgh: University of Pittsburgh Press, 1982); Maud Ellmann, *The Poetics of Impersonality: T. S. Eliot and Ezra Pound* (Cambridge, Mass.: Harvard University Press, 1987); Paul Smith, *Pound Revised* (London: Croom Helm, 1983); John Lauber, "Pound's Cantos: A Fascist Epic," *Journal of American Studies* 12 (April 1978); Andrew Parker, "Ezra Pound and the 'Economy' of Anti-Semitism," *boundary 2* 11 (1983); and Richard Sieburth, "In Pound We Trust: The Economy of Poetry / The Poetry of Economics," *Critical Inquiry* 14, no. 1 (1987).

15. Arguably anti-Semitic lines occur even as late as Canto 113: "As to sin, they invented it—eh? / to implement domination / eh? largely" (803).

16. For mention of Quisling, see *RS,* 402–5; Laval and Petain are encoded in the following line:

L.   P.   gli onesti [the honest ones].

C 76, 474

17. Pound refers to this in his prose: "I have heard faith once over the radio, and it was concentrated in the two syllables *Schicksal*, uttered in a context that might have been taken from the testament of Kang Hi" (*SP*, 66).

18. See Casillo, *Genealogy of Demons*, 339, for a critique of an attempt to defend Pound from charges of anti-Semitism on statistical grounds. Hugh Kenner writes, "If Mussolini was not altogether the seamless factive intelligence Pound imagined him to be, it was necessary, we may say, for Pound to invent him." *The Poetry of Ezra Pound* (Lincoln: University of Nebraska Press, 1985), 301.

19. In Terrell, *Companion to the Cantos*, 551.

20. Leon Surette, *Light from Eleusis*, 223. See also 219–22.

21. Leon Surette, "Ezra Pound's Fascism: Aberration or Essence? The Correspondence with William Bird," in *Queen's Quarterly* 96, no. 3 (1989): 602–3, 620. Also see Surette's "Pound, Postmodernism, and Fascism," in *University of Toronto Quarterly* 59, no. 2 (1989–90).

22. Surette, "Ezra Pound's Fascism," 609.

23. Charles Olson, *Charles Olson & Ezra Pound: An Encounter at St Elizabeths*, ed. Catherine Seelye (New York: Grossman, 1975), 53.

24. Charles Olson, *The Maximus Poems*, ed. George Butterick (Berkeley: University of California Press, 1983), 32.

25. See especially Alan Durant, *Ezra Pound: Identity in Crisis* (Totowa, N.J.: Barnes & Noble, 1981).

26. Jean-Michel Rabaté, *Language, Sexuality, and Ideology in Ezra Pound's "Cantos"* (Albany: State University of New York Press, 1986), 32.

27. While Pound is referring to Talleyrand's memoirs, the language is his own. See Terrell, *Companion to the Cantos*, 666.

28. See Sieburth, "In Pound We Trust," 168–69, for discussion of this passage in terms of digestion and incorporation.

29. Quoted in Noel Stock, *Reading the "Cantos": A Study of Meaning in Ezra Pound* (New York: Pantheon, 1966), 75–76.

30. See Casillo, *Genealogy of Demons*, for thorough documentation of Pound's notion of the Jewish parameters of language; also Sieburth, "In Pound We Trust."

31. The observation of Roland Barthes on language in authoritarian regimes, quoted in Nicholls, *Ezra Pound*, is very much to the point: "In the Stalinist world, in which *definition*, that is to say the separation between Good and Evil, becomes the sole content of all language, there are no more words without values attached to them . . . there is no more lapse of time between naming and judging, and the closed character of language is perfected" (102).

32. Kenner, *The Poetry of Ezra Pound*, 13.

33. Quoted in Redman, *Ezra Pound and Italian Fascism*, 265.

34. Kenner's summation of Major Douglas's theorem is "Total cost exceeds total purchasing power." *The Pound Era*, 307; see 301–17 for a discussion of Douglas.

35. See Bernstein, *Tale of the Tribe,* 40.

36. Ian Bell sees the Poundian ideogram as "structured not along the lines of restrictive grammar but from a series of pictures that were communally accessible." *Critic as Scientist: The Modernist Poetics of Ezra Pound* (London: Methuen, 1981), 103.

37. One can read Pound's anxieties over authorship in such metaphors, which also appear in the use of the word "Drafts" in the titles of installments of *The Cantos.* See Sieburth, "In Pound We Trust."

38. Antonio Gramsci, *Selections from the Prison Notebooks,* ed. and trans. Quintin Hoare and Geoffrey Nowell Smith (New York: International Publishers, 1971), 23.

39. For example, after quoting a sentence of the original, Pound writes, "This is followed, v. 6, by a very cheap and shoddy suggestion. Arry is here a tin-horn professor. A *Manchester Guardian* product" (*GK,* 316). Perhaps the suggestion is Aristotle's advice that "We ought, then, to feel towards pleasure as the elders of the people felt towards Helen . . . for if we dismiss pleasure thus we are less likely to go astray." *The Basic Works of Aristotle,* ed. Richard McKeon, trans. W. D. Ross (New York: Random House, 1941), 963–64. Compare Pound's use of the same Homeric moment in Canto 2.

40. Kathryne V. Lindberg, in *Reading Pound Reading: Modernism after Nietzsche* (New York: Oxford University Press, 1987), sees Pound's reading procedures as much more deliberately disruptive and anticanonical than I do here.

41. Quoted in E. Fuller Torrey, *The Roots of Treason: Ezra Pound and the Secret of St. Elizabeths* (San Diego: Harcourt Brace Jovanovich, 1984), 201.

42. See Pierre Bourdieu, "Flaubert's Point of View," *Critical Inquiry* 14 (Spring 1988): 539–62.

43. Peter Makin, *Pound's "Cantos"* (London: George Allen & Unwin, 1985), 210; Kenner, *The Poetry of Ezra Pound,* 300.

44. See the section "MONEY," in "A Visiting Card," where Pound writes that money "is a certificate of work done within a system, estimated, or 'consecrated', by the state" (*SP,* 311).

45. See Casillo, *Genealogy of Demons,* 329, for a discussion of this.

46. See Maud Ellmann, *The Poetics of Impersonality,* 170–77.

47. Laughlin, *Pound as Wuz,* 7.

48. *Ezra Pound, The Spirit of Romance* (New York: New Directions, n.d.), 7.

49. The best-known example of this is "With usura the line grows thick." See Michael André Bernstein, "Image, Word, and Sign: The Visual Arts as Evidence in Ezra Pound's *Cantos,*" *Critical Inquiry* 12 (Winter 1986): 347–64.

50. Mussolini's "oratory" is also "worth study" (*JM,* 65).

51. At its extreme, the heroic word is purely magical: "There is no need for the President's taking ACTION, IF he will show . . . that muddled thought is NOT the straight road. . . . It doesn't require appointments, jobs, commissions to untangle these clots and clogs. He can commit this en[o]rmous ACT of enlightenment over the radio in three minutes." Quoted in Flory, *The American Ezra Pound,* 87.

52. See Ernest Fenellosa, *The Chinese Written Character as a Medium for Poetry*, ed. Ezra Pound (San Francisco: City Lights Books, 1983), 41. The phrase is a touchstone for Allen Ginsberg, who quotes it in his "Wichita Vortex Sutra" in *Planet News* (San Francisco: City Lights Books, 1968), 119.

53. According to Kenner and Davenport, Pound recited either this dialect passage or the one from Canto 35 to Mussolini, prompting the response of "divertente." See Hugh Kenner, *The Pound Era* (Berkeley: University of California Press, 1971), 540, and Guy Davenport, *Cities on Hills: A Study of I–XXX of Ezra Pound's "Cantos"* (Ann Arbor: UMI Research Press, 1983), 69. It seems appropriate that Pound would display the deformed matter of history to the genius who was to reorder and purify it.

54. Ezra Pound, *Confucius* (New York: New Directions, 1951), 20. The lance could also be wielded by a genius:

> I have written more than once that Gaudier-Brzeska was the most complete case of Genius I have ever encountered. Put it creative genius, fully equipped, but Gaudier was a danger to everyone in the room. You could have slept or dreamt for twenty minutes while Gaudier was hammering the butt end of a chisel, but you had not the excitement of mental peril which accompanied Francis Picabia. There was never a rubber button on the end of his foil. It wasn't a foil, it was a razor sharp at the point and had thereby the greater pedagogical value.
>
> *SP*, 459

55. "The sum of human wisdom is not contained in any one language, and no single language is CAPABLE of expressing all forms and degrees of human comprehension"; "the maximum of **phanopoeia** . . . is probably reached by the Chinese . . . the maximum of **melopoeia** is reached in Greek, with certain developments in Provençal" (*ABC*, 34, 42). "Narrative not the same as lyric; different techniques for song and story. 'Would, could,' etcetera: Abbreviations save *eye* effort. Also show speed in mind of original character supposed to be uttering" (*L*, 322).

56. A similar progress toward the visual can be seen in Olson's *Maximus Poems*.

57. Jacques Lacan, *Ecrits: A Selection*, trans. Alan Sheridan (New York: Norton, 1977), 171–73.

58. For Pound even his own name was phallic: "the phonetic translation of my name into the Japanese tongue is so indecorous that I am seriously advised not to use it, lest it do me harm back in Nippon. (Rendered back *ad verbum* into our maternal speech it gives for its meaning, 'This picture of a phallus costs ten yen' " [*LE*, 259].) The adjective "maternal," rare for Pound, is certainly "worth study" in this context.

59. Lacan, *Ecrits*, 198.

60. Ezra Pound, *Impact: Essays on Ignorance and the Decline of American Civilization*, ed. Noel Stock (Chicago: Henry Regnery, 1960), 144.

61. Olson, *Charles Olson and Ezra Pound*, 55.

62. See Casillo, *Genealogy of Demons*, 38–49, for more discussion.

63. Cf. "His true Penelope was Flaubert" in "Mauberley" (*P*, 187).

64. See Humphrey Carpenter, *A Serious Character: The Life of Ezra Pound* (Boston: Houghton Mifflin, 1988), 494.

65. The following passage from *JM* (quoted in Casillo, *Genealogy of Demons*, 139), also indicates how Pound's idealization of the people could flip over into disgust: "It is possible the Capo del Governo wants to go slow enough so as not to see in his old age, an Italy full of fat peasants gone rotten and a bourgeoisie stinking over the peninsula as Flaubert saw them stinking through Paris."

66. See Alice Yaeger Kaplan, *Reproductions of Banality* (Minneapolis: University of Minnesota Press, 1986), 25–35, for a discussion of Fascism as a "polarity machine."

67. There are many similar moments in *The Cantos.* Throughout, there is the close equivalence of the genius and the Jew, one fecundating the world, the other infecting it. The Bank of England creates its spurious riches out of nothing; Dionysus in Canto 2 also creates his divine beasts out of nothing. The image of poet gazing upon the body of his beloved is inverted in Canto 35, poorly pronounced, sloppily expressed, recorded in verse whose somnolent line breaks hardly distinguish it from prose:

> Mr Elias said to me:
> "How do you get inspiration?
> "Now my friend Hall Caine told me he came on a case
> "a very sad case of a girl in the East End of London
> "and it gave him an i n s p i r a t i o n . The only
> "way I get inspiration is occasionally from a girl, I
> "mean sometimes sitting in a restaurant and
> looking at a pretty girl I
> "get an i-de-a, I-mean-a-biz-nis i-de-a?"
>
> C 35, 173–74

68. Gramsci, *Selections*, 138–39.

69. "When a code ceases to be regarded as an approximate expression of principles, or of a principle, and is exalted to the rank of something holy in itself, perversion ineluctably sets in. . . . Code-worship appertains properly to tribes arrested at nomad level"—i.e., to Jews (*GK*, 164).

70. Quoted in Nicholls, *Ezra Pound*, 95.

71. See Homberger, ed., *Ezra Pound*, 14–22.

72. Ronald Bush, in *The Genesis of Ezra Pound's "Cantos"* (Princeton: Princeton University Press, 1976), demonstrates that Pound's hesitancy with regard to any epic inheritance was much stronger in the Ur-*Cantos*.

73. See Bernstein, *Tale of the Tribe*, and Bush, *Genesis*, 123–24.

74. Pound wrote that the Hell Cantos were "specifically LONDON, the state of the English mind in 1919 and 1920" (*L*, 239).

75. This narrative of submission forms the keystone of Matthew Arnold's cultural arch. The touchstone of touchstones is "In His will is our peace." See Matthew Arnold, *Selected Prose*, ed. P. J. Keating (New York: Penguin, 1982), 348. Arnold's touchstones are precursors of Pound's ideogram, but it is precisely the narrative of submission that differentiates the two patterns:

in the will of the genius is peace for the genius and bafflement for the "man with the abacus."

76. For a discussion of the differences between Pound's Homeric and Dantean hells, see Jerome McGann, "The *Cantos* of Ezra Pound, the Truth in Contradiction," in *Critical Inquiry* 15 (Autumn 1988): 1–25.

77. See Terrell, *Companion to the Cantos*, for identifications.

78. See Kenner, *The Pound Era*, 465.

79. Bourdieu, "Flaubert's Point of View," 555.

80. Paul Smith in *Pound Revised* calls the phallic quality of the third image listed here "almost comic" (43).

81. See Marjorie Perloff's essay, "The Contemporary of Our Grandchildren" in *Poetic Artifice* (Evanston, Ill.: Northwestern University Press, 1990), 119–44, for discussion of just how wide Pound's influence has been.

CHAPTER THREE

1. Franco Moretti's "The Spell of Indecision," in *Marxism and the Interpretation of Culture*, ed. Cary Nelson and Lawrence Grossberg (Urbana: University of Illinois Press, 1988), which expresses reservations about *Ulysses*, or Leo Bersani's "Against Ulysses," in *The Culture of Redemption* (Cambridge, Mass.: Harvard University Press, 1990), are important exceptions. But Bersani's chapter, an actual attack, acknowledges the book's cultural prestige; it ends "to stop working on *Ulysses* is like a fall from grace" (178).

2. For reference to *The Lamplighter*, see Don Gifford with Robert J. Seidman, Ulysses *Annotated: Notes for James Joyce's "Ulysses,"* 2d ed. (Berkeley: University of California Press, 1988), 384.

3. Consider the effect when any of the three tries to use dialect. Pound uses idiosyncratic versions of Black and crackerbarrel dialect throughout his letters and at times in *The Cantos*, where they are tolerable at best. In "*A*," Zukofsky's uses stick out glaringly:

> He's but
> A coof for a' that: he'll break his whip that guiltlesse
> Smals must die—I spec it will be all 'fiscated.
> De massa run, ha! ha! De darkey stay, ho! ho!
> So distribution should undo excess—(chaseth),
> Shall brothers be, be a' that, Child, lolai, lullow.
>
> *A 8, 50*

The effect of instant anomaly is somewhat similar (though much milder) in *Ida* when Stein calls Ida a "suicide blonde," has a general say "hell . . . yes I know Ida" (40), and has a suitor who is giving Ida swimming lessons exclaim as she kicks him, "Jesus Christ my balls" (113). What looks like dialect in "Melanctha" and *Brewsie and Willie* is closer in syntax if not orthography to Stein's own narrative style than to the speech of the fictional parties in question. By contrast, Joyce's use of dialect is subtle and highly specific.

4. Samuel Beckett, "Dante . . . Bruno. Vico . . Joyce" in *Our Exagmination Round His Factification of Work in Progress* (New York: New Directions, 1962),

13. Beckett goes on to compare conventional reading habits to dogs salivating over their food.

5. "Introduction," unsigned, in *Coping with Joyce: Essays from the Copenhagen Symposium*, ed. Morris Beja and Shari Benstock (Columbus: Ohio State University Press, 1989), xii.

6. Julia Kristeva, *Desire in Language: A Semiotic Approach to Literature and Art*, ed. Leon S. Roudiez, trans. Thomas Gora, Alice Jardine, and Leon S. Roudiez (New York: Columbia University Press, 1980), 151.

7. Jacques Derrida, "Two Words for Joyce," in *Post-Structuralist Joyce*, ed. Derek Attridge and Daniel Ferrer (Cambridge: Cambridge University Press, 1984), 147. Immediately prior to the sentences quoted, Derrida seems to be contradicting the assertion my quotation attributes to him. He writes that not only Joyce's potential readers but Joyce himself suffered under "the Babelian act of war" that his writing represents, and that "there can be no simple confusion between him and a sadistic demiurge, setting up a hypermnesiac machine, there in advance." But this denial of simple identity tends to evaporate during the remainder of the paragraph, which expatiates on the qualities of this malign, sublime, impossible person-mechanism, ending with the assertion that any supercomputer capable of dealing with *Finnegans Wake* "would only be the double or the simulation of the event 'Joyce', the name of Joyce, the signed work, the Joyce software today, joyceware" (148).

8. Hélène Cixous, "Joyce: The (r)use of writing," in Attridge and Ferrer, eds., *Post-Structuralist Joyce*, 16–17.

9. "The artist, like the God of the creation, remains within or behind or beyond or above his handiwork, invisible, refined out of existence, indifferent, paring his fingernails" (*PA*, 215). Jean-Michel Rabaté's recent study of Joyce begins, "More than any writer of this century, Joyce has forced criticism to acknowledge its theological nature." *James Joyce, Authorized Reader* (Baltimore: Johns Hopkins University Press, 1991), 1.

10. Reproduced in Sylvia Beach, *Shakespeare and Company* (New York: Harcourt, Brace, 1959), 117.

11. Hugh Kenner, *Ulysses* (London: George Allen & Unwin, 1980), 76. Cf. "Some mind, it is clear, keeps track of the details of this printed cosmos, and lets escape from its scrutiny the fall of no sparrow" (64).

12. Clive Hart, "Wandering Rocks," in *James Joyce's "Ulysses,"* ed. Clive Hart and David Hayman (Berkeley: University of California Press, 1974), 194.

13. Beach, *Shakespeare and Company*, 35–36.

14. Pound's disgust with *Work in Progress* is well known. He continually associated it with drunkenness, introspection, excrement, and feminine lability: "this flow of conSquishousness Girtie/Jimmee stuff has about FLOWED long enuff." Quoted in *Pound/Joyce: The Letters of Ezra Pound to James Joyce*, ed. Forrest Read (New York: New Directions, 1970), 256. Less obvious, I think, is his nostalgia for the narrative of *Ulysses*. He wanted Joyce to write a sequel: "It would be jolly to see ole Poldy Bloom wakin up in the

morning with his frowsy head beatin' the foot board. It would be jolly to see Cissy Caffrey gettin out a clean set of diapers for that dirthy young spalpeen young whatshisname. It would be jolly to hear the Croppy boy bein' orated over with the voice of all the sonzofbitches that ever made speeches in the lowsy louses of Parliament, and Poldy's new weepin meditations about the new measures in Ireland and the sacredness of the censorship and the rights of free fahrtin in public" (ibid., 240).

15. See David Lloyd, *Anomalous States: Irish Writing and the Post-Colonial Moment* (Durham, N.C.: Duke University Press, 1993), 88–115, for complication of the notion of heteroglossia. Lloyd sees Joyce's language as hybrid, not merely dialogic.

16. Hugh Kenner, *Joyce's Voices* (Berkeley: University of California Press, 1978), 37.

17. *Corrections of Misprints in "Finnegans Wake" by James Joyce as Prepared by the Author after Publication of the First Edition* (New York: Viking, 1945).

18. Karen Lawrence, *The Odyssey of Style in "Ulysses"* (Princeton: Princeton University Press, 1981), 125.

19. Patrick Parrinder, "From Telemachus to Penelope: Episodes Anonymous?" in *Assessing the 1984 "Ulysses,"* ed. C. George Sandulescu and Clive Hart (Totowa, N.J.: Barnes & Noble, 1986), 140.

20. Bersani, *Culture of Redemption,* 155.

21. See Derrida, "Two Words for Joyce," 148.

22. T. S. Eliot, "Ulysses, Order, and Myth," in *James Joyce: Two Decades of Criticism,* ed. Sean Givens (New York: Vanguard Press, 1948), 201–2.

23. Hart, "Wandering Rocks," 215. Subsequent references in the text.

24. See Roland Barthes. "The Reality Effect," in *The Rustle of Language,* trans. Richard Howard (Berkeley: University of California Press, 1989). 141–48.

25. Gifford, *Annotated,* 272.

26. See Frank Budgen, *James Joyce and the Making of "Ulysses"* (Bloomington: Indiana University Press, 1960), 67–68.

27. Harold Bloom, introduction to *James Joyce's "Ulysses,"* ed. Harold Bloom (New York: Chelsea House, 1987), 1.

28. David Hayman, *"Ulysses": The Mechanics of Meaning* (Madison: University of Wisconsin Press, 1982), 21.

29. A. Walton Litz, *The Art of James Joyce: Method and Design in "Ulysses" and "Finnegans Wake"* (London: Oxford University Press, 1961), 35.

30. Ibid., 35–36.

31. Stanley Sultan, *The Argument of "Ulysses"* (Middletown, Conn.: Wesleyan University Press, 1987), 18.

32. See Lawrence, *Odyssey of Style* (136–37) for a discussion of Sultan's thesis.

33. Michael Grodin, *"Ulysses" in Progress* (Princeton: Princeton University Press, 1977), 159–60.

34. See Sandulescu and Hart in *Assessing the 1984 "Ulysses"* for convincing rebuttal of Gabler's claims to have produced the definitive edition. In

"A Crux in the New Edition," 28–34, Richard Ellmann discusses the phrase in question, reversing his earlier approval in the preface to the Gabler edition, xii.

35. See David Hayman, "The Empirical Molly," in *Approaches to "Ulysses": Ten Essays*, ed. Thomas F. Staley and Bernard Benstock (Pittsburgh: University of Pittsburgh Press, 1970), 103–35, for refutation of the (now fading) view of Molly as whore.

36. David Hayman, in "Stephen On the Rocks," *James Joyce Quarterly* 15 (1977): 5–18, argues that Stephen masturbates at the end of "Proteus." Whether Hayman is right or wrong, his article seems a confirmation of the opacity of the narrative in *Ulysses*, even early on. Either a highly respected Joyce scholar is "guilty" of remarkable projection or Joyce has created a character in whom orgasm causes no interruption of mental monolog.

37. One could argue that both Bloom's memories of love making on Howth (9.904–16) and Molly's at the end of the book indicate a mutual mental and physical consummation, at least for those moments years before. She does mete out occasional high praise: "I saw he understood or felt what a woman is," though the next words undercut any pure communion: "and I knew I could always get round him" (18.1578–80). But a marriage of true minds between them is hard to substantiate in the face of the constant blending, in Molly's mind, of Bloom with other men. Take these lines from near the close, referring first possibly to Boylan, then to Mulvey and then to Bloom: "or shall I wear a red yes and how he kissed me under the Moorish wall and I thought well as well him as another" (18.1603–5).

38. Richard Ellmann, preface, in the Gabler edition of *Ulysses*, xiii. Hugh Kenner, on the other hand, calls Bloom's statement "perhaps his most fatuous remark of the day"; it "seems like a pearl of wisdom" only in contrast with the primary narrator's "endless talk." *Joyce's Voices*, 34.

39. Colin MacCabe, *James Joyce and the Revolution of the Word* (New York: Barnes & Noble, 1979); Patrick McGee, *Paperspace: Style as Ideology in Joyce's "Ulysses"* (Lincoln: University of Nebraska Press, 1988); Frances L. Restuccia, *Joyce and the Law of the Father* (New Haven: Yale University Press, 1989); Vicky Mahaffey, *Reauthorizing Joyce* (Cambridge: Cambridge University Press, 1988); Jean-Michel Rabaté, *James Joyce*.

40. MacCabe, *James Joyce*, 14; McGee, *Paperspace*, 194.

41. She also sees an overall tendency for the first and second halves of *Ulysses* to refer to the Old and New Testaments respectively. See Restuccia, *Joyce*, 20–72.

42. Ibid., 40, 70. Bloom may be a type of Moses and of Elijah (who are types of Christ), but when a rocket in "Circe" signifies the "second coming of Elijah" (15.2175–76) Joyce is making a dirty joke: the rocket in "Nausicaa" signified Bloom-Elijah's first coming.

43. *Oakland Tribune*, May 12, 1990, C7.

44. Bloom at 8.907, Molly at 18.1574.

45. Thunder is interpreted in this way by Stephen (though not Bloom) in "Oxen of the Sun" and by Molly in "Penelope."

46. Budgen, *Joyce and the Making of "Ulysses,"* 19–20.

47. Ibid., 215.

48. That to reassert these norms means the slaughter of hundreds is a primary contradiction. See Max Horkheimer and Theodor Adorno, *Dialectic of Enlightenment,* trans. John Cumming (New York: Continuum, 1986), 43–80.

49. In this, "Circe" backs up MacCabe's claim that *Ulysses* "has no metalanguage." See Rabaté, *James Joyce,* for discussion of the narrative mechanisms of "Circe," and Cheryl Herr, *Joyce's Anatomy of Culture* (Urbana: University of Illinois Press, 1986) for discussion of how music-hall elements endemic to the episode function as cultural critique.

50. See the letters to Budgen on Joyce's search for equivalents for *moly* (*LJ,* 147–49).

51. See Kenner's discussion of Joyce's version of free indirect style, which Kenner labels "The Uncle Charles Principle," *Joyce's Voices,* 15–38.

52. Lawrence, *Odyssey of Style,* 208.

53. Franco Moretti, *Signs Taken for Wonders* (London: Verso, 1988), 205. Moretti's emphasis differs from McGee's and Lawrence's in that he sees Joyce as writing out of a much less powerful position. Joyce, for Moretti, depicts the end of liberal capitalism without being able to imagine any society to put in its place.

54. Mark Shechner speculates that the style stimulated Joyce: "Joyce was playing in this chapter, but the game involved his own erotic propensities, his libidinal clichés . . . the chapter is an act of exorcism that affirms an old commitment even while denying it." *Joyce in Nighttown: A Psychoanalytic Inquiry Into "Ulysses"* (Berkeley: University of California Press, 1974), 161.

55. One of the many examples of "Circe" quoting previous chapters is the following: *"Kitty unpins her hat and sets it down calmly, patting her henna hair. And a prettier, daintier head of winsome curls was never seen on a whore's shoulders"* (15.2586–88). This does not contradict my point that the chapter styles are not portable. "Circe" is not written in Gerty's style—far from it. The extreme incongruity of the second sentence is what provides the shock of humor.

56. Compare the syntax of these two passages: "At four she. Winsomely she on Bloohimwhom smiled. Bloo smi qui go. Ternoon" (11.309–10) and *"Bloom walks on a net, covers his left eye with his left ear, passes through several walls, climbs Nelson's Pillar, hangs from the top ledge by his eyelids, eats twelve dozen oysters (shells included)"* (15.1841–43).

57. Lawrence, *Odyssey of Style,* 207–8.

58. Fredric Jameson, " 'Ulysses' in History," in *James Joyce and Modern Literature,* ed. W. J. McCormack and Alistair Stead (London: Routledge & Kegan Paul, 1982), 140–41. Rabaté makes a similar statement, placing Molly "after the collapse of the book. Joyce thought his novel was finished but not completed after 'Ithaca' and was duty-bound to append Molly's signature at the bottom of his logbook." *James Joyce,* 100.

59. *Dubliners* ends with a moment to which Joyce's "scrupulously mean" style does not apply: "His soul swooned slowly as he heard the snow falling

faintly through the universe and faintly falling, like the descent of their last end, upon all the living and the dead." Such writing, referring to what it cannot register denotatively and contain morally, is unusual in *Dubliners*. The other stories end with ironic resolutions—the coin in Corley's palm, the cry "Daybreak, gentlemen"—but with no change in the characters or in the writing. Paralyzed humans have been displayed by prose which remains uninfected. The *mot juste* is on one side of the equation, on the other, a futile society.

The mildest hint of cuckoldry is enough to change that. Gretta has hardly been "unfaithful"; Michael Furey was a far cry from Blazes Boylan: diffident, adolescent, tubercular, and soon dead. But the thought of Gretta's feelings for another male is enough to send Gabriel (and with him, Joyce's style) beyond controlled rationality into lyricism.

In "A Painful Case," Joyce creates a character who refuses this type of lyricism, and who exemplifies the connection between control of language and male fear of female sexuality. Mr. Duffy is a walking allegory of a naturalist narrative sentence, with his "odd autobiographical habit which led him to compose in his mind from time to time a short sentence about himself containing a subject in the third person and a predicate in the past tense" (*D*, 134–35). He is also a textbook case of gynephobia, starting away in disgust when Mrs. Sinico grabs his hand passionately (*D*, 139). He breaks off relations and reenters solitude in order to pen such apothegms as: "Love between man and man is impossible because there must not be sexual intercourse and friendship between man and woman is impossible because there must be sexual intercourse" (*D*, 140).

The barrenness of Mr. Duffy's fate and the dryness of his prose form a vicious circle; the mysterious passion which Gabriel at least hears of serves as a partial way out of this stasis. The end of "The Dead" can appear coincidental: Bartell D'Arcy just happened to sing the song he did when he did, etcetera. But in *Exiles* the opportunity for Bertha's infidelity is arranged most determinedly; the connection between cuckoldry and aesthetic creation is made very clear by Richard Rowan, an artist less ironized than Gabriel or Stephen and thus more of a stand-in for Joyce. There are intricacies involving love and free will behind Richard's decision to send his wife off with Robert. But Richard's need to write is key to his behavior, as he insists on telling Robert afterward:

Richard:	Do you want to know what I did?
Robert:	No.
Richard:	I came home at once.
Robert:	Did you hear Bertha return?
Richard:	No. I wrote all the night.

E, 109

At the end Richard is sexually wounded but literarily potent.

60. When I say this, I am not referring to his private emotional investments in writing about cuckoldry. It is true, as Restuccia states (*Joyce*, 131), that some of Joyce's letters contain passages that parallel Bloom's maso-

chistic fantasies in "Circe." But "Circe," if read as the expression of Joyce's personal masochism, becomes less interesting than it is in context of *Ulysses.*

61. "Quietly he read, restraining himself, the first column and, yielding but resisting, began the second. Midway, his last resistance yielding, he allowed his bowels to ease themselves quietly as he read. . . . Hope it's not too big bring on piles again. No, just right. . . . Life might be so. It did not move or touch him but it was something quick and neat. Print anything now" (4.506–12).

62. See Gifford, *Annotated,* 404 and Restuccia, *Joyce,* 47.

63. Mulligan, "chewing and laughing," says "He is going to write something in ten years" (10.1089–90).

64. See Gifford, *Annotated,* 254.

65. The assessment is repeated in "Oxen of the Sun" (14.1456–57). Joyce had written just such a review as Mulligan criticizes Stephen for producing. And Yeats had written, concerning Lady Gregory's *Cuchulain of Muirthemne: The Story of the Men of the Red Branch of Ulster,* "I think this book is the best that has come out of Ireland in my time." See Gifford, *Annotated,* 254. One could speculate that the literary paybacks in "Scylla and Charybdis" might have had as much to do with Yeats not being able to finish *Ulysses* as the newness of Joyce's writing techniques.

66. Restuccia, *Joyce,* 106.

67. J. S. Atherton, "The Oxen of the Sun," in Hart and Hayman, eds., *Joyce's "Ulysses,"* 334.

68. I am not counting the fantasy sections of "Circe." We do "really" see her in "Wandering Rocks" as she throws a coin out a window to the one-legged sailor. But the phrase "a generous white arm from a window in Eccles street flung forth a coin" (10.220–21) presents us with flesh not character.

69. "When Bloom 'narrated' about Stephen at such length before falling asleep, he did not expect him to return, and he apparently had no other purpose than to displace Boylan in Molly's thoughts." Sultan, *Argument,* 440.

70. Father Robert Boyle, S.J., "Penelope," in Hart and Hayman, eds., *Joyce's "Ulysses,"* 412.

71. Consider the sexual-geometric symbolism concerning ALP in *Finnegans Wake.* See Mahaffey, *Reauthorizing Joyce,* 32–50.

72. There is a general consensus as to which parts of "Circe" occur on the narrative level. See Kenner, "Circe," in Hart and Hayman, eds., *Joyce's "Ulysses,"* 361–62.

73. Herr, *Joyce's Anatomy of Culture,* 96, 284–85.

74. Gifford, *Annotated,* 602.

75. S. L. Goldberg, in *The Classical Temper: A Study of James Joyce's "Ulysses"* (London: Chatto and Windus, 1969), makes a good case against the believability of her character, 290–300.

CHAPTER FOUR

1. For readings of *Three Lives* as going beyond representation, see, among others, Norman Weinstein, *Gertrude Stein and the Literature of Modern Con-*

sciousness (New York: Frederick Unger, 1970); Marianne DeKoven, *A Different Language: Gertrude Stein's Experimental Writing* (Madison: University of Wisconsin Press, 1983); and Lisa Ruddick, *Reading Gertrude Stein: Body, Text, Gnosis* (Ithaca, N.Y.: Cornell University Press, 1990).

2. See, among others, Ruddick; Neil Schmitz, *Of Huck and Alice* (Minneapolis: University of Minnesota Press, 1983); Marjorie Perloff, *The Poetics of Indeterminacy* (Evanston, Ill.: Northwestern University Press, 1983); and Wendy Steiner, *Exact Resemblance to Exact Resemblance* (New Haven: Yale University Press, 1978).

3. See James E. Breslin, "Gertrude Stein and the Problems of Autobiography," in *Critical Essays on Gertrude Stein,* ed. Michael J. Hoffman (Boston: G. K. Hall, 1986), 149–59; Schmitz, *Huck and Alice,* 226–39; and Harriet Scott Chessman, *The Public Is Invited to Dance: Representation, the Body, and Dialogue in Gertrude Stein* (Stanford: Stanford University Press, 1989), 167–98.

4. Bruce Comens writes that "Stein is one of the major literary theorists of the century." " 'What I Thought of the Atomic Bomb': Invention and Intervention in Gertrude Stein" (Paper delivered at the Modern Language Association meeting, Washington, D.C., December 29, 1989), 2. For Hejinian's views, see "Two Stein Talks," *Temblor* 3 (1986), 128–39.

5. A note on the back cover of the reissue of *How To Write* (West Glover, Vt.: Something Else Press, 1973) calls Stein's more conventional lectures "self-defeating" and labels the pieces in *How To Write* "essays . . . from the thick of the battle against old baggage."

6. John Ashbery, "The Impossible," in *Gertrude Stein Advanced,* ed. Richard Kostelanetz (Jefferson, N.C.: McFarland & Company, 1990), 111.

7. Wyndham Lewis, *Time and Western Man* (Boston: Beacon Press, 1957), 61.

8. B. L. Reid, *Art by Subtraction: A Dissenting Opinion of Gertrude Stein* (Norman: University of Oklahoma Press, 1958), vii.

9. See Joyce's letter to Harriet Weaver in which he gives seven highly complex "translations" of "L'Arcs en His Cieling Flee Chinx on the Flur." Quoted in *JJ,* 594.

10. This is not strictly true: a knowledge of William James helps in reading *Three Lives.* See Ruddick, *Reading Gertrude Stein,* 12–54.

11. Even in the case of the (relatively) conventional *Three Lives,* members of the firm that published it thought that Stein was a foreigner unfamiliar with English. See *CC,* 127.

12. "It seems to me that Miss Stein is a vulgar genius talking to herself, and if she is talking to herself, she is not an artist." B. L. Reid, quoted in Schmitz, *Huck and Alice,* 160.

13. Quoted in *GSIP,* 62–63.

14. Quoted in *CC,* 117.

15. Ruddick, *Reading Gertrude Stein,* 67.

16. Ibid., 77. *Americans* in Ruddick's account is far from simply anal— the anality is read as a component in Stein's struggle against patriarchy and

as an exemplification of the anality that is at the base of all literary form: "All literary genres depend on repetition of one sort or another; as Stein . . . attends to the sound of that repetition . . . she is playfully discovering something about the link between (all?) literary repetition and the primitive pleasure people take in filling up with and excreting matter" (81). David Antin writes of the final pages of the book—in Ruddick's terms the most completely anal—"There is probably nothing in the English language to compare with the seemingly infinite series of meaningful distinctions about living and aging and dying that Stein draws phrase by phrase for nearly twenty-one pages out of minute shifts in the aspect of the English verb in the litany that closes *The Making of Americans."* "Some Questions about Modernism," in Kostelanetz, ed., *Stein Advanced,* 209. For another extremely high evaluation also see Charles Bernstein's "Professing Stein/Stein Professing" in *A Poetics* (Cambridge, Mass.: Harvard University Press, 1992).

17. "Stein's pursuit of a quixotic dream of total knowledge ends in inevitable failure, but *this* story [Stein's struggle for self-realization through writing], which gradually unfolds in the text, makes more compelling reading than the family chronicle it displaces." Jayne L. Walker, *The Making of a Modernist: Gertrude Stein from "Three Lives" to "Tender Buttons"* (Amherst: University of Massachusetts Press, 1984), 54. Ruddick also discusses such narratives with considerable finesse.

18. DeKoven, *A Different Language,* xvii.

19. See Julia Kristeva, "Revolution in Poetic Language," in *The Kristeva Reader,* ed. Toril Moi, trans. Margaret Waller (New York: Columbia University Press, 1986), 89–136.

20. DeKoven, *A Different Language,* 151.

21. "I was alone at this time [in 1910] in understanding him, perhaps because I was expressing the same thing in literature." Gertrude Stein, *Picasso,* ed. Edward Burns (Boston: Beacon Press, 1985), 42.

22. See Schmitz, *Huck and Alice,* 162–99.

23. Perloff, *Poetics of Indeterminacy,* 102–7. See also her discussion of "Milk" in *The Dance of the Intellect* (Cambridge: Cambridge University Press, 1985), 190–92.

24. "So I am pulling a poem out of this BOX. The words on the page do not contain it, but their conundrum does." William Gass, "Gertrude Stein and the Geography of the Sentence," in *The World Within the Word* (New York: Alfred A. Knopf, 1978), 97, 98. See also Ruddick's reading of *Tender Buttons* in *Reading Gertrude Stein* as embodying a feminist gnosticism.

25. Steiner, *Exact Resemblance,* 6, n. 3.

26. Ibid., 204.

27. Chessman, *The Public Is Invited to Dance,* 4.

28. Alice B. Toklas, *What Is Remembered* (New York: Holt, Rinehart, and Winston, 1963), 54; Stein, *MOA,* 485, quoted in Chessman, *The Public Is Invited to Dance,* 146.

29. Things weren't uniformly ecstatic. Bridgman points out some of the complexities that resulted from *Toklas.* He speculates that Toklas may have

had a significant role in writing it; whether she did or not, the fact that Stein's success resulted from a Toklasesque writing may have contributed to the temporary writing block that followed publication. See *GSIP*, 209–37. In *A Stein Reader* (Evanston: Northwestern University Press, 1993), 568–69, Ulla Dydo examines the manuscripts of *Stanzas* and finds evidence of a quite bitter quarrel between Stein and Toklas. Stein had, in 1932, recently unearthed the manuscript of *Q.E.D.* and with it the memory of her passion for May Bookstaver. This infuriated Toklas, who, in typing *Stanzas* changed most *may*s to *can*s. At one point Stein seems to mock Toklas's censorship by writing, with unusual care, the word *may* and placing the letter *n* between and above the *a* and the *y*, thus producing the uncensorable but nasty *many*.

30. Chessman, *The Public Is Invited to Dance*, 3.

31. Ibid., 100–101, 107.

32. Schmitz, *Huck and Alice*, 200–201. Also see Bridgman, *Stein in Pieces*, for whom Stein's reticence over her sexual identity is central to her work, and Catherine R. Stimpson, "The Mind, the Body, and Gertrude Stein," *Critical Inquiry* 3, no. 3 (Spring 1977), quoted in Schmitz, 199.

33. Schmitz, *Huck and Alice*, 162, 165–66, 172–73.

34. *The New York Review of Books*, January 18, 1990.

35. Quoted in Fredric Jameson, *The Ideologies of Theory: Essays 1971–1986*, vol. 1, *Situations of Theory* (Minneapolis: University of Minnesota Press, 1988), 180.

36. "Rose is a rose is a rose is a rose" first appears in "Sacred Emily" (1913) in *Geography and Plays* (New York: Something Else Press, 1968). "Sacred Emily" is not, by conventional criteria, a poem at all, but a ten-page prose piece where most of the paragraphs contain one to four words. Occasionally ten or twelve words will extend past the right-hand margin back to the left-hand margin of the next line, demonstrating that the paragraphs are indented. The New Critical unity that Stein invokes is not easily detectable.

> Night town.
> Night town a glass.
> Color mahogany.
> Color mahogany center.
> Rose is a rose is a rose is a rose.
> Loveliness extreme.
> Extra gaiters.
> Loveliness extreme.
> Sweetest ice-cream.
> Page ages page ages page ages.
> Wiped Wiped wire wire.
> .   .   .   .
> Pussy pussy pussy what what.
> Current secret sneezers.
> Ever.
> Mercy for a dog.
> Medal make medal.
> Able able able.

A go to green and a letter spoke a go to green or praise or
Worships worships worships.
Door.
Do or.

187

37. If Toklas didn't write *Toklas* herself, the book was written in her language. See note 29 above.

38. Schmitz, *Huck and Alice*, 206–19, gives a very insightful account of *Toklas* and *Everybody's Autobiography* as a battle of geniuses between Stein and Picasso.

39. Stein's love for Toklas and its creative outcome can be seen as a much more successful enactment of Pound's Propertian credo, *Ingenium nobis ipsa puella facit*, the girl makes me a genius.

40. Note how in the following passage, Stein has a second writer removed from the roll: "I remember once coming into the room and hearing Benard Faÿ say that the three people of first rate importance that he had met in his life were Picasso, Gertrude Stein and André Gide and Gertrude Stein inquired quite simply, that is quite right but why include Gide. A year or so later in referring to this conversation he said to her, and I am not sure you were not right" (*SW*, 231).

41. See *LIA*, 225, 237. Also "Henry James" in *FIA*.

42. "It is very like a frog hopping he cannot ever hop exactly the same distance or the same way of hopping at every hop. A bird's singing is perhaps the nearest thing to repetition but if you listen they too vary their insistence" (*LIA*, 167).

43. In the case of one of the other excerpts she read, "A little monkey goes like a donkey that means to say that means to say that more sighs last goes. Leave with it. A little monkey goes like a donkey." Decoding and recreating the thing would have been easier since she supplied the title, "A DOG." A possible scenario would be: a puppy, a "little monkey," jumping and scrabbling at its master's knees, begging (successfully) to be taken out for a walk. But such easy cuteness is very much the exception in *Tender Buttons*.

44. See Schmitz, *Huck and Alice*, 192–98.

45. The chronology is slightly more tangled: *FIA* was written before the lectures. Nevertheless, in its meditations on the contingencies of biography and fame—what if Grant had been Hiram Grant a leader in religion?—it clearly shows the impact of *Toklas*.

46. In "Composition as Explanation" Stein's claims seem more tentative and the writing in general feels vaguer and more mystified than in her other lectures, written after she had become, as she puts it in *EA*, "a real lion a real celebrity" (143).

47. The other mention of the war occurs at *YGS*, 4; "When we read about a boat we know that it has been sunk."

48. A rather exact analogy to Stein's reading method here occurs when Etta Cone is typing the manuscript of *Three Lives*. Out of delicacy, not having been given explicit permission by Stein to read the manuscript, Cone was

"faithfully copying the manuscript letter by letter so that she might not by any indiscretion become conscious of the meaning" (*SW*, 49). Because Cone is not a genius, the implications of her procedure are of course utterly different. Again, compare Cézanne's valued method of painting, where each part of the canvas was given equal importance, with Marie Laurencin's comic method of viewing paintings: "bringing her eye close and moving over the whole of [the picture] with her lorgnette, an inch at a time" (*SW*, 57).

49. One of the key words Stein uses in describing obstacles to her aesthetic progress is "bother":

> The Velaquez bothered me as I say because like the Cazins of my youth they were too real and yet they were not real enough to be real and not unreal enough to be unreal.
>
> *LIA*, 73

> What was the first play I saw and was I then already bothered bothered about the different tempo there is in the play and in yourself and your emotion in having the play go on in front of you.
>
> *LIA*, 94

> Listening and talking do not presuppose resemblance and as they do not presuppose resemblance, they do not necessitate remembering. Already then as you see there was a complication which was a bother to me in my conception of the rhythm of a personality. I have for so many years tried to get the better of that the better of this bother. The bother was simply that and any one may say it is the bother that has always been a bother to anybody for anybody conceiving anything.
>
> *LIA*, 175

Perhaps this is a stretched point, but for me these "bothers," especially when repeated, evoke "brother." They arise over aesthetic qualities that are intended to be analyzable, conventional, and portable—not unique to the place of the genius. They seem related to the aesthetic qualities that Stein's brother missed in her work. The aggressive "explaining" about which Stein complains in the following passage in the text is also the downfall of Ezra Pound, the "village explainer." See *SW*, 189.

50. See *EA*, 11–12, where the same realization is described as "the most awful moment of my life."

51. See *EA*, 86. Also: "There is more back and forth in war than there is even in dancing or in kissing and so war is interesting" (*FIA*, 50).

52. Fredric Jameson, *The Political Unconscious: Narrative as a Socially Symbolic Act* (Ithaca, N.Y.: Cornell University Press, 1981), 102.

53. William Wordsworth, preface to *Lyrical Ballads*, in *William Wordsworth*, ed. Stephen Gill, The Oxford Authors (London: Oxford University Press, 1984), 603, 608.

54. Stein claims the work is "romantic" in the advertisement to *LCA*.

55. Wordsworth, preface to *Lyrical Ballads*, in *Wordsworth*, 605.

56. Ibid., 606.

57. Ibid., 657–59.

58. Ibid., 607.

59. The sentence referred to in the extract is: "A ring around the moon is seen to follow the moon and the moon is in the center of the ring and the ring follows the moon" (*WAM,* 46).

60. Immanuel Kant, *The Critique of Judgment,* trans. J. H. Bernard (New York: Hafner Press, 1951), 161–62.

61. David Lloyd, "Kant's Examples," in *Representations* 28 (Fall 1989): 41–42.

62. Kant, *Critique of Judgment,* 152, 150.

63. Ibid., 150.

64. Lloyd, "Kant's Examples," 45, 39.

65. Paul de Man, "Hegel's *Aesthetics,*" *Critical Inquiry* 8 (Summer 1982): 773, 769, 770.

66. In "An Instant Answer or A Hundred Prominent Men," Stein repeats "and one" one hundred times. Gertrude Stein, *Useful Knowledge* (Barrytown, N.Y.: Station Hill Press, 1988), 150–51.

67. Also see *EA,* 49–50, 67.

68. See Schmitz, *Huck and Alice,* 226–39.

69. Gertrude Stein, *Narration* (Chicago: University of Chicago Press, 1935), 16.

CHAPTER FIVE

1. An index of his continuing neglect by the poetic mainstream: he does not appear in the latest *Norton Anthology of Modern Poetry,* ed. Richard Ellmann and Robert O'Clair, 2d ed. (New York: Norton, 1988).

2. Of the Black Mountain school, Robert Creeley, Robert Duncan, and Cid Corman were particularly appreciative. See Creeley's essays in *A Quick Graph* (San Francisco: Four Seasons Foundation, 1970), 121–42; Duncan's memoir in *Paideuma* 7 (1978), 421–28; and Corman's contribution to *MAP,* 305–36. Olson, who would have been a rival for the position of Pound's number one son, had no use for Zukofsky. Zukofsky's work has had considerable prestige among language writers, especially at the outset of the group's development. See Ron Silliman's "Z-Sited Path," in *The New Sentence* (New York: Roof, 1987), 127–146, and Barrett Watten's "Social Formalism: Zukofsky, Andrews, and Habitus in Contemporary Poetry," *North Dakota Quarterly* 55 (1987): 365–82. In "Talks," *Hills* 6–7 (1980), Watten refers to Zukofsky as "the greatest poet of the century," 179.

3. Barry Ahearn, in *Zukofsky's "A"* (Berkeley: University of California Press, 1983); Joseph M. Conte, in *Unending Design* (Ithaca, N.Y.: Cornell University Press, 1991); Guy Davenport, in *The Geography of the Imagination* (San Francisco: North Point Press, 1981); Michael Heller, in *Conviction's Net of Branches* (Carbondale: Southern Illinois University Press, 1985); Hugh Kenner, in *The Pound Era* (Berkeley: University of California Press, 1971); Michele J. Leggott, in *Reading Zukofsky's "80 Flowers"* (Baltimore: Johns Hopkins

University Press, 1989); and Peter Quartermain in *Disjunctive Poetics: From Gertrude Stein and Louis Zukofsky to Susan Howe* (Cambridge: Cambridge University Press, 1992) stand out as celebrators of Zukofsky's technical achievements. Despite its title, Eric Mottram's "1924–1951: Politics and Form in Zukofsky," *Maps* 5 (1973): 76–103, is more concerned with the political dimension of Zukofsky's work; Eric Homberger in *American Writers and Radical Politics, 1900–39* (New York: St. Martin's, 1986) and Burton Hatlen in "Art and/as Labor: Some Dialectical Patterns in *"A"*-1 through *"A"*-10," *Contemporary Literature* 25, no. 2 (1984) also focus on Zukofsky's politics. Paul Smith's *Pound Revised* (London: Croom Helm, 1983) devotes a chapter to a post-Lacanian, politicized reading of Zukofsky. Norman Finkelstein, in *The Utopian Moment* (Lewisburg, Pa.: Bucknell University Press, 1988), assesses Zukofsky's poetry in terms of its relevance to its place in history. Watten's essay, "Social Formalism," anticipates some of my concern here as to the formal outcomes of Zukofsky's political positions.

4. See Davenport, *Geography of the Imagination*, 107.

5. Silliman, "Z-Sited Path," 146, 143.

6. Davenport, *Geography of the Imagination*, 103.

7. Louis Zukofsky, *All: The Collected Short Poems, 1923–64* (New York: Norton, 1971). Now collected in *CSP* along with *Catullus* and *80 Flowers*.

8. See Leggott, *Reading Zukofsky's "80 Flowers,"* 66–67.

9. Paul de Man, "The Rhetoric of Temporality," in *Blindness and Insight* (Minneapolis: University of Minnesota Press, 1983), 187–228; Joel Fineman, "The Significance of Literature: *The Importance of Being Earnest*," in *October* 12 (1980): 79–90, and "The Structure of Allegorical Desire," in *Representation and Allegory*, ed. Stephen J. Greenblatt (Baltimore: Johns Hopkins University Press, 1981), 26–80.

10. See the opening chapter of Barry Ahearn's *Zukofsky's "A"* and Terrell's introduction to *MAP*.

11. In *CSP*, 8–20. Zukofsky wrote that " 'The' was a direct reply to *The Waste Land*" (*PZ*, 78).

12. Numbering every line has reminded some readers of frames in a film. See Duncan in *Paideuma* 7 (1978):424.

13. Celia Zukofsky's year-by-year bibliography (*MAP*, 385–92) gives 1926 as the date "Poem beginning 'The' " was composed; however, slightly faulty memory on her part or last-minute revision on his could account for what certainly reads like a conscious echo.

14. T. S. Eliot, "Philip Massinger," in *Selected Essays* (New York: Harcourt, Brace, and Co., 1950), 182. Throughout his life Zukofsky remained touchy about the question of his being imitative. In the late talk about Stevens he applies Stravinsky's Eliotic remark to himself: "I must trust myself then as a poet, and like Stravinsky accused of imitating Mozart, answer (at least to myself) *no, I stole Mozart*." In "For Wallace Stevens," *PR*, 31.

15. In a letter to Pound, Zukofsky mentions, as an obvious fact, that he can't teach at Columbia because he is Jewish (*PZ*, 147).

16. Louis Zukofsky, *A Test of Poetry* (New York: Jargon/Corinth Books, 1964).

17. See Ahern, *Zukofsky's "A,"* 177–80. *Pericles* was published as a companion volume to *Bottom.*

18. See Ezra Pound, *Women of Trachis* (New York: New Directions, 1957). Pound calls the play "the highest peak of Greek sensibility" (3), but more personal motives can also be discerned in his decision to translate it. "What / SPLENDOUR / IT ALL COHERES" is, in Pound's words, "the key phrase, for which the play exists" (50), but in the original context the line expresses Herakles' contentment at the thought that death puts a stop to labor—hardly a Poundian sentiment. SPLENDOUR and COHERENCE are, of course, important in Pound's work as expressions of his desire to produce total(itarian) illumination. In a crasser register, the hero's marital troubles in the original rhyme with Pound's at the time he made the translation. *"A"*-21 is similar in its transformation of the original. It is hard to imagine that Zukofsky found the play, with its evil pimp, freeborn Athenian girl almost sold into slavery, slapstick action, and coincidence-laden plot "the highest peak" of anything, but as an expression of a family reunited through the power of love (the action takes place around the shrine of Venus), *Rudens* matched Zukofsky's personal concerns well.

19. Zukofsky's relation to William Carlos Williams makes an interestingly inverse parallel to his relationship with Pound. While Pound would barely read Zukofsky's work, especially after the early thirties, Williams valued Zukofsky's editorial skills highly and often sent his own work to Zukofsky for editing. See Neil Baldwin, "Zukofsky, Williams, and *The Wedge*" in *MAP* (129–42) for an account of Zukofsky's extensive revisions of Williams's poems.

20. See *PZ*, 178–99.

21. Paul Smith, overoptimistically in my view, sees Zukofsky's printing of the poem as an implied criticism: "possibly a signal to the reader as to what faults Pound can be accused of." *Pound Revised*, 134.

22. Hatlen writes that the last words of the first half of *"A"*-9 "are perhaps the last Marxian words that Zukofsky ever wrote." "Art and/as Labor," 230.

23. Zukofsky did write some short poems during the war. See Finkelstein, *The Utopian Moment*, 34–35, for a discussion of "A Song For the Year's End," where Zukofsky's despair is much more qualified, and in Finkelstein's view, measured by an undercurrent of utopian hope:

> Then I shall go and write of my country,
> Have a job all my life
> Seldom write with grace again, be part of the world,
> See every man in forced labor,
>
> *CSP*, 112

24. In his first letter to Pound after the war, Zukofsky identifies *"A"*-11 as "after Perch' io non spero" (*PZ*, 206), the same source as Eliot's "Ash Wednesday"—another example of Zukofsky following in a master's footsteps.

25. See *MAP*, 50–51. As an index of the pressure of the McCarthy years, compare Celia's post-World-War-Two reminiscences depicting Zukofsky as an absent-minded, apolitical poet, "Louie was never a member and he couldn't even remember when he had been in Wisconsin and of course Louie was so mixed up that the FBI was correcting him" with Zukofsky's reaction in 1938 to Pound's dedication of *Guide to Kulchur* to him and Bunting: "Can't guess what *Kulchah* is about, but if you want to dedicate yr. book to a communist (me) and a British-conservative-antifascist-imperialist (Basil), I won't sue you for libel" (*PZ*, 195). (Note that Zukofsky's communism is the small-*c* variety. In 1933 he wrote Pound, saying "I am not here writing as a member of the U.S. Communist Party—I am sure that as far as they're concerned papa & childt & Unk Bill Walrus [Pound and Zukofsky and Williams] are in the same gallery" [*PZ*, 148].)

26. See "Work/Sundown" in *PR*, 165–66.

27. Quoted in *A Big Jewish Book*, ed. Jerome Rothenberg (Garden City, N.Y.: Anchor Press/Doubleday, 1978), 610.

28. See his wife's bibliography in *MAP*, 385–92.

29. *"A" 1–12* (New York: Doubleday, 1967), v.

30. *"A,"* 126–27, 231–61. Don Byrd notes that Zukofsky makes a similar claim for the unity of all of Shakespeare's writing in *Bottom*. See "The Shape of Zukofsky's Canon," in *MAP*, 163.

31. It is probably excessive to read echoes of Hester Prynne's *A* into *"A."* But the color of her letter would fit his Marxist leanings; the filigree she elaborated around it makes an appropriate emblem for some of his verbal tracery; and her sin of adultery is somewhat related to Zukofsky's own apostasy: in *"A"*-4, he has his Fathers chastise him: "We had a Speech, our children have evolved a jargon" (12).

32. I took part in a series of performances of *"A"*-24 in 1978 and thus write from experience.

33. Zukofsky had a strong sense that poetic recurrence made poetry into music. His lines, printed at the end of the *L. Z. Masque*, make recurrence the principal feature of *"A"*:

> the gift—
> she hears
> the work
> in its recurrence
> A, 806

Poetry's uneasy social position has motivated a number of similar displacements: compare Pound's oft-cited but not terribly meaningful division of poetry into word-painting (phanopoeia), word-music (melopoeia), and word-poetry (logopoeia) (*ABC*, 37), or Olson's claim that what a poet must do is "dance / sitting down." Charles Olson, *The Maximus Poems*, ed. George F. Butterick (Berkeley: University of California Press, 1983), 39.

34. See Kenneth Cox, "Zukofsky and Mallarmé: Notes on *"A"*-19," in *Maps* 5 (1973): 1–13.

35. See Watten, "Social Formalism," for an analysis of Zukofsky's similar metaphorization of science.

36. See Hugh Kenner, "Oppen, Zukofsky, and the Poem as Lens," in *Literature at the Barricades: The American Writer in the 1930s,* ed. Ralph F. Bogardus and Fred Hobson (Tuscaloosa: University of Alabama Press, 1982), 162–74.

37. Pound wrote to Zukofsky, "My model historian is the chink whose name I forget. sic 'Then for nine reigns there was no literary production' " (*PZ,* 74).

38. Ricky, Whittaker Chambers's brother, was eulogized in "*A*"-3.

39. Louis Zukofsky, ed., *An "Objectivists" Anthology* (New York: To Publications, 1932), 25. Through his introduction, Zukofsky uses the word "job" to describe a poem.

40. Ibid., 139.

41. Ibid., 118.

42. See William Harmon, "Louis Zukofsky: Eiron *Eyes,*" in *American Poetry 1946 to 1965,* ed. Harold Bloom (New York: Chelsea House, 1987), 67–81, for a discussion of "traduction" as well as "Zoo-zoo-caw-caw-of-the-sky."

43. In *Bottom,* Zukofsky reveals a surprisingly Poundian twist on this motif. There, Bach's work is said to be as distant from the (feminized) populace as is higher mathematics: "Hamilton's mathematics [noncommutative algebra] was not more natural to Anglo-Irish dames than the music of Bach's *Matthew Passion* to Leipzig ladies in 1729" (*B,* 61).

44. See Burton Hatlen, "Art and/as Labor," especially 226–27, for further discussion of these motifs.

45. The reading cited is in Don Byrd, "The Shape of Zukofsky's Canon," in *MAP,* 173.

46. These lines seem autonomous not least because they imitate Pound's "ply over ply" figure.

47. Watten, "Social Formalism," 378.

48. At the end of his career, Zukofsky indicated that his early attempts at classical forms resulted from the challenge of the difficult. In an interview with L. S. Dembo he said, "But what I'm saying in " 'Mantis': An Interpretation" is not that the sestina is the ideal form; rather that it's still possible ["Mantis" itself is a sestina]. Williams said it was impossible to write sonnets. I don't know whether anybody has been careful about it. I wrote five hundred sonnets when I was young and threw them away" (*MAP,* 276). In an early letter to Pound, Zukofsky wrote, "Think, if I may humbly say so, that *A*-7 performs the revolution in the sonnet I hinted at elsewhere" (*PZ,* 42).

49. This obsession with horses runs throughout Zukofsky's writing, starting with "Poem beginning 'The' "—"238 If horses could but sing Bach, mother" (*CSP,* 17) and continuing through "*A.*" In the index, the entry for "horse" is one of the longest. Typical of the deficit underlying Zukofsky's assertions of totality, the source for "As true as truest horse" (*A 12,* 132)

turns out to be especially conflicted. In *A Midsummer Night's Dream*, Thisby's declamation is intended as ridiculously malaprop: "Most brisky juvenal, and eke most lovely Jew, / As true as truest horse . . . I'll meet thee, Pyramus" (2.1.85–87).

50. See Hatlen, "Art and/as Labor," for more detailed discussion.

51. The two letters spell the capitalized word "AM" and suggest Jehovah's I AM THAT I AM, or at least Coleridge's "primary IMAGINATION . . . a repetition in the finite mind of the eternal act of creation in the infinite I AM." *Biographia Literaria*, ed. J. Shawcross, 2 vols. (Oxford: Oxford University Press, 1907), 1:202. The first letter is of course the title of the poem. In a related gesture, in one short poem in *All* Zukofsky transmutes the number 25 into a divine bird-boat: "Forget the number / Think of an entablature of snow / Engraved there 2 a bird-prow / Taking 5 in tow" (*CSP*, 80). (The next poem comments sardonically, *"God the man is so overweening / He would prolong / A folly of thought see 2 as a bird"* [*CSP*, 81].)

52. I owe the observation that follows to Hatlen, "Art and/as Labor," 219.

53. Louis Zukofsky, *The First Half of "A"-9* (New York: privately published, 1940), 37. Subsequent references in text.

54. See Ahearn, *Zukofsky's "A,"* and Quartermain, *Disjunctive Poetics*, for discussions of conic sections and the poetics of the poem.

55. Michael Davidson, "Dismantling 'Mantis': Reification and Objectivist Poetics," *ALH* 3, no. 3 (Fall 1991): 534.

56. I assume the British pronouncer of "capitalism" is Basil Bunting. The humor seems his.

57. Peter Quartermain, in " 'Not at all Surprised by Science': Louis Zukofsky's *First Half of "A"-9,"* writes over twenty pages on the piece, concluding, a tad disingenuously, "Exegesis should not be necessary" (*MAP*, 225).

58. Louis Zukofsky, *Little* (New York: Grossman, 1970), 4.

59. Louis Zukofsky, *Autobiography* (New York: Grossman, 1970), 43, 59.

60. An especially bitter diatribe occurs during an interpolation in the *Rudens* translation (*A*, 499–500).

61. See Paul Smith, *Pound Revised*, for a discussion of the way Zukofsky weaves Melanesian myth, familial concerns, etymological analysis of "napalm," and quotations from *The New York Times* and Samuel Johnson into *"A"*-18.

62. See Peter Quartermain, " 'Actual Word Stuff, Not Thoughts for Thoughts': Louis Zukofsky and William Carlos Williams" in *Credences* 2, no. 1 (1982): 108.

63. De Man, "The Rhetoric of Temporality," 191. Subsequent page references in the text.

64. In the original version, the face was Rimbaud's. Zukofsky, ed., *An "Objectivists" Anthology*, 131–32.

65. In this region of *"A,"* "Wrigleys" exerts a minor fascination. The one line Pound singled out for left-handed praise in the early version of

"A" 1–7 he published in his *Active Anthology* (London: Faber & Faber, 1933) was "Outwriggling the wriggling Wrigley boys" (*A*, 21). "In his *tour de force* L. Zukofsky gives a phonetic representation of an American chewing-gum" (*SP*, 325).

66. A history of the twentieth-century American literary avant-garde could be written tracing uses of epideictics such as "this" and "here." Among many examples: "A SOUND: Elephants beaten with candy and little pops and chews all bolts and reckless reckless rats, this is this," in *Tender Buttons* (*SW*, 474); "Here here / here. Here," in Robert Creeley's *Pieces* (New York: Scribners, 1969), 14 (the word is stressed in many of his poems); *This* magazine was one of the founding journals of the language writing movement.

67. Fineman, "Significance," 2–83, 86.

68. See Burton Hatlen, "Zukofsky as Translator," in *MAP*, 345–64.

69. It is interesting to compare the reactions of Basil Bunting, the other dedicatee of *Guide to Kulchur*, to Catullus's poems. Bunting published few translations; one of them translates the first few lines of Catullus's longest and most mannered poem (64) and then breaks off:

> Health to you, heroes, brood of the gods, born in the prime season,
> thoroughbreds sprung of thoroughbred dams, health to you aye, and again
>   health!
> I will talk to you often in my songs, but first I speak to you, bridegroom
> acclaimed with many pinebrands, pillar of Thessaly, fool for luck, Peleus,
> to whom Jove the godbegetter, Jove himself yielded his mistress,
> for the sea's own child clung to you
> *—and why Catullus bothered to write pages and pages of this drivel mystifies me.*
>   Basil Bunting, *Collected Poems*
>   (London: Fulcrum Press, 1970), 139

70. David Melnick, "The 'Ought' of Seeing: Zukofsky's *Bottom*," in *Maps* 5 (1973): 55–65.

71. Both the examples here are taken from Melnick. Subsequent references to his article included in the text.

72. Kenneth Burke's remark in "Lexicon Rhetoricae" on literary perfection—a key term for Zukofsky—is apropos here: "Perfection could exist only if the entire range of the reader's and the writer's experience were identical down to the last detail. Universal and permanent perfection could exist only if this entire range of experiences were identical for all men forever." In *Counter-Statement* (Berkeley: University of California Press, 1968), 179.

73. The quote is from Fineman, "The Structure of Allegorical Desire," 52.

74. See Ahern, *Zukofsky's "A,"* 177–80.

75. It also occurs as a grounding motif throughout the "Chaconne" of *"A"*-24, 637–80.

76. The interview is in *MAP*, 265–82; the poem in *CSP*, 222–31.

77. For an extensive unpacking of all that Zukofsky put into this passage, see Leggott, *Reading Zukofsky's "80 Flowers,"* 34–72.

78. See Ahearn, Zukofsky's "A," 185; and Leggott, *Reading Zukofsky's "80 Flowers,"* 37–47.

AFTERWORD

1. As Barrett Watten has pointed out, writers have not imitated Duchamp or the asymptotic distance toward which his career points. See *Total Syntax* (Carbondale, Ill.: Southern Illinois University Press, 1985), 215–17.

2. With many poets, the life can supplant the writing as the principal focus. The cases of Charles Olson, Sylvia Plath, Anne Sexton, and Philip Larkin are charged instances.

3. Immanuel Kant, *Critique of Judgment,* trans. J. H. Bernard (New York: Hafner Press, 1951), 146.

4. See Ahern, Zukofsky's "A," 191.

5. For instance, the end of *Lucy Church Amiably* is not particularly different from the texture throughout: "They like them and with it there and with beside which can as if as pleasing before it with all of it not more than as an advantage for them. They like it they say how do you do. Very well I thank you" (*LCA,* 240).

6. Gertrude Stein, *Picasso,* ed. Edward Burns (Boston: Beacon Press, 1985), 90–91.

7. Gertrude Stein, *Paris France* (New York: Charles Scribner's Sons, 1940), 120.

8. Wallace Stevens, *Opus Posthumous,* ed. Samuel French Morse (New York: Vintage, 1957), 80.

9. Basil Bunting, "On the Fly-Leaf of Pound's Cantos," in *Collected Poems* (London: Fulcrum Press, 1970), 122.

10. Rosalind Krauss, "Poststructuralism and the 'Paraliterary,' " *October* 13 (1980): 40, quoted in Gregory L. Ulmer, "The Object of Post-Criticism," in *The Anti-Aesthetic,* ed. Hal Foster (Port Townsend, Wa.: Bay Press, 1983), 107–8.

11. Ulmer, "The Object of Post-Criticism," 108.

12. Antony Easthope and John O. Thompson, eds., *Contemporary Poetry Meets Modern Theory* (Toronto: University of Toronto Press, 1991), vii.

13. Michel Foucault, "What Is An Author?" in *Language, Counter-Memory, Practice: Selected Essays and Interviews,* trans. Donald F. Bouchard and Sherry Simon (Ithaca, N.Y.: Cornell University Press, 1977), 138.

14. Samuel Beckett, "Texts for Nothing," in *Stories & Texts for Nothing* (New York: Grove Press, 1967), 96–97.

15. Ibid., 92–93.

16. But it is interesting that Ginsberg's relations with Pound have, on occasion, led him to suggest that his utterance has a magical potency. See "Wichita Vortex Sutra," in which Ginsberg pronounces the end of the Vietnam War in 1966. Pound's sense of the morally pure and efficacious word is prominent in the poem. I discuss this in *The Marginalization of Poetry* (Princeton: Princeton University Press, forthcoming).

17. I am thinking here of some of the early celebrations of the polysemy of Stein and Zukofsky by language writers. But on the other hand, language writing on the whole represents the most thoroughgoing exploration of the social consequences of writing techniques since modernism. A controversial claim—and one for which I can certainly be accused of partiality. I discuss the issues at length in *The Marginalization of Poetry*.

Index

Compositor: Impressions
Printer: Edwards Brothers, Inc.
Binder: Edwards Brothers, Inc.
Text: 10/13 Palatino
Display: Palatino